Commonsense Copyright

Commonsense Copyright

A Guide for Educators and Librarians

SECOND EDITION

by

R. S. Talab

McFarland & Company, Inc., Publishers
Jefferson, North Carolina, and London

Disclaimer: The author provides information and guidance on a wide variety of topics. For legal advice the reader is advised to seek the assistance of a qualified attorney.

Author's Note: Web site information and addresses change periodically.

Library of Congress Cataloguing-in-Publication Data

Talab, R. S., 1948–
    Commonsense copyright : a guide for educators and librarians /
by R. S. Talab.— 2d ed.
        p.   cm.
    Includes index.
    ISBN 0-7864-0675-5 (sewn softcover : 50# alkaline paper) ∞
    1. Copyright — United States — Popular works.   2. Fair use
(Copyright) — United States — Popular works.   I. Title.
KF2994.T36   1999
346.7304'82 — dc21   99-12915
                                                                CIP

British Library Cataloguing-in-Publication data are available

Manufactured in the United States of America

McFarland & Company, Inc., Publishers
  Box 611, Jefferson, North Carolina 28640
    www.mcfarlandpub.com

This book is dedicated to my mother Inga;
sisters Shirley and Julie; husband
Dan; and my sons Grant and Farbod.

Table of Contents

Part V. Permissions and Policy Development

Part VI. Notes and Resources

Part VIII. Appendices

Preface to the
Second Edition

Since the original edition of this book was published in 1986, the field of copyright has undergone substantial change. Not only has the law been amended, but advances in technology have given rise to new issues and created some confusion about old ones.

Why should I know about copyright? Having accurate information can mean the difference between using something for "fair use" purposes at no cost or not using it all. For example, an elementary teacher requested the use of a short segment of a song from a music company for a student to use in an in-class-only multimedia project. The company requested $5,000 for permission. A school library media director requested the use of a short video clip for a teacher to use in a class presentation on a one-time-only basis. The film company requested $1,000 for permission. In both cases such uses, if once-only and of a sufficiently brief or insubstantial amount, would have been considered "fair use" and not subject to any fees at all, but these educators did not know it. Not having accurate copyright information can also be costly. The Los Angeles Unified School District in 1998 paid roughly $300,000 to the Software Publishers Association for infringing software uses that were prohibited to teachers in the district policy manual but which the District did not wish to waste precious resources on in litigation.

How often has the Copyright Act been amended? There have been 31 amendments to the Copyright Act, not including the provisions added by the Semiconductor Chip Protection Act of 1984 which are not a part of the Copyright Law. The latest two occurred in the latter part of 1998. Regular updating must be part of copyright compliance procedures. The need for the United States to comply with changes in the international arena is playing an increasingly important part of national copyright policy, as well. A growing number of changes to the copyright law are the result of compliance with international treaties, which were of little concern even fifteen years ago.

What changes are there in the second edition? Additions to this edition include sections at the end of each chapter called "can do," "cannot do," "tried and true," and sometimes "beware" or "tips," as are question-and-answer sections. Resource sections are provided on videos, off-air taping of broadcast, cable, and satellite programming, software, periodicals, books, Web sites, discussion groups, licensing societies, reference materials, and permissions. Simplified guidelines and charts can be consulted for quick reference. Example lessons from teachers and librarians also provide help in teaching ethical use of copyrighted works, as well.

Why is copyright important? In a time in which information is accessible all over the world instantaneously it is a privilege to live in a country which sees the need to reward innovation through intellectual property rights. The United States and other countries which recognize intellectual property rights receive tangible, economic benefits from this system. On a personal note, countries in which copyright does not exist have been observed by the author to have far less innovation than those that do, made evident through interactions over the years with university scholars in these countries. What is the incentive to create when efforts of months or years can be quickly copied and sold by someone other than the author? This is copyright's dilemma; to provide economic incentives for creation and to provide limited exemptions for the public good. It's a very worthwhile balancing act.

Part I
Copyright Primer

1
A Copyright Primer

Introduction

The photocopier, the personal computer, videocassette recorder and videodisc player, compact disc (CD-ROM) reader and recorder, cable television, satellite, and the Internet enable more people to self-publish and repackage knowledge and information at a limitless pace.[1] Fast becoming site-independent, electronic publishing increasingly influences the politics of information access.[2] For these reasons public access and individual rights have become a more fluid balancing act, involving not only authors and users but intellectual property professionals whose business it is to protect copyright owners through encryption and other software engineering techniques and devices.[3] It is now possible for an author to take five years to complete a work and anyone who is interested five minutes to duplicate it and place it on the Internet where anyone on the planet can download it.

Nicholas Negroponte in *Being Digital* (1996) stated that

> As we interconnect ourselves, many of the values of a nation-state will give way to those of both larger and smaller electronic communities. We will socialize in digital neighborhoods in which physical space will be irrelevant and time will play a different role... Reading about Patagonia can include the sensory experience of going there.[4]

The intriguing corollary of this dynamic arrangement is that proper remuneration should accrue to its creators to ensure that someone, somewhere, will take the risk of creating a new original work.

Important Amendments to the Act

The scope of copyright has enlarged considerably over the years. The first United States Copyright Act was enacted in 1790.[5] The first statute that Congress

3

enacted was an almost exact copy of an earlier English statute.[6] With later revisions of the act in 1831, 1879, 1909, and 1978, as well as many revisions since then, the scope of "writings" widened to include technological developments.[7] Now covered are literary, dramatic, and musical works, letters, maps, lectures, paintings, photographs, designs, sculpture, film, computer-readable databases, computer programs, and architectural works.

The Copyright Act has been amended 31 times and still counting, since the major revision act of 1976.[8] Each year several new copyright bills are introduced. Anyone possessing the original 1976 act has an historical document with limited current use. While all of these changes can affect educators and librarians, those of greatest importance have been included in this section (for information on new and pending copyright legislation, see http://lcweb.loc.gov/copyright). See Appendix H for a complete list of these revisions.

Copyright Notice Optional and Infringement Fines Raised

The Berne Convention Implementation Act of 1988 (P.L. 100-568) enacted several changes. The most important ones were that the copyright notice was made optional for published works and that registration was made a requirement of bringing suit for U.S. works (subject to a grace period) but was made optional for foreign works.

The notice requirement was abolished for all works first published on or after March 1, 1989. For such works no copyright notice is required. Notice, however, is still required on all copies of works first published before that date. Notice will still be widely used even when it is not required to inform the world of the copyright status of the work. The position of the copyright notice has to "give reasonable notice of the claim of copyright" [Section 401(c)]. This means that it must be easy to locate but that there is no assigned position.

The act also raised statutory damages from $500 to $20,000 (raised from $250 and $10,000) and if the copyright owner sustains the burden of proof and the infringement was committed willfully, then statutory damages can be raised to $100,000 (raised from $50,000). The fine for the innocent infringer (one who is unaware and has no reason to believe that copying something is an infringement) was raised to $200 (raised from $100). (Fines were raised for other infringements in later amendments.)

Architectural Works a Copyrightable Category

The Architectural Works Copyright Protection Act (Title VII of the Judicial Improvements Act of 1990, P.L. 101-650) created a new category of copyrightable subject matter for architectural works.

An "architectural work" is the design of a building as embodied in any tangible medium of expression, including a building, architectural plans, or drawings. The work includes the overall form as well as the arrangement and composition of spaces and elements in the design, but does not include individual standard features.

Repeal of Five-Year Reports of the Register of Copyrights

Section 108(i) was repealed (P.L. 102-307), which required that five-year reports be submitted on the "balancing of the rights of creators, and the needs of users."

Term Extension for Certain Works

The Copyright Renewal Act (P.L. 102-307) allowed an extension of the copyright term for works first published between January 1, 1964, and December 31, 1977, for another 47 years.

Fair Use Applicable to Unpublished Works

This Amendment (P.L. 102-492) changed the law so that fair use could be made of unpublished works.

The fact that a work is unpublished shall not of itself bar a finding of fair use if such finding is made upon consideration of all of the above factors [Section 107].

Restoration of Copyright to Foreign Works

North American Free Trade Agreement Implementation Act (NAFTA)
The change most important for educators and librarians in this Act (P.L. 103-182) was the restoration of copyright to films in the public domain because of compliance problems. The General Agreement on Tariffs and Trade (GATT) later added a "more comprehensive renewal provision."[9]

General Agreement on Tariffs and Trade (GATT)
GATT (P.L. 103-465) restored copyright to foreign works which had fallen into the public domain in the U.S. but not in the originating country because of copyright registration formalities. Works in World Trade Organization countries (WTO), if they are less than 75 years old and are still protected in the country of their origin, were "automatically reinstated when GATT took effect in the U.S."[10] The Copyright Office keeps restoration lists for these foreign works. Copyrights in the U.S. cannot be recaptured. GATT changed the law so that computer programs could be rented and made the recording and

trafficking of sound recordings and music videos "actionable," subject to a copyright infringement lawsuit.[11]

Digital Audio Transmission Protected

This act (P.L. 104-39) defined a "digital transmission" as "a transmission in whole or in part in a digital or other non-analog format" [Section 101]. The owners of sound recordings have a new right in public performance in the limited context of digital transmission.[12] It also added several paragraphs to Sections 114 and 115 protecting the transmission and licensing of sound recordings.

Exemptions for Literary Works for Blind and Disabled

This act (P.L.104-97) added Section 121 to the act which allowed greater latitude in the "fair use" of literary works in specialized formats for the blind and disabled.

> it is not an infringement of copyright for an authorized entity to reproduce or to distribute copies or phonorecords of a previously published, nondramatic literary work if such copies or phonorecords are reproduced or distributed in specialized formats exclusively for use by blind or other persons with disabilities [Section 121(a)].

Excluded materials are

> norm-referenced tests and related testing material ... computer programs, except the portions thereof that are in conventional human language (including descriptions of pictorial works) and displayed to users in the ordinary course of using computer programs [Section 121(b)(2)].

An "authorized entity"

> means a nonprofit organization or a governmental agency that has a primary mission to provide specialized services relating to training, education, or adaptive reading or information access needs of blind or other persons with disabilities" [Section 121(c)(1)].

Special education and library media teachers who serve these students also qualify as "authorized entities." A "specialized format" means

> Braille, audio, or digital text which is exclusively for use by blind or other persons with disabilities [Section 121(c)(3)].

The Copyright Technical Amendments Act (P.L. 105-80)

Several changes were made to the act. Of importance to educators and librarians were that it further defined copyright in certain motion picture restored works, allowed the Copyright Office to raise fees, and redefined phonorecord distribution as constituting publication only after January 1, 1978.

Copyright Term Extension Act (P.L. 105-278)

Key provisions include extending the term of copyright from life plus 50 years to life plus 70 years for individual authors and to extend the term from 75 years for corporate entities to 95 years to conform to WIPO treaties. This extension applies to works still under copyright on the bill's effective date as well as to future works. An exception permits libraries, archives, and nonprofit educational institutions to treat a copyrighted work in its 20-year extension of protection as if it were in the public domain for noncommercial purposes under certain conditions.

Digital Millennium Copyright Act (P.L. 105-304)

This act had several components that updated copyright law in the digital environment and conformed it to the World Intellectual Property Organization (WIPO) treaties of 1996. Major sections include **Title 1:** Prohibitions on the circumvention of protection technologies (password or encryption) used by the copyright holder to prevent access to material and the prevention of the manufacturing of devices which defeat this protection (in a two-year and 18-month time frame). The Librarian of Congress will study the effect of "anti-circumvention" measures on the use of copyrighted works. Nonprofit libraries, archives, and educational institutions were exempted from criminal penalties and civil fines under certain conditions. **Title II:** Limitations were placed on online service provider (OSP) liabilities, including nonprofit educational institutions and a mechanism was created for this purpose when storing infringing information with an OSP, using "information location tools" and hyperlinks. An OSP does not have to monitor its service or seek out information about infringement of its service. Nonprofit libraries, archives, and educational institutions are now allowed access to commercial works to determine whether or not to acquire a work. **Title III:** Exemptions were made for certain types of computer maintenance and repair. **Title IV:** Broadcasters were allowed the same exemptions for digital recordings that they have for analog ones. Section 108 was updated to permit authorized institutions to make up to three digital preservation copies of a copyrighted work and to "loan" those copies to other qualifying institutions. Digital preservation of works in obsolete formats was allowed. The Register of Copyrights was charged with reporting to Congress by May 1999 on how to "promote distance education through digital technologies" and to formulate them into statutory proposals. **Title V:** Vessel hull designs have *sui generis* protection for 10 years.

Copyright Basics

Handling copyright questions can be enhanced through knowledge of its purpose, the area of coverage, and the differences among common law, statutory copyright, agreements, and administrative law.

Copyright. The copyright clause of the Constitution gives Congress the power to grant authors exclusive rights to their writings in order to "promote the progress of science and the useful arts" (article 1, section 8, clause 8). The primary purpose of copyright is to foster the dissemination of intellectual works for the public welfare. Giving authors exclusive rights to their works for a limited period of time is seen as a way of rewarding them for their contribution to society. "Copyright" literally means the exclusive right to make copies of a work. It could be described as a practical way of uniting publication with profit. By this method authors are given a "headstart" as a monetary incentive to creative production.

Statutory Law. Copyright law is governed by two aspects: statutory law and common law. They are of equal importance.[13] Statutory law is enacted federal law. Federal copyright law (enacted by Congress as "statutes") supersedes state copyright law. If there is a difference between the federal and the state law, then the federal statute takes precedence. What is not mentioned in a federal copyright statute devolves to state jurisdiction.[14]

Common Law. Common law is based on local customs as they are interpreted by court decisions. Statutory law is interpreted through court decisions. Court decisions are very important in copyright law, because it requires a greater degree of interpretation by the courts. *Stare decisis* or "let the decision stand" means that once a decision has been made in a type of case, then later decisions tend to be decided in that way. This allows educators some measure of prediction in how a use will be viewed by the courts in similar circumstances.

Agreements. Agreements negotiated by producers and educators for off-air taping, music, print, and multimedia have an impact on how the law is interpreted in court decisions (see Appendices A–F). When a case is brought to court, the judge examines the applicable federal and state law, the contract, case law (court cases), and any agreements that might affect the involved parties. While agreements apply only to those groups that agree to them, they do provide a measure of guidance in deciding a case.

Contracts. The nature of the contract is an extremely important consideration in copyright law. A contract is a legally binding agreement.[15] While every contract is an agreement, not every agreement is a contract. The three elements that must be present are:

1. **Consideration**—a legal term for what one party to a contract gives to another. A contract could state that one party would pay the other party

a certain amount of money for the purchase of a book, a software program, an article, etc.

2. **A time frame** — the contract should specify the date of delivery, completion, or performance, and any starting or ending dates, if the contract is for a specific duration.

3. **Signatures** of all parties.[16]

Everything is negotiable in a contract, including copyright. While contract law and copyright law are distinct, a contract can assign or transfer copyright. Once someone has signed over copyright in a valid contract it cannot be retrieved. A qualified attorney should work with the prospective author/producer to ensure an equitable contract, particularly with regard to licensing issues. Copyright owners have multiple rights — reproduction, distribution, adaptation, public performance, and public display. Any one of them can be signed away, individually or in part. (See Rights of the Copyright Owner, page 14.)

Subject Matter of Copyright [Section 101]

There are eight broad categories of copyright:

1. **Literary works** — books, periodicals, manuscripts, computer programs (including source code, programmable–read only memory chips [PROMS], as well as support manuals and documentation), phonorecords, film, audiotapes, disks, and computer punch cards.

2. **Musical works** (including any accompanying words) — songs, operas, and musical plays.

3. **Dramatic works** (including music) — plays and dramatic readings.

4. **Pantomimes and choreographic works.**

5. **Pictorial, graphic and sculptural works** — fine and applied art, photographs, prints and art reproductions, maps, globes, charts, technical drawings, diagrams, and models and boat hulls.[17]

6. **Motion pictures and audiovisual works** — slide/tape, multimedia presentations, filmstrips, films, videos, film loops, and film cartridges.

7. **Sound recordings and phonorecords** — disks, tapes, and cassettes.

8. **Architectural works** — the design of a building, architectural plans or drawings.

These categories overlap so that a motion picture may contain choreography and music which require separate (and in the case of music, several) licenses which must be obtained. A computer program might have copyrighted graphics by various artists and several songs by different performers, for which separate permissions and licenses must be obtained.

Ownership of Copyright as Distinct from Ownership of Material Object [Section 202]

A distinction is made between the original work of authorship and the material object. For example, a book is not an original work. It is one of a number of copies. The original work could be made into many types of copies — hardback books, paperback books, serializations in periodicals, audiotapes, phonorecords, videotapes, computer disks.[18]

Duration of Copyright [Sections 302–305] [As Amended by P.L. 105–278]

Term — The terms of copyright for the majority of works vary according to the type of authorship, the type of work, whether it was created before or after the 1976 act, before or after the 1998 Copyright Term Extension Act, and whether the work is published or unpublished. There is a difference in the term for copyrights under the 1909 law, the 1978 law and the 1998 law, the notable exceptions being motion pictures in the U.S. and Canada and other restored works, affected by NAFTA and GATT.

1998 Law

Basic Term — The life of the author plus 70 years for a work created after January 1, 1978 [Section 302(a)].

Expiration — All copyrights uniformly expire on the 31st day of December, 70 years after the author's death.

Joint Works — A work by two known living writers written after January 1, 1978, or in its first copyright term, would be the life of the last living author plus 70 years, dating from the surviving author's death [Section 302(c)].

Works for Hire — Works produced after January 1, 1978, by a company or institution are copyrighted for 95 years from publication or 120 years from creation, whichever is shorter. In this category are all print and nonprint materials by corporate authors or companies, such as Warner Bros. motion pictures [Section 101][Section 201(b)].

Pre–1978

Copyrights — A work by a known living writer in the first or renewal term of copyright at the time of the 1998 act has been extended to 95 years from the date that the copyright was originally secured.

Unpublished Works—Unpublished works existing before January 1, 1978, endure for the life of the author plus 70 years, but in no case will expire earlier than December 31, 2002. If a work is published on or before December 31, 2002, then it is protected until December 31, 2047 [Section 303].

There are additional provisions regarding sound recordings made before February 15, 1972, termination of grants and licenses, presumption of author's death, and reproduction by libraries and archives.

Registration [Sections 408–412]

Because of the Berne Convention Implementation Act (P.L. 100-568, 102 Stat. 2853) registration requirements have been relaxed. Registration can be made during the first copyright term for any published work or for any unpublished work secured after January 1, 1978.

Inducements to registration. Subject to a grace period, the chief inducement to registration is that it is a prerequisite (except for Berne Convention works whose country of origin is not the U.S.) to an infringement action [Section 411] and to the awarding of statutory damages and attorney's fees [Section 412]. For registrations made within five years after publication the court is obliged to treat the certificate of registration as "prima facie evidence of the validity of the copyright" [Section 410(c)].

Compilations and Derivative Works [Section 103]

A **compilation** is a collection of materials put together by an editor with or without the addition of annotations, introductions, supporting material, and criticism. In a compilation, only the *collection* of materials that the author chooses, their arrangement, and any contributions made by the compiler are copyrightable, not the individual works.

John Smith decides to compile a collection of poetry from 1900 to the present. He collects the poetry, arranges it, writes an introduction, annotates each of the poems involved, and writes an index and bibliography. All authors would have to lawfully agree to permission and/or payment [Section 201(c)]. This collection of poetry, including any additions, would then be registered as a compilation.

A **derivative work** is one in which the new author adapts or transforms a previous work, making a new version of it. The author of a play, in this case, would grant permission to someone to make an adaptation for film, compact disc, videodisc, or other media. For the work to be copyrightable by the person doing the derivative work, it must be made lawfully with the consent of the original author.

New Versions

New versions of works are those in which material is added to an existing work. The copyright in a new version of an existing work covers only new material. The addition of the new material does not change the expiration date of the original material to which the new material was added.[19]

Contributions to Collective Works [Section 201(c)]— Copyright Retention

Contributions to collective works (periodicals, books, anthologies, compilations) are copyrighted by a journal, for example, as a collection. There are two possible copyrights — one for the individual contributor and one for the collection. The individual copyright on the separate work may be retained by the author. While the periodical publisher may ask to retain copyright or make copyright retention by the periodical a condition of publication, the author also may wish to retain copyright and can make this request. In this way the author, and not the periodical, will be contacted by those wishing to make reprints or other requests.

Uncopyrighted Works [Section 102(b)]

There are several kinds of materials which are not eligible for protection by copyright. There are also many kinds of materials for which copyright protection is not requested.

Works in the Public Domain. There are two types of public domain works: those for which copyright protection has expired and those for which copyright protection was not requested. With the exception of Canadian or Mexican "motion pictures and works embodied in motion pictures" made by U.S. nationals between January 1, 1978, and March 1, 1989 [Section 104(a)], when copyright protection has ended for a work it falls into the public domain.[20] There are no restrictions of any kind on the use of the work. Works that ended their copyright protection before December 31, 1976, went into the public domain and copyright cannot be retrieved.

Ideas, Methods, Systems, and Principles. Copyright does not apply to ideas, methods, systems, principles, processes, or concepts. The "theory of relativity" can and should be used by anyone wishing to apply it in an article or book. In the educational context, concepts such as "accountability" and "information literacy," or other such ideas, are free to be used by anyone regardless of whose original idea it was. What can be copyrighted is the presentation of the idea in a book, article, game, and so forth.

Trademark Law. It should be noted that a trademark may be appropriate in instances in which it is desired that a name or design be protected. A trademark is:

> a word, phrase, symbol or design, or combination of words, phrases, symbols or designs, which identifies and distinguishes the source of the good or services of one part from those of others.[21]

Unlike copyrights and patents which protect original artistic or literary works, trademarks protect inventions and have 10-year renewable terms. A request for information and application can be made to the United States Patent and Trademark Office in Washington, D.C., by phone (1-800-PTO-9199) or by the Web (http://www.uspto.gov).

Common or Standard Works. Works which contain no original authorship can be freely used. Standard calendars, height and weight charts, tape measures and rulers, and lists of tables taken from public documents or other common sources are not subject to copyright protection. What can be copyrighted is the method of presentation, such as a growth chart for children consisting of height measured in inches, with each foot depicting a taller animal with a special rhyme.

Devices and Blank Forms. Devices for measuring or computing or for use in conjunction with a machine are not subject to copyright protection. Slide rules, wheel dials, nomograms, mathematical principles, formulas, equations, and devices based on them are not copyrightable. The printed material of which a device usually consists (lines, numbers, symbols, calibrations) cannot be copyrighted because the material is necessary for the idea, principle, formula, or standard of measurement involved to be used. Blank forms, or any forms designed to record rather than to convey information, cannot be copyrighted, either.

Works of the United States Government [Section 105]. Works produced by the U.S. Government are not copyrighted. Exceptions include works of the National Technical Information Service, which may have a limited copyright of up to five years, government contractors, and postage stamps.[22] In other cases U.S. government works have been republished commercially. New work that is added, such as an introduction, illustrations, or explanations, is copyrightable by the new contributor. The notice must identify those parts of the work which are not copyrighted when a work is "preponderantly" that of the U.S. Government.

Author as Source of Copyright Ownership

The source of copyright ownership is the author of the work.[23] Any work by an author in which ownership can be proven has copyright protection whether published or unpublished. The author's work is eligible for copyright protection from the time it is written or recorded in a "tangible medium of expression" [Section 101]. These two concepts are of increasing importance in electronic publishing and communications, particularly the Internet.

Rights of the Copyright Owner [Section 106]

There are five separate and exclusive rights which are granted to the copyright owner, each of which may be transferred separately or jointly. They are:

1. **Reproduction** —the right to reproduce the first or original embodiment and any copies; this right prevents anyone other than the copyright owner to make copies.

2. **Preparation of Derivative Works** —the right to produce a new version of the author's work. Derivative works include translations from one language to another, including computer languages, musical arrangements, dramatizations, fictionalization, motion picture adaptations, sound recordings, art reproductions, abridgments, condensations, or any other form in which the work is altered or adapted.

3. **Public Distribution** —the sale, gift, or other transfer of ownership, rental, lease, or lending of the author's work. If an owner chooses to sell a publisher the manuscript, then the right of public distribution is sold so that copies of the work can be distributed. In this type of transfer, the author generally contracts to be given certain royalties on the sale of the work to the public. Types of distribution, such as hardback and paperback rights and foreign distribution, are contractual.

4. **Public Performing Rights** —literary, musical, dramatic, and choreographic works, pantomimes, motion pictures, and other audiovisual works. The following would constitute a performance of a work: live renditions that are face to face, renditions from recordings, broadcasting, retransmission by cable or microwave. To "perform publicly" is defined as a performance at an establishment open to the public or where a substantial number of persons outside of a normal circle of a family and its social acquaintances is gathered.

5. **Public Display** —to display a work by means of film, slide, television image, or any other type of device. Motion pictures and other audiovisual works are considered exhibitions rather then displays. Public display applies to any work embodied in a manuscript or in printed matter, and in pictorial, graphic, and sculptural works, including motion picture "stills."[24]

Works for Hire [Section 101][Section 201(b)]

A "work for hire" is a work produced by an employee or contractor within the scope of employment. The statute does not define "employee" for work-for-hire purposes, although several factors are taken into consideration, such as the hiring party's right to control the "manner and means by which the work is done," skills required, duration of employee-hiring party's relationship, etc.[25] In such a case the copyright is owned by the person or entity who hired the employee to produce the work.

In the case of librarians and educators a work for hire could include a syllabus, library information pamphlet, Web site, or other materials created within the normal scope of duties. Works produced at home or without substantial use of institutional facilities are generally considered to be the property of the author, although there is no "clear, bright line."[26]

If an independent author produces a print or non-print work, whether or not the resulting work will be a "work for hire" depends on the type of contract. The employment contract for a school district, college, university, or other educational institution may have an institutional ownership clause or refer to the faculty or student handbook, which may also have such a clause. Otherwise, the terms of the individual contract would apply, if there is one. If the independent author signs a contract that the resulting work is a "work for hire," then the independent author does not retain copyright because the agreement stipulated that this was to be so.[27] It is best to ask for a contract in any situation in which the terms of work creation are unclear.

If a work is "specially ordered or commissioned" [Section 101] for use as one of the categories of works enumerated in the statute and the parties "expressly agree" in writing, then the work is to be considered a "work for hire." These categories are: a contribution to a collective work (such as a periodical), part of a motion picture or other audiovisual work, a translation, a supplementary work (see Section 101 for the definition of "supplementary work"), a compilation, an instructional test, a test, answer material for a test, and an atlas, for example.

> [C]omputer programs can be works made for hire *only* if they are created by an employee within the scope of her employment.[28]

When a work is commissioned by an institution or other entity, rather than produced within the scope of the employee's normal work activities, then it is in the best interest of the employee to ask for a written contract that should be signed by the parties stating the purpose of the work commissioned by the institution and the rights and obligations of the author and the institution.[29] Otherwise, such a work would fall into the "work for hire" category under the terms of most employee yearly contracts.

Fixation

The most basic concept in copyright law is that of fixation.[30] Any work has copyright protection eligibility the minute it is "fixed in a tangible medium of expression." This does not mean that copyright protection is assured even though a work has not been registered with the Copyright Office. Fixation is a device to ensure that both published and unpublished works in all lawfully protected copyright categories are protected by federal statute whether the form is in words, numbers, notes, graphic or symbolic indicia, sculpture, architectural drawings, etc.

Copies

According to Section 101:

> "copies" are material objects, other than phonorecords, in which a work is fixed by any now known or later developed method and from which the work can be perceived, reproduced, or otherwise communicated, either directly or with the aid of a machine or device. The term "copies" includes the material object, other than a phonorecord, in which the work is first fixed.

"What is a copy?" constitutes an almost metaphysical discussion when connected not only with traditional reprographics but also compounded with the concept of "fixation" when used in conjunction with computers, compact discs, e-mail, listservs and electronic journals published via the Internet.[31]

There is, in Section 102, the stipulation that works may be fixed in different ways "in a tangible medium of expression, *now known or later developed*" (italics are added). This provision provides Congress "considerable room for technological advances in the area of fixation" as noted by the Information Infrastructure Task Force (1995 September).[32] According to this definition copies can be fixed in any tangible medium, whether by print, videotape, e-mail or the Internet. Moreover, according to the *House Report 94-1476* accompanying the Copyright Act of 1976, Congress intended the terms "copies" and "phonorecords" to comprise all of the material objects in which copyrightable works are capable of being fixed.[33]

However, the 1998 act has provided a "safe harbor" for various kinds of transitory copies in the digital environment. Nonprofit libraries, archives, and educational institutions may gain access to a commercial copyrighted work in order to make a good faith determination of whether or not to acquire the work [Section 402]. Broadcasters are also allowed to make permitted ephemeral reproductions. Title II of the 1998 act also limits online service provider's liability for copyright infringement in several important situations. Liability for transitory copies — the storing of material at user request, referring users to material at other online locations (such as through links), system caching (in which the online service provider makes a temporary copy of material at the request of the user) and transmission and routing (providing connections for material through the service provider's system and for intermediate and transient storage of material in such activities)— have all been exempted if monetary, and injunctive relief has been limited if certain conditions are met.

Infringement [Sections 501–510]

To "infringe" copyright means to violate any of the five exclusive rights: reproduction, preparation of a derivative work, public distribution, public performance, and public display. An infringer could unwittingly violate one or more of the copyright owner's rights. For example, if the drama teacher bought one copy of a play, reproduced several copies for the cast, and later performed the play for the public without paying performance royalties and charged admission, then the teacher would be guilty of two separate violations: reproduction and public performance.

Remedies for an infringement include: injunction [Section 502], impounding and disposing of infringing articles [Section 503], actual or statutory damages and profits [Section 504], costs and attorney's fees [Section 505], and criminal offenses [Section 506], which include forfeiture and destruction, fraudulent copyright notice, fraudulent removal of copyright notice, false representation, and rights of attribution and integrity. States and governmental entities can be sued for copyright infringement.[34]

In pursuing an infringement suit, the copyright owner could choose two avenues — actual damages, including additional profits made by the infringer, or statutory damages [Section 504]. The penalties increase if the defendant is found guilty of criminal infringement (see Criminal Infringement, page 18).

Actual damages— The copyright owner could choose to recover actual damages and any profits of the infringer that are attributable to the infringement. For example, the costs of copies of a play distributed to cast members by photocopying, the royalty for the number of nights that the play was shown, and perhaps all or a percentage of the profits that the play took in could be requested as damages, and a fine could be imposed.

Statutory damages — The copyright owner could collect from one or more infringers, depending on whether or not the infringement was deemed criminal and the type of offense (circumvention of copyright protection systems, phonorecordings, and so forth, not less than $500 or up to $1,000,000 [Section 504 and Section 1204]. "In a case where the copyright owner sustains the burden of proving" a willful infringement [Section 504(c)(2)], then the court can increase the award to not more than $100,000. "In a case where the infringer sustains the burden of proving, and the court finds, that such infringer was not aware … that his or her act constituted infringement … [the fine may be reduced] to a sum of not less than $200" [Section 504(c)(2)].

Court costs and attorney's fees could be awarded at the court's discretion [Section 505]. If the defendant lost, he or she could be ordered to pay court costs and attorney's fees for both sides. Time lost due to court appearances can be a major consideration. In most cases, the institution or business would be named as co-defendant in the suit. In addition, the employee or corporate officer could also be liable for contributory infringement.[35]

The "Innocent Infringer" Provision [Section 504(c)(2)][36]

Help for nonprofit users in the form of the "innocent infringer" provision was widely discussed before its adoption into law. It was designed to provide broad insulation for teachers, librarians, archivists, public broadcasters, and the nonprofit institutions of which they are a part.

> The court shall remit statutory damages in any case where an infringer believed and had reasonable grounds for believing that his or her use of the copyrighted work was a fair use under section 107, if the infringer was: (i) an employee or agent of a nonprofit educational institution, library, or archives acting within the scope of his or her employment who, or such institution, library, or archives itself, which infringed by reproducing the work in copies or phonorecords; or (ii) a public broadcasting entity which or a person who, as a regular part of nonprofit activities of a public broadcasting entity (as defined in subsection b(g) of section 118) infringed by performing a published nondramatic literary work or by reproducing a transmission program embodying a performance of such a work.

In this case, statutory damages will be waived. In these cases, the "burden of proof" would be on the defendant to prove good faith and innocence of any wrongdoing.

Criminal Infringement

Criminal infringement occurs when any person infringes a copyright willfully and for purposes of "commercial advantage or private financial gain"

[Section 506(a)]. The educational or nonprofit infringer would rarely be found guilty of such a use. However, it is important to note that the penalties for criminal infringement are: 1) imprisonment for 1 to 10 years, depending on the type of infringement [Section 2319(a)(1–3)]; and 2) the "maximum fine for an individual who has been found guilty of an offense is $250,000; the maximum fine for an organization that has been found guilty of an offense is $500,000" [Section 3571ff. of Title 18, U.S.C.] and for circumvention of copyright protection systems it can be as high as $1,000,000 [1204(a)(1)].[37]

Cease and Desist Letters

As a first step before a court action is begun, an attorney for the copyright owner (plaintiff) would likely (1) write a "cease and desist" letter to the person(s) and/or the institution; and (2) the attorney would ask that he/she cease the infringing activities and not do them anymore (desist). The letter would enumerate the activities/use of copyrighted materials in question, may state the consequences of further use of the materials, ask that materials be purchased or erased, or state resulting legal action and fines that the copyright owner will take should such activities continue. Most often educational institutions halt such activities and court action is not initiated as a consequence. As a condition of such cessation the violations are often not made public.

The Two Questions to Ask About a Questionable Use

It is helpful to always remember that when using copyrighted materials one must envision oneself on the witness stand in a court trial. Any instance of alleged copyright infringement ultimately will come down to two attorneys in a court room with a judge and possibly a jury. Inevitably, because the circumstances of each case are different and open to interpretation, there will be a contest between which side presents the best case. While envisioning oneself on the witness stand, one should ask oneself these questions:

1. Is this an unethical use?
2. Could this use harm the author's market?

If the answer to either of these questions is "yes," then it is best not to proceed.

Steps in Developing an Infringement Case

While there are many steps and avenues in litigations that are dependent upon the individual circumstances of each case, below is a brief listing of what a school or institution could face at a trial. There are two main elements of copyright infringement: ownership of a valid copyright and copying by the defendant of protectable material.[38]

According to Robert C. Osterberg[39] the steps in preparing a copyright owner's case include:

Initial evaluation — Witnesses are interviewed, and the copyright is evaluated. Except for foreign works and pending registrations, "no action for infringement of the copyright in any work shall be instituted until registration of the copyright claim has been made" [Section 411(a)].

Selecting the defendants — This includes choosing people involved in the chain of command, such as the instructor/librarian/employee, principal, superintendent, board of education or regents, and any employees involved directly or indirectly in the alleged infringement.

Pretrial remedies — preliminary injunctions, seizure, impounding of articles.

Pretrial preparation — depositions (taking written statements of witnesses to the infringement), contacting any experts.

Trial presentation — There are five elements to a plaintiff's case: copyright ownership and its validity, access of the accused author, copying, use of the original protected portion, and substantial similarity, if it applies. The purpose of these elements is to show that the resulting work was based on using the copyright owner's original work.

Other **copyright owner** aspects are: actual damages, infringer's profits (if any), statutory damages (if applicable), a permanent injunction (use has to be stopped not just now but also in the future), destruction of materials seized and impounded, costs, and a reasonable attorney's fee.

Other **copyright user** aspects are: offering the burden of proof that profits and damages did not exist, usually through expert testimony.

An "**innocent infringer**" in a nonprofit educational institution [Section 504(c)(2)], may avoid statutory damages by offering the burden of proof that the person had no knowledge that this was illegal use.

While there are many other aspects to a trial, these should make the copyright owner and user more knowledgeable about some of the aspects of a trial should court action be initiated.

Searching for Copyright Information Online

Search the Copyright Office by Internet — Copyright Office records of works cataloged or indexed from 1978 to date are available over the Internet. These include information concerning registrations and documents that have been recorded. To connect by Web go to http://lcweb.loc.gov/copyright or

Telnet to 140.147.254.3 or marvel.loc.gov and login as "marvel" to access the system. Then select the "Copyright" menu.

Pay the Copyright Office to Search — The Copyright Office will search for the copyright status of a work upon request. There is a fee.

Copyright Office Information —

Forms Hotline (202) 707-9100 (24 hours a day)

Forms and Information (202) 707-3000

Fax on Demand for Circulars and/or Announcements (202) 707-2600

TTY (202) 707-6737

Can Do

You may:

1. Make fair use of unpublished works.

2. Reproduce or distribute copies or phonorecords of previously published, nondramatic literary works, if they are in specialized formats for the blind or persons with other disabilities, as long as it is a nonprofit organization or governmental entity.

3. As a copyright owner, transfer one or any combination of your five rights to another party.

4. Register a work for copyright protection in order to sue for infringement and to receive statutory damages and attorney's fees.

5. Freely use works in the public domain or works for which copyright was never requested.

6. Freely use U.S. Government works, excluding the National Technical Information Agency (five-year copyright), government contractor works, and postage stamps.

7. Request, as a faculty or staff member, that a contract be signed, either for separate compensation or "work for hire" purposes, to clarify your legal rights with respect to works initiated or requested outside your normal scope of employment.

8. Make three digital copies of a work to preserve it if the machinery to view the work is no longer available through standard commercial outlets.

Cannot Do

You may not:

1. Assume that because you have a copy of something you own the work. You only own the copy.

2. Sue for copyright infringement without applying for copyright registration first.

3. Make a compilation and copyright anything other than the collection itself, its arrangement, and your own contributions. Permission is still required for the separate works included.

4. Make a derivative work without permission from the author.

5. Copyright an idea. Only the presentation of that idea can be copyrighted.

6. Copyright a blank form, equation, or principle.

Tried and True

1. A work is eligible for copyright protection once it is written or recorded in a "tangible medium of expression." This includes e-mail.

2. Copyright notice has not been necessary since 1989.

Beware

Ask yourself two questions before you copy a work:

1. Is this an ethical use?
2. Could this use harm the author's market?

If either answer is "yes," then don't proceed.

Part II
Uses of
Copyrighted Materials

2

Exceptions to Author's Rights: Section 107, "Fair Use"

The fair use doctrine, codified for the first time in Section 107 of the 1976 law, is over 150 years old.[1] It can be defined as a public usage for which the copyright owner is not remunerated, presumably because it is minimal and because it is in the public interest. Such a use balances the "dissemination of knowledge with the negligibility of use."[2] Copyright authority Saul Cohen, in perhaps the definitive expression of what constitutes fair use, expressed the feeling of the courts:

> This is really a pretty trifling and insignificant thing the defendant has done; he acted reasonably, he meant no harm, he has not profited greatly and the plaintiff is not really hurt; so, we will not find any infringement by this use.[3]

Fair use was developed as all judicial doctrines are, by precedent. Historically, it has developed from a little-used defense in infringement cases to a widely-accepted doctrine of important use and scope.[4] The Supreme Court has ruled only four times on fair use.[5] In recent years, however, there has been a growing number of university faculty and librarians that believe that "fair use" has been eroded through narrow interpretation.[6]

Sinofsky (1995) summarized this position:

> [T]hese new [multimedia] guidelines ... provide a standard — a much needed one — against which to judge copyright-related matters. However, somewhere along the way, the original two guidelines (print and music) have become set in stone, the flexibility to handle special instances seemingly abandoned. Reread their introductory matter. Both refer to stating *minimum*, not maximum fair-use standards. When was the last time you heard anyone refer to these guidelines as "minimum"?[7]

The author concurs.

The doctrine draws its substance from the same constitutional clause as copyright, because it is believed to be necessary in order to "promote the progress of science and the useful arts."[8] This concept was evident in the first Copyright Act of 1790, which closely resembled the English copyright statute.[9] It was called "an act for the encouragement of learning." The purpose of the "fair use" doctrine was the public good.[10] While each case is different, the law's purpose was not complicated use computation. Fair use is an "equitable rule of reason."[11] Responsible use requires some knowledge, some consideration, and a practical, flexible policy.

The Four Criteria

The thrust of the four fair use criteria is most often found to be economic.[12] However, each of the four criteria is important in fair use considerations.[13] An understanding of these four factors can help provide an answer to the question "How can I comply with the law?" and it is often just common sense.[14] While technology and circumstances change, the basic rationale remains essentially the same.[15]

The four factors of the fair use doctrine act as weighted measures.[16] In some cases the purpose of the use would be sufficient to make a use unfair. In another situation, the amount of the use, while small in quantitative terms, might be so qualitatively essential to a copyright owner's market that such a use could harm the potential market of an author. Each of these four factors should be considered in using both print and nonprint materials.[17]

1. **Purpose and character of the use**—This is how the material is used, such as for profit or nonprofit purposes, and the intent for which it was made. If the purpose of the use of a work is to make a profit, such as taking a copyrighted graphic from a commercial Web site and putting it on your own commercial Web site, then that use requires permission or licensing. A nonprofit use would depend more on the particular circumstances of the use.[18]

2. **Nature of the copyrighted work**—This is the expectation of the author and society of the work's value and use, as well as whether or not the work is scholarly or commercial.[19] If the work is scholarly, then the expectation of the author and publisher would be that the work would be used for educational or research purposes. While the author isn't generally paid, and often must pay for defraying the cost of publication in some fields, it is a professional courtesy to request permission for uses over the guidelines. Historically, fair use of scholarly/informational work is accorded greater latitude, except when the copying is systematic and large scale (see *American Geophysical Union v. Texaco* case in Library Reproduction Rights, Chapter 11). Permission requests

gauge the acceptance of the author's work professionally and in most cases are part of the merit system of an institution.

The expectation of an author who writes articles for *Atlantic Monthly* or produces films or music, is that fair use will be made of the work in the non-profit/educational context and that the work will not be substantially used by another writer to make a profit.

3. ***The amount and substantiality of the material used***—This is how much of the work is used, both qualitatively and quantitatively. Amount is an important factor for all materials, particularly print materials.[20] The "substantiality" of a work is considered in terms of how important the portion used is in relation to the work as a whole. This factor is very important in music, for example. A line or melodic phrase could be the identifying or key part of the song. A particular algorithm could be the key to a certain type of program. While amount is usually considered to be length, substantiality is a qualitative judgment and is concerned with the importance of the amount taken in relation to the entire work.[21]

4. ***The effect of the use on the potential market of the work***—This involves an estimate of the expected purchasing audience of the work. While all the rest of the factors deal indirectly with economics, this criterion deals specifically with actual or estimated market loss.[22] In fact, this factor is in many cases the determining factor for fair use.

A "fifth" factor is good faith. Courts take all four factors into consideration. However, in recent years these factors have also been balanced with that of good faith and the "public interest" when deciding on the evaluation of fair use. "Courts may weigh the propriety of the defendant's conduct in the equitable balance of a fair use determination."[23]

The Three Fair Use Tests

The three tests as described in the *House Report*—brevity, spontaneity, and cumulative effect—are increasingly important in determining the parameters of uses that are considered fair.[24] Computer networks, distance education, ISDN, and wide area networks, make copying small amounts into a large aggregate amount unlike a class of 25 students in one classroom or, at most, several sections of a class taught by one instructor in a classroom. These three tests are:

1. **Brevity**—The relative amount of what is copied should be brief, for example, 250 words for poems, 2,500 words or 10 percent of articles, stories, and so forth as given in the fair use charts (see Appendix A) for various types of print and nonprint material uses.[25]

2. **Spontaneity**—For a work to be considered spontaneous it must not

be needed enough ahead of time that reprints or permission could be acquired. This criterion is designed to capture the "teachable" moment when something is needed for the classroom immediately. It is concerned with the intent in making copies and emphasizes responsible use and "good faith."[26]

3. *Cumulative effect*—This is aggregate use, the combination of small uses that rise to such a proportion that economic harm is done to the potential market of an author. Cumulative effect is the result of many one-time or class-sized unauthorized uses of a chapter of a book or an article, for example, across a large district, college, company, or network.[27]

Because this test is the most difficult to evaluate, someone, whether in the central administration, the library, audiovisual department, copy center, continuing education division or elsewhere, should be designated to take an overall look at the copying practices of the institution, as the American Library Association has recommended (1995).[28]

Coursepaks and the Three Fair Use Tests

Two cases involving the use of "coursepaks," reading packets requested by professors from copying services, were pivotal for the educational community in terms of the application of the three tests and illustrate the increasing reliance upon these tests in fair use determinations when large numbers of copies are involved. *Princeton University Press v. Michigan Document Services* (1994) and *Basic Books, Inc. v. Kinko's Graphic Corp.* (1991) both involved the making of coursepaks for students in universities.[29] The defendants argued that their service was fair use since no economic benefit was received by the professors. Also, more than 100 authors indicated that monetary rewards were secondary. However, the courts rejected the fair use argument in the context of high-volume, organized, and repetitive copying by the copy shops. This decision, along with the *Texaco* decision,[30] illustrates that the limits of professional fair use, even without monetary gain, do not extend beyond these tests, which will play an increasingly larger part of fair use determinations in electronic distribution systems, particularly the Internet.

The Sliding Scale

Copyright law seeks to balance owner's rights with user's rights. As such, it is a dynamic balance which changes with technology and usage. The four fair use factors are always weighed individually and also on a continuum of profit/nonprofit uses and profit/nonprofit works, much like a sliding scale. It is helpful in copyright determinations to view usage in this fashion. For example, a nonprofit work, such as a scholarly article, used for a nonprofit use, such as a classroom one, would be among the most acceptable of fair uses. A profit work, such as a popular song, used by a producer of a commercial for television during the Super Bowl, would clearly not be fair use and would need to be licensed. All other works fall in between. The three fair use tests must also be taken into consideration.

Can Do

You may:

1. Consider the four fair use criteria when deciding upon the use or reproduction of copyrighted materials:
    a. purpose and character of the use,
    b. nature of the copyrighted work,
    c. amount and substantiality of the material used, and
    d. effect of the use on the potential market of the work.
2. Consider the sliding scale when deciding to make fair use of a work.
3. Consider the three tests when deciding to make fair use of works for large courses, particularly over unsecured electronic, satellite, or other networks:
    a. brevity,
    b. spontaneity, and
    c. cumulative effect.

Cannot Do

You may not:

1. Assume that because a use is for educational purposes it is a fair use.
2. Copy a part of a commercial work for a commercial purpose and consider it to be a fair use.
3. Assume that a key (substantial) part of a work is a fair use just because the amount is small.

Tried and True

Fair use is for purposes of research, scholarship, criticism, or parody.

Tip

Don't reproduce copyrighted cartoon characters on school newspapers or on the walls of school buildings. "Where Disney characters have been painted on walls, the schools have been ordered to repaint the wall in order to erase the Disney characters."[31]

3

Print Materials

Educational Guidelines for Nonprofit Copying

The "Agreement on Guidelines for Classroom Copying in Not-for-Profit Educational Institutions" (see Appendix D) was developed by the Ad Hoc Committee on Copyright Law (representing many educational associations) and two author-publisher groups. The guidelines were meant to be stated as a "reasonable interpretation of the minimum and not the maximum standard" for use.[1] In recent years there has been criticism from some experts that the guidelines have been used as a maximum instead of a "rule of thumb."[2] They were drawn in accordance with the policies of a large number of authors and users for the majority of instances.[3] Chart 1 in Appendix A provides a simplified interpretation of usage for print materials.

Reproduction of Print Material — Usage Examples

Examples of usage for print, special print, and nonprofit materials are provided alphabetically within these categories. When more than one type of material is listed, the use should be treated the same for all types listed in that category; for example, essay collections, anthologies, and encyclopedias are listed as one category, and their use is the same.

1. *Architectural drawings*—May an instructor make an overhead transparency of a drawing from a book of drawings for use in art class? *Yes. Leave artist's name on the transparency.

2. *Children's books and "special works"*—To illustrate a point in story telling, may an instructor photocopy a page of the children's book being discussed for each student in the class to evaluate? *Yes. Special works can be children's books or any work which combines a comparatively small amount of prose and many illustrations, such as Shel Silverstein's *The Giving Tree*.

3. *Encyclopedias and anthologies*—A teacher wants to photocopy two

essays, totaling 3,000 words, from a current encyclopedia volume to be distributed to students in a creative writing class. ***Maybe.** The general rule for excerpts from this type of material is 2,500 words in an excerpt or essay. This amount exceeds the guidelines, though not to a great degree. The *House Report* notes that there may be instances which legitimately exceed the guidelines; however, caution is advised.

4. ***Government documents***—For a fifth-grade project on soil testing, the teacher wants to copy five pages from a 20-page U.S. government pamphlet, for students to use. There was no copyright mark. Is this permissible? ***Yes.** Government pamphlets are generally free to be used because they are in the public domain. The only exception would be if there was a copyright symbol. This generally means that the work was contracted and given copyright. Fair use rules would have to be followed as with other copyrighted materials. Government documents, pamphlets, books, etc., are nearly always copyright free.

5. ***Lectures, sermons, speeches***—A history instructor wishes to photocopy an 1100-word speech of Alfred North Whitehead for a unit on World War II. The speech is in a collection of published speeches found in the library. It will be distributed to a history class. ***Yes.** Fair use can be made of speeches found in a published work. Section 107 was amended in 1992 so that unpublished speeches, lectures, and sermons existing before January 1, 1978, are subject to fair use.[4] However, unpublished works, not yet in the public domain, are protected for the life of the known author plus 50 years. Works under the new law for which the life plus 50 term has expired or would expire soon are still protected until the year 2002.

6. ***Maps, charts, graphs, cartoons***— To illustrate the change in political maps for a class, the instructor would like to take two maps each out of two textbooks and two periodicals to make overhead transparencies for class. ***No.** The rule for these materials is one per issue or one per book. However, if the use was spontaneous, the circumstance would be different and could exceed the rule somewhat.

7. ***Newspapers, current news sections of periodicals***—For a current events project, the teacher requires the students to keep a notebook on some aspect of world affairs. At the end of the unit, would it be permissible to have each student copy the materials in the folder and distribute them to their classmates? All the students would then have a bound folder for further reference during the next two units. ***Yes.** Both newspapers and current news sections of periodicals are subject to free use — any amount can be legally copied for any purpose.

8. ***Novels, nonfiction, textbooks, theses***—In a current-trends-in-fiction class, students are encouraged to copy 250-word, one-page excerpts from the novels that they are studying. May the students be allowed to collect the excerpts and distribute them to other members of the class? Four excerpts would be required for criticism and comment. ***Yes.** A 1,000-word excerpt is

allowed twice per class per term. Four 250-word excerpts, while not in line with the cumulative rule, add up to the amount rule for term use. Other copying should be curtailed. On the other hand, one 2,000-word excerpt takes more from an individual author, and therefore could potentially do more harm; so more caution would have to be used in taking a larger amount from an individual author than small amounts from different authors.

9. *Photographs, pictures*—To illustrate different kinds of Pacific Northwest flora, a biology instructor would like to make two transparencies from a current periodical that has pictures of various kinds of plants. *Yes, as long as the photographs are not individually copyrighted. If there is a copyright on each picture, then none of the pictures could be used without permission. (This is most often the case in print works.)

10. *Poetry*—For a modern poetry section, an instructor would like to make photocopies of small portions of song lyrics of four songs and also copy two entire songs in order to illustrate rhyme schemes. The entire songs would be made into transparencies for one-time classroom use. The smaller portions of songs would be used as portions of test questions for a quiz. *Yes. The entire songs would not be distributed to the class, and the number of songs used for transparencies was small. Multiple copies of entire songs should not be made. Using only a small amount of each song would put the use within the guidelines if treated as lyrics only. If the instructor used more than a small amount, or handed out copies of several complete songs for students to use, then it would be considered unfair use. If, on the other hand, students were encouraged to bring one or more copies of songs that they had chosen individually for study and comment, this would be better because one author's song has not been distributed to an entire class.

11. *Short stories, essays*—A seventh-grade English teacher would like to take two stories, totaling 7,500 words, from a living writer's one-volume story collection. The teacher would then like to distribute them to students in a creative writing class. *No, the rule is a 2,500-word excerpt or story, although this may vary according to the "spontaneity" test. However, 7,500 words clearly exceeds the guidelines. Using reprints would be wiser, both in terms of time and expense.

Special Categories in the Educational Setting

Student Publications

Campus student publications, such as the newspaper or literary magazine, should follow the fair use guidelines closely. If these publications are sold, then greater care should be used. Occasionally, there are cases involving infringement in student publications, generally involving the newspaper, so faculty advisors should make sure that fair use is followed.[5]

The liability of the school for the content of the publications of its students is largely dependent on the relationship of the institution to the publication. If the publication is featured as part of a school or university activity, if it is supported by the institutional treasury, and if the institution has the right to review articles, then the university or school's liability for what is printed is increased. Student editors should be instructed that quotes of a substantial part of a work should require permission, which will generally be granted with a fee. Journalism departments are well-versed in these issues.

Classes of College and University Works

The ownership of faculty and student work is a matter with both philosophical and practical, monetary consequences.[6] Most large universities have a clause which states that when substantial university resources are used in developing intellectual property or for data collection then these products are the property of the university.[7] It is generally the case that professors own the copyright to works they produce, even on academic time, if they do not use substantial university resources.[8] "Substantial" is not always defined in policies but it means facilities, such as labs, equipment, media facilities, and computer centers, which are university-owned or supported. Unsponsored research which does not use substantial resources could fall under "work for hire" or be excluded through a specific statement for certain categories. Some universities state that certain categories of works are not claimed as university property by their nature — monographs, literary, and artistic creations. Technological works typically involve substantial resources even if unsponsored (see section in Internet chapter). In large universities there is a procedure to handle inventions and proprietary works but copyrighted materials, with few exceptions, such as computer software, typically do not involve heavy university expenditures. In the case of federally-sponsored research, federal law, the Bayh-Dole Act (35 U.S.C. 200), provides for the university ownership of intellectual properties.

Live Performances of Dramatic Works

Performances would be exempt where the performers contributed their time. If admission was charged, "after deducting the reasonable costs of producing the performance," the proceeds must be "used exclusively for educational, religious, or charitable purposes and not for private financial gain."[9] In the event of an admission charge, the copyright owner must be given an opportunity to decide "whether and under what conditions the copyrighted work should be performed."[10] If the copyright owner objected in writing at least seven days before the performance, then that performance would be canceled.[11]

Photocopying in the College and University

The role of the university is that of vanguard, forming the "cutting edge" of intellectual advancement. Because of higher education's greater need for up-to-date materials, the formulation of the guidelines for educational copying caused some concern in higher education when they first appeared.[12] The *House Report 94-1476*, which contained the guidelines, addressed this concern. The *Report* noted that the Association of American University Professors and the Association of American Law Schools had written the committee "strongly criticizing" the guidelines as being too restrictive for classroom teaching at the university and graduate level.

In reply, the *Report* reaffirmed that the purpose of the guidelines was to state the "minimum and not the maximum standards" of educational fair use and that the agreement acknowledged that "there may be instances in which copying which does not fall within the guidelines ... may nonetheless be permitted under the criteria of fair use. The committee believes the guidelines are a reasonable interpretation of the minimum standards of fair use."[13] The elasticity of the guidelines, particularly in the college and university setting, was clarified, The Ad Hoc Committee replied:

> The guidelines are intended as a "safe harbor," assuring the teacher who stays within their scope that he or she will not be liable for infringement. They do not speak at all to the possible additional uses that are still protected by the fair use doctrine.... In short, there is potentially a great deal of educational photocopying beyond that set forth in the guidelines that will clearly be lawful in the future as it has been in the past.[14]

Copyright Clearance Center

The Copyright Clearance Center (CCC) is a nonprofit organization established in 1971 by authors, publishers, and users of copyrighted material. The CCC grants permissions for print materials through the Academic Permissions Service (APS) and the Transactional Reporting Service (TRS). The APS provides permission and fee information for over 9,200 publishers. The TRS provides instant photocopy authorizations for more than 1.75 million publications: scholarly, technical, medical, legal, and trade journals. Users may obtain clearance for use of copyrighted materials on corporate internets. Web-based licensing and permissions are available at http://www.copyright.com/ and their annual service fee is nominal.

The CCC initiated the Comprehensive Rightsholders' Photocopy Agreement. This consolidates contracts into one inclusive agreement and places the CCC into position for adding multiple levels of rights across a wider range of media. Online licensing of photographs began in 1997 — Media Image Resource Alliance (MIRA) in partnership with the American Society of Media Photographers and Applied Graphics Technologies, Inc. The address is: Copyright Clearance Center, Inc., 222 Rosewood Drive, Danvers, MA 01923, 508-750-8400.

Can Do

You may:

1. Copy articles for course purposes, provided that the copying limitations of the Simplified Guidelines for Print Materials are followed (see Appendix A, Chart 1).[15]
2. Make single copies of articles for instruction and research.[16]
3. Make multiple copies of an article for classroom use.

Cannot Do

You may not:

1. Make copies of workbooks, study guides, manuals, standardized tests and test booklets.[17] Fair use does not apply to "consumables."
2. Photocopy poems, stories, and essays to substitute for an anthology.
3. Distribute electronic copies of an article to all company employees through the company intranet without copyright permission.

Tried and True

Photocopying small amounts of material is advertising. Photocopying small amounts repeatedly or large amounts of material is theft (and it's expensive).

Beware

1. Publisher representatives will check a campus copy center's copyright compliance anonymously.
2. Because a work is "out-of-print" does not mean that it is also out of copyright protection.

4
Music

Five Basic Rights of the Copyright Owner

Under the copyright law, there are five basic rights of the copyright owner which apply to songwriters.[1] They have the right to:

1. Make copies or phonorecords of the song. This includes recording the song, using the song in movie sound tracks, print sheet music, and music sampling.
2. Distribute copies or phonorecords of the song. Typically, distribution rights are included with the mechanical, synchronization, and print licenses which the publisher issues.
3. Perform the song publicly. Performance venues and broadcasters pay license fees to ASCAP, BMI, and SESAC, the three U.S. performing-right societies for this right. The money is then paid to publishers and writers.
4. Make derivative versions of the song. Most often this applies to print arrangements and advertising jingle versions.

An additional right for license purposes is the:

5. Digital audio transmission right for owners of sound recordings.[2]

Nonprofit Uses of Music

Classroom uses of music and certain types of performances are exempt in nonprofit educational institutions (see Appendix A).[3] It is not necessary for schools to secure rights to give performances of nondramatic musical works (plays and operas are dramatic works). However, if admission is charged at a nonprofit performance, the proceeds must only be used for educational or charitable purposes.[4]

The Emergency Performance Rule

The one exception to copying is the emergency performance rule. Emergency copies can replace purchased copies, which for any reason are not available for imminent performance, provided that purchased copies are substituted later. For example, shortly before a school band is to play a concert, the music teacher learns that six students have lost their music. The teacher is then entitled to make replacement copies for that performance. Later, the lost music would have to be purchased again.[5]

Musical Excerpts in Books

References to musical excerpts in books require that a publisher obtain permission for such a use by an author, since a few bars of a song can constitute the melodic line. Apart from a specific limitation, fair use of music is beset with peril and should only be done with great caution, for the principles are clear enough but their application in specifics is not.[6] It should also be noted that infringement cases in music, both religious and secular, occur frequently.[7] F.E.L. Publications, Ltd., won a decision over the Catholic Bishop of Chicago Archdiocese in the amount of $3,000,000 in actual damages and $1,000,000 in punitive damages.[8] The highest profile case in recent years involved someone posting many of a church's works on the Internet.[9] Even though the amounts used were small in some cases, they were the "heart" of the work. Another such case involved uploading and downloading music to and from CompuServe by subscribers. CompuServe had to pay $500,000 in damages for over 550 music compositions used in this manner and had to work with publishers to develop licensing for online users.[10]

College and University Satellite Distance Education Music Licensing

Most university campus distance education providers purchase sets of compact discs from various producers which are licensed for a time period. Such use is considered "non-broadcast"; this type of licensing service is available and is advertised in satellite periodicals. Newer satellite systems have a PIN system which restricts reception, thereby controlling reception and further limiting liability for "non-broadcast" use.

Music Licensing — Overview

Music licensing has many elements. While music may be used within the classroom for educational purposes (see Multimedia and the Fair Use Guidelines, Chapter 8), using music in other instances requires licensing or permission. Licensing music for these other uses is complex, expensive, and a number of entities control parts of the music. There are performers, songwriters, and instrumentalists who create the music. There is a record company that produces the recording. A song consists of the composition (the notes), written by one or more persons, and the lyrics (the words sung to the notes), written by another person or persons. The vocal and instrumental performance of a song makes up a third aspect of music. Each of these elements must be cleared for reuse in a new production."[11] In addition, U.S. law allows arrangements of musical works to be copyrighted separately from the original work.[12]

It should also be noted that a short clip of music in the classroom for a one-time project that is erased is fair use. In some cases, educators have called record companies for this permission, not knowing that such use was legal, and have received responses from "yes" to a $1,500 charge for such a use. It is best to be familiar with music fair use.

Commercial Music Distribution

Ephemeral Recordings

Several changes were made in these two acts to conform to transmission, licensing, and use in the commercial digital music environment. In brief, Title II of the Term Extension Act, "Fairness in Music Licensing Act of 1998," allows exemptions for the transmission of retransmission of audiovisual works by satellite or cable and nondramatic musical works by radio or television broadcast station for food service and drinking establishments under 2,000 gross square feet with less than six loudspeakers, no more than four in one room, not more than four audiovisual devices, and so forth, and there must be no admission charge. Guidelines for reasonable rates for license fees for individual proprietors were also included. The Digital Millennium Copyright Act extends to broadcasters the same privilege to transmit that they have with analog broadcasts [Section 402]. Section 405 amends Section 114 and tries to ensure that recording artists and recording companies will be protected with new technologies and the create better licensing systems for digital audio services. Section 405 also amends Section 112 offers a statutory license for certain types of digital reproductions called "ephemeral recordings" and facilitates licensing for such recordings by Internet music services.

License Types

Nonclassroom and/or commercial uses of music have several license types which are available from several sources. If a student or faculty member wished to develop a project that would eventually be available commercially, then some knowledge of these types of licenses would be helpful. In most instances, however, the NMPA/Harry Fox Agency (see Appendix B and page 42) would prove helpful for music licensing purposes. NMPA/Harry Fox has a Web site at the http://www.nmpa.org/hfa.html address. Licenses available from Harry Fox and other record labels and agencies include:

A **mechanical** license needs to be obtained when a song is to be played without being synchronized to a video. For example, music would be played as a background for a montage of photos. If an album includes one or more cover songs, then a mechanical license is required.[13] Recording artists and record companies who secure mechanical rights are licensed to record and distribute a song owner's music. They usually pay the royalties in advance. The cost is then passed on to the consumer when buying the compact disc.

A **synchronization** license would need to be obtained when music is synchronized to video for commercials, films, etc. These rights may be obtained from The Harry Fox Agency or from Copyright Management, Inc. A master recording use right would be obtained, as well, if the original song was used (see master recording license).

A **video application** license is needed when music is synchronized with video and distributed on tape or disk (such as CD-ROM and videodisc).

A **public performance** license is required to perform a musical composition publicly. These are available from ASCAP, BMI, and SESAC. A public place would be a trade show, concert, etc.

A **master recording** license is required to reproduce and distribute a particular recording of a musical composition by a specific artist. For example, if a producer of a film wanted to use the song "My Girl" by The Temptations, in whole or in part, then that master use right must be negotiated with the record company. This right would be obtained from the record label.

A **live stage** license permits a performer to perform music in a live stage performance.

An **electrical transcription** license permits the use of music for syndicated radio programs, background music, in flight music, etc.

An **import license** permits the use of musical compositions in recordings made outside of the U.S. and imported into this country for sale.

Music — Usage Examples

Following are some questions and answers on fair use of music:

1. A high school music teacher wants to make some small edits to a purchased sheet music song for use with the choir. Is this permissible? *****Yes.** Making edits of a purchased sheet music song, as long as the work is not distorted

or the lyrics (if there are any) are not altered or lyrics added where there are none, is acceptable for school use.

2. In evaluating student work, is it permissible for the professor to make a copy of the musical work performed by each student for his or her final grade, that is then kept in a music library for subsequent student evaluation and comparison? *Yes. A copy may be made of a performance by students for evaluation or rehearsal purposes, and either the teacher or the institution may retain it.

3. For a lesson on Renaissance music, may a music teacher make a copy of an aria of a song that is only available in a collection? *Yes. Making a single copy of a performable unit, such as a section, movement or aria, if the music is out of print or unavailable except in a larger work, for research or class preparation, is permissible.

4. For a unit on contemporary music, may a music teacher make a copy of a song for the purpose of constructing a series of questions on the use of lyrics? *Yes. Copying a copyrighted sound recording for use in constructing aural exercises or examination is permissible.

5. The school hires an acting troupe to present selections from *West Side Story* for an assembly. Neither the troupe nor the school has paid royalties for this presentation. No admission is charged. Is this a permissible use? *No. If an outside group of performers is paid to present an assembly, even a religious or charitable one, royalties have to be paid. It makes no difference if admission is charged or not. If outside performers are hired, the performance is not exempt [Section 110(4)].

6. In constructing each student's electronic portfolio, a 30-second clip of popular music is played in the background of the introduction for each student. Each project will be used only in the classroom and then erased at the end of the semester. Is this a permissible use? *Yes. According to the Fair Use Guidelines for Educational Uses of Multimedia, such a use is permissible, if credit is given to the artists and producers involved.

Please note that Web site information changes over time. Consult each particular site for specific information.

American Society of Composers, Authors, and Publishers (ASCAP)

With over 68,000 members, ASCAP has many services available on their Web site (http://www.ascap.com/). The ASCAP Clearance Express (ACE) System provides information on titles, performers, writers, and publishers in the ASCAP repertory. Information of use at this site includes ACE FAQ (frequently asked questions), list of works to which copyright protection has been restored, publisher information for ASCAP publishers when a work is co-published with a non–ASCAP entity, copyrighted arrangements of public domain works, ASCAP licensing-rate schedules for Internet performance, and radio licensing (blanket and program).

Also under licensing is a section on copyright information/music. The site is updated weekly. Other sections include songwriter workshops and seminars, legal and legislative updates, *Playback* (an electronic version of their magazine), and *What's New* (an explanation of what is available on the site).

Broadcast Music, Inc. (BMI)

BMI represents more than 180,000 songwriters, composers, and music publishers with more than 3,000,000 works in all areas of music. Its Web site (http://www.bmi.com) provides useful information. *Songwriter's Toolbox* has data for songwriters about BMI, performing rights, music publishing, and copyright. *News and Events* features a current events section. *Events Catalog* is the Internet song title database searchable by song title or writer, with writer and publisher information on songs licensed by BMI. *Legislation* includes a copyright column, legislative information, news announcements, copyright legislation information, links, and press releases. *Licensing* provides licensing information for public performance on radio, TV, cable, the Internet, and in business establishments. It includes downloadable license agreements for meetings, conventions, trade shows, and expositions; and FAQs on using music on the Internet. The Copyright Royalty Commission adjusts royalty rates and distributes royalty fees according to Sections 108–109.

Society of European Songwriters and Composers (SESAC)

The smallest of the performing rights organizations, SESAC was founded in 1930 and is the second oldest performing rights organization in the United States. SESAC, which used to be limited to European and gospel music, now includes popular music, rock classics, Latina, jazz, and Christian music. Its Web site (http://www.sesac.com) has these features: SESAC repertory online (online licensing), who is SESAC, current news, songwriter profiles, licensing information, top ten links, request information, TV/film writers, *Focus Magazine*, and mail.

The site does not have a legislative section or copyright information other than that for prospective affiliates at the time of this writing.

The Harry Fox Agency, Inc.

This agency handles most music licensing. It currently represents more than 20,000 music publishers. It licenses music nationally and internationally in several formats. Its Web site has excellent links to other useful music right societies, licensing, and copyright sites (http:www.nmpa.org).

Note: Please see music section of Library Reproduction Rights, Chapter 11, for information on copying phonorecords for internal library use, including music on obsolete equipment.

Can Do

You may:

1. Make a copy of a performable unit (movement, aria) for personal or nonprofit use.

2. Make multiple copies for classroom use of a small amount of any performable unit.

3. Make emergency copies to replace purchased copies, which for any reason are not available for imminent performance, provided that the purchase copies are substituted later.

4. Allow students to use 30-second clips of music for student-produced classroom multimedia projects. These projects may be exhibited at open house or at a professional conference for up to two years after creation.

Cannot Do

You may not:

1. Play tape, compact disc, or radio music on a cable channel owned by the district without permission or licensing. Because of changes in the law in 1998, permission might be easier to obtain for the retransmission of radio music in limited instances.

2. Use popular music in satellite or cable distance education programming without licensing or permission.

Tried and True

1. Encourage students to use royalty-free music on compact discs as much as possible, but don't discourage them from using popular music if the use is appropriate for in-class presentations and will be erased after completion.

2. Kindergarten through sixth grade students are not held to the 30-second clip of music stipulations for multimedia presentations according to the Educational Fair Use Multimedia Guidelines. They may use more as needed.

3. Music uses that are appropriate to student project content and educational outcomes are generally fair use.

4. If a student is considering a commercial venue for a project, then the student should: a) use original music, b) use copyright-free music, or c) gain permissions/licensing for the work at the time of creation. Much time and effort is saved, and the work would not need to be changed, should permission/licensing efforts fail later.

Beware

1. The major music associations have investigators in large cities that check music uses at schools and colleges, as well as at restaurants and other commercial establishments.

2. BMI searches the Internet for unauthorized uses of music.

3. "Watermarking" and other devices can detect Internet music copying.

Tips

1. Public domain music on compact disc is available in computer stores. Most of these discs are free to be used in school projects. For Internet or Web use, read the license.

2. There are public domain music sites on the World Wide Web. Try using Yahoo! to find them.

3. The Music Educators National Conference (MENC) has a Web site at http://www.menc.org. It also has the following helpful copyright booklet available online:

> Alhouse, J. *The United States copyright law: A guide for music educators.*

This booklet costs $10 to members and $12.50 to nonmembers.

4. The Kohn Web site called "Kohn on music licensing," is excellent, with much music information. They have a book and yearly supplements (*Kohn on music licensing*), as well as online supplements. Their Web site has court cases, copyright, licensing, and music law information. See http://www.kohnmusic.com.

5. The Music Librarians Association also has an excellent site with copyright information at http://www.musiclibraryassoc.org/Copyright/copyhome.htm.

5
Audiovisual Materials

Audiovisual works, as defined in Section 101, are works that:

> consist of a series of related images ... shown by the use of ... projectors, viewers or electronic equipment, together with accompanying sounds, if any.[1]

Audiovisual works can be filmstrips, slide sets, multi-media kits, motion pictures, video games, motion picture (16 or 35 mm) film or videotape, cassettes, laser discs, compact discs or digital video discs.[2,3] Audiovisual works are **dramatic** literary or musical works. Because of this clause, performance or display of audiovisual works may only be exempted: (1) for teaching and systematic instruction, (2) for home use (time shifting), and (3) with the copyright proprietor's permission.

Home-Use Taping and the School

The question of whether or not a teacher or librarian in a nonprofit educational institution can tape a program at home and then use it in teaching has yet to be answered in court. The *Sony* decision was a ruling on home use only, and it is the only decision of its kind on these issues to date.[4] Section 106 gives the copyright owner the right to "display a work publicly." According to the *House Report* a work is displayed in public if it is in a "place open to the public or at any place where a substantial number of persons outside of a normal circle of a family and its social acquaintances is gathered."[5] The *Report* states that performances at "clubs, lodges, factories, summer camps and schools" are to be considered "public."[6]

While it may be permissible for a teacher to copy a work at home or to request that a media specialist tape a show for viewing at school one time to capture a "teachable moment," any use after that does not fall within the Off-Air Taping Guidelines (Appendix A, Chart 3) and permission or a license

44

must be obtained. "Librarying" of small portions of videotapes of commercial programming, whether on broadcast television, cable, or satellite segments, constitutes copyright infringement.[7]

Teacher Local Video Rental

Because of the ease and convenience of renting videos from local retail outlets, teachers have been renting videos for classroom use. While most uses for this purpose are legally permissible, some are not. In addition, administrative law applies to these uses. If a board or other policy-making body has approved guidelines which prohibit the use of teacher rental videos in the classroom, then the teacher cannot do this.

One of the conditions of Section 110(1) is that motion picture and video exhibition must be a part of "systematic instructional activities." This means that any showing of a video for purely entertainment purposes would be an infringement. For example, showing a video of *Romeo and Juliet* in an English class during a unit on Shakespeare would be permissible. Showing *Mr. Bean* or other such entertainment features on a dull Friday afternoon without an instructional rationale would not. The key is that it is a viable part of a lesson plan. *House Report 94-1476* states:

> The "teaching activities" exempted by the clause encompass systematic instruction of a very wide variety of subjects, but they do not include performances or displays, whatever their cultural value or intellectual appeal, that are given for the recreation or entertainment of any part of their audience.

A display of a rented video for instructional purposes would include a library, gym, auditorium, or workshop, provided it is used as a classroom.[8]

Use in Nonprofit Educational Institutions

Use of audiovisuals in schools and other nonprofit endeavors must meet Section 110 criteria. Showings in fraternity and sorority houses, student recreation lounges, and in "video" theaters require licensing, either on a title-by-title basis or on a video blanket licensing program. Audiovisuals must be shown:

1. *As part of "systematic instructional activities"*—in a teaching or learning environment of a classroom or library and not as a recreational or diversionary endeavor [Section 110(2)(a)].

2. *"Directly related ... to teaching"*—again, this is a prohibition against competition with movie houses or rental companies [Section 110(2)(b)].

3. *"In classroom or similar places"*—for example, a school or library could not rent a hall and show motion pictures not directly related to "systematic" teaching activities.

4. *"Without any purpose of direct or indirect commercial advantage"* [Section 110(4)].

5. *"Without payment of any fee or other compensation ... [to] performers, promoters, or organizers"* [Section 110(4)].

Because of these stipulations, benefit performances where performers are hired would not qualify as an educational exemption, nor would recreational showings of motion pictures, whether on video or film, for employees, students, or guests of nonprofit institutions.

Closed Circuit Viewing

Still Images

A "displayed" work would be a photograph or other artwork. Section 109 defines the ways in which the owner of a copy of a copyrighted work may use it. Section 109 states that a copy may be displayed "to viewers present at the place where the copy is located." The *House Report* defines this phrase as:

> generally intended to refer to a situation in which viewers are present in the same physical surroundings as the copy, even though they cannot see the copy directly.

Obvious meanings for this situation would be a classroom, auditorium, or other such room. The *Report* states that:

> Display of a visual image of a copyrighted work would be an infringement if the image were transmitted by any method (by closed or open circuit television, for example, or by computer system) from one place to members of the public located elsewhere.[9]

Closed Circuit Use of Audiovisual Works

A work that is "performed" would be audiovisual (moving images), with or without accompanying sound. While the meaning of the language is still unclear, using closed circuit to display or perform a work campus-wide in a college or other large institution with multiple buildings or to transmit to colleges, as in a university setting, would probably be an infringement of copyright. However, through time the common practice has been for schools to request closed circuit viewing on the purchase order. In practice refusals are quite rare.[10]

The Off-Air Taping Guidelines

The "Guidelines for Off-Air Recording of Broadcast Programming for Educational Purposes," cover commercial broadcast programs, including those simultaneously broadcast on cable, and PBS programs cleared for taping. Cable programming is not subject to copyright law or these guidelines. However, many educational media producers do not want any part of their work reproduced because their materials are designed for education.[11] In addition, categories of programs which cannot be taped are those available for purchase and rental and those on subscription television, which requires a user fee, and is not subject to fair use.

There can be little doubt that the impetus for these guidelines came from a suit brought against the Board of Cooperative Educational Services (BOCES) of Erie County, New York, by three film companies — Encyclopaedia Britannica, Learning Corporation of America, and Time-Life Films — in 1978. Off-air taping had been done by BOCES over several years. In the 1976-77 school year alone BOCES duplicated approximately 10,000 tapes of copyrighted motion pictures. It maintained videotape equipment worth a half million dollars and employed five to eight people. Educational services were provided to over 100 public schools. No records were maintained of how many times each videotape was viewed or its disposition after use.[12]

The court ordered that BOCES cease taping the companies' educational films off the airwaves and obtain proper licenses for such use that were available. Other films which had been videotaped and incorporated into the curricula were allowed to be distributed as long as a plan was implemented to monitor the use of the tapes and require their return and erasure within a specified time period.

In keeping with this decision, the guidelines made it clear that duplication of programs available through licensing, inadequate record keeping, and retention of tapes after use add up to infringement. "Intentional substitution" of a program taped off-air to avoid rental is not only a cause for a lawsuit, but it is also unethical. Quite often the licensing fee for use of a program is a necessary way of figuring the profit to be made in its production.[13] The Association for Information Media and Equipment (AIME) is the educational media producers' association. It has a toll-free number to report illegal videotaping. According to Botterbusch (1996):

In more than one case, a whistle-blower with the school district alerted AIME to illegal taping by a teacher. AIME has received settlements from several schools whose teachers were involved with off-air taping violations.[14]

The Provisions of the Guidelines

Program showing — The period of time during which a program may be shown is ten consecutive days. During that time a program may be shown once "in the course of relevant teaching activities," and then repeated once only for reinforcement purposes. No definition is provided for what constitutes "the course of relevant teaching activities," whether it includes a class for which a teacher has more than one section or not. However, practice has shown that a teacher who instructs more than one section of a class, such as three sections of English 101, would be in keeping with the guidelines if a tape was shown to those sections, as long as proper use records were kept.

Program review — After the initial ten-day period, the instructor has 35 more days in which to review the tape. This 45-day holding period does not include weekends, examination periods, or other scheduled interruptions. In effect, the holding period lasts around two months. At the end of that period the tape must be erased or destroyed immediately.

Copies made by media specialist — A "limited number" of copies may be made to meet the "legitimate needs" of requesting teachers, but each request must be initiated by the teacher. The term "limited number" serves to remind users that an unlimited number of copies, particularly those not specifically requested, would not be within the guidelines. The media specialist and teacher should make sure that a tape is requested for "legitimate needs" which can be defined as being part of systematic instructional activities, directly related to teaching content, and intended to be shown in the classroom. Copies should not be made indiscriminately [Section 110].[15] The media specialist may alert faculty of programs that might be beneficial. Regardless of the number of times a program is broadcast, it can only be taped once for that teacher.

Other provisions are:

1. Tapes can only be used in "classrooms and similar places of instruction" for nonprofit educational institutions. Uses outside the classroom during the ten-day showing or the 35-day holding periods would require authorization. Such uses would include student exhibition during the holding period, use in a library, showing for parent-teacher and student groups, etc.

2. A tape may be used only "within a single building, cluster, or campus, as well as in the home of students receiving formalized home instruction." Loaning of tapes, or distribution of tapes off-campus, is prohibited."[16]

3. While the program does not have to be shown in its entirety, it cannot be altered from the original content, or physically or electronically merged to constitute a compilation or anthology.

4. All copies of a program must include the notice of copyright on the broadcast program as recorded.

5. Lastly, institutions are expected "to establish appropriate control procedures" to ensure that the guidelines are followed. This could be interpreted to mean that adequate record keeping of the name of the requester, the date it was taped, the name of the program, and the class it was used for is maintained. A mechanism to prevent retaping or reshowing a tape should be initiated, whether it is a check-out system or some other device, to ensure that the guidelines are followed.

These guidelines have been a reasonable solution for off-air taping needs over the years.[17]

Regular Broadcast Programming. Regular broadcast programming, as seen on the major broadcast stations, such as NBC, ABC, CBS, and programs cleared for taping through PBS which are simultaneously rebroadcast, are permissible under the "Guidelines for Off-Air Recording of Broadcast Programming for Educational Purposes" (see Appendix A, Chart 3). Satellite and cable programming from such programmers as The Disney Channel and The Discovery Channel require licenses of varying amounts.[18]

Satellite Programming. Satellite programmers are not subject to copyright law. This programming is governed by the Communications Act of 1934 (488 Stat. 1064), as amended (P.L. 98-549, Cable Communications Policy Act of 1984), to include satellite programming and falls under the jurisdiction of the Federal Communications Commission (FCC). This act does not employ the concept of "fair use," and use is subject to licensing. Educational television satellite networks transmit a variety of programming from other copyright owners. Many have their own Web sites, such as SATLINK and Sea World.[19] Remember, Web site information and addresses may change.

Mind Extension University (MEU)	http://www.meu.edu
NASA Select TV	http://www.nasa.gov
SATLINK	http://www.msba.gen.mo.us/satlink.htm
Sea World	http://www.seaworld.org/

Cable Programming. Cable programmers have their own policies on off-air taping. Fair use may not be made of this programming. *Cable in the Classroom* and other journals usually have information on off-air taping policies. Many have their own Web sites and viewing guides, such as A&E, C-SPAN, CNN, The Learning Channel, and The Discovery Channel. Some also have lesson plan guides as well.

A&E	http://www.aetv.com
C-SPAN	http://www.c-span.org
CNN	http://www.cnn.com
The Discovery Channel	http://www.discovery.com

Obsolete Equipment and Format Changes

In some instances, making a copy in another format is necessitated by obsolete equipment. In others the producer is out of business or does not have a replacement copy available in another format or will not respond to queries. "Obsolete" is defined in Section 404, as amended, as "no longer manufactured or is no longer reasonably available in the commercial marketplace." Three copies of these works may be reproduced in digital format. Section 404 allows three copies of a work currently in the library's or archives' collections to be made for preservation purposes, as long as a "reasonable attempt" has been made to contact the producer to obtain permission and the copies are not used off the premises. A "reasonable effort" would be, for example, three phone calls with follow-up letters, copies of which would be placed in files, and documentation of the phone calls, with pertinent information about the phone number not being a working one.

In many instances, 16 mm films, videocassettes, filmstrips and audio-cassette tapes may be exchanged for new formats at a discount, depending on the producer. An instructor who regularly makes copies of purchased tapes or slides, for example, is performing illegal acts, whether he or she is sued or not.[20] (See Library Reproductions Rights, Chapter 11.)

Audiovisual Materials — Usage Examples

The following are some examples of fair use of audiovisuals.

1. An instructor would like to make small excerpts on cassette audio-tapes for use in demonstrating various music styles. Is this permissible? *Yes. Small excerpts for use in teaching and scholarship is fair use.

2. A teacher wants to illustrate a talk with small clips from current television shows to illustrate theme and context. Is this permissible? *Yes. Small clips for instructional purposes are exempt and considered fair use.

3. Only the audio portion of a television documentary is taped from a program on PBS and is kept permanently by the teacher for classroom use. Is this permissible? *No. The off-air taping or audio taping of a television program for a one-time classroom use is permissible under the off-air taping

guidelines. However, a tape (including audio) **must be erased** no later than 45 days after taping. It cannot be kept without permission or rental. It is possible that permission would be granted for audio only. Retaining a small portion of the documentary is fair use.

4. A teacher makes a copy of a program on commercial television at home and uses the program at school for instructional purposes. Is this permissible? *Yes. While this is acceptable once, depending on district policy, any further viewing of the program past the guidelines requires a licensed copy.

5. A teacher would like to show a rented video of *Star Wars* on the last day of school. Is this permissible? *No. Only uses which are part of "systematic instructional activities" are permissible. Because this video would be presented for entertainment the classroom exception would not apply.

Change of Format — Usage Examples

1. A school district buys one copy of a 16 mm film and would like to make five tapes for use in its schools. Is this permissible? *No. Making copies of a film without license or agreement is infringement.

2. A media department regularly converts phonograph records into audiocassettes for individual teachers. Is this permissible? *No. Conversion of records on a regular basis without license or permission is illegal.

3. A media center has six one-inch videotapes that are 15 years old. The videotape machine that was used is no longer in working condition; and buying a new one is impractical since one-half inch formats are being used exclusively by the center. The librarian tried to contact the producer but found out that the company was out of business. Can the one-inch tapes be converted to one-half inch tapes? *Yes. Under most circumstances, copying a tape still protected by a copyright would be an infringement. However, if the librarian tried to contact the producer and the producer was out of business, then conversion could not harm sales. If the equipment is obsolete then the producer should be contacted to see if a new version is available at a fair price. If it is not, then the tape may be converted.

4. An art instructor needs 50 slides for an art history class. Because they are unavailable for purchase, he would like them to be copied from an art book that the library owns. May we do this for him? *No. The large number of slides and the likelihood that they will be used from term to term make this an illegal use. Permission should be requested.

5. For a class in physiology, the instructor purchased a set of slides. She has requested that five duplicate sets be made from it for use in lab sessions. Is this legal? *No. If five sets of slides are needed, then five sets of slides should be purchased.

6. Is it permissible for an instructor to make a copy of a 1903 copyrighted silent film for classroom use? *Yes. A film copyrighted in 1903 is in the public domain.

7. An instructor wishes to have the school library media specialist play a video that she taped at home two years ago on the new media retrieval system. Is this legal? *No. The school library media specialist must tape within the time restrictions of the off-air taping guidelines. This tape does not fall within that time frame so permission or licensing must be obtained. The *Video Locator* or the *Videohound* can be used to locate most videos and television programs for this purpose.

Can Do

You may:

1. Tape a program off-air, except cable (unless it is a retransmission) or satellite, and keep it 45 days, according to the off-air taping guidelines — 15 days for classroom use and 30 days for evaluation.

2. Tape news programs (except magazine format news programs, such as *60 Minutes*) and retain them indefinitely for teaching, scholarship and research.

Cannot Do

You may not:

1. Archive copies of videotapes or clips of videotapes in the media center or library. There is no right to archive videotapes.

2. Copy satellite programs without permission. Look in the satellite periodicals for their taping guidelines. Satellite programming is not subject to copyright law or to fair use.

3. Copy subscription cable programs without permission, such as HBO, Cinemax, and Showtime. The Discovery Channel, The Learning Channel, and others allow taping for up to two years, and some have teacher guides. However, the program may not be taped without permission unless either it is stated so during the program or such information is consulted in cable guides.

4. Bring in old videos from home for which the off-air taping guidelines limit has expired and show them, either in an individual classroom or through a media distribution system managed by the library media specialist.

Tried and True

1. Tape programs and show them to students. Evaluate them for 45 days and then ask the media specialist to get permission to keep it. This way you may then show it yourself or have the librarian show it for you.

2. If you have a tape that you copied at home then don't ask the librarian to archive it for you at school. Librarians are not allowed by the law to archive such a video in the library, unless it has been licensed or permission has been granted.

3. In the long run, it's cheaper to be legal.

Beware

Video vendors report illegal copies that they see in institutions to their companies. Disgruntled teachers and librarians do, too. (They have told this to the author!)

Part III
Computer-Based Systems

6

Computers

The computer software industry is a cornerstone of American trade; however, piracy, particularly at the international level, is also a widespread and growing problem, as well. The Business Software Alliance (BSA) operates 35 hotlines around the world for callers to seek information about piracy or to report suspected piracy.[1] While there are other forms of protection commonly used by producers, such as trade secret, "unfair competition" provisions, and patents, copyright is the most common protection for programs used by the general public.[2] Software engineering — special codes, counters, and other technical devices — are increasingly used to protect software from theft.

Copyright protection was available as early as 1964, when the U.S. Copyright Office began issuing certification of registration for copyright of computer programs, and in that year programs were first mentioned in a revision bill.[3] Section 117 of the 1978 Copyright Act extended protection to computer programs. Over the years other amendments have been made as technology has advanced.[4] Case law has upheld copyright in computer programs regardless of their form, purpose, or fixation.[5] As with other literary works under the copyright law, computer programs are eligible for copyright protection as soon as they are written or recorded in a medium of expression, such as on a tape, compact disc, floppy disk, or chip.[6] Copyright protection applies to the program on the tape or disk, accompanying manuals, lessons, or guides, as well.

Computer Maintenance Provisions

Sections of the Digital Millennium Copyright Act (P.L. 105-304), particularly Section 1201 and Title III, apply to computer maintenance in schools, universities, and other institutions:

— Temporary copies of computer programs may be made during computer maintenance.

— Unauthorized access to a work through circumventing a technological protection measure put in place by the copyright owner is prohibited, as well the manufacturing and associated services of devices solely aimed at circumvention.

— Exceptions to this prohibition are reverse engineering, security testing, encryption research, law enforcement, and intelligence activities.

Title III of the act amends Section 117 to ensure that services responsible for computer maintenance to do not become inadvertently liable when turning on computers for this purpose. This was done in response to *MAI Systems Corp. v. Peak Computer, Inc.* (991 F. 2d 511 [9th Cir. 1993]). A computer servicing company used software which was licensed to, but not owned by the customer when it loaded the program into the computer's random access memory (RAM), thereby making a reproduction of the program. The *MAI* court ruled that licensees could not make copies, only owners could. Title III overrules *MAI* by allowing the owner or the licensee of a machine to make or authorize the making of a copy of a computer program under certain conditions for computer hardware repair or maintenance.

The Rights of the User

While "fair use" and other exemptions are referred to as "rights," they are technically limitations on the rights of the copyright owner.[7] The *Vault* case helped to clarify user rights.[8] The individual or institution that purchases a program has the right:

1. to make an archival copy to guard against destruction or damage through mechanical failure,
2. to make the necessary adaptations in order to use the program correctly on a computer or peripheral,
3. to use a commercial copy program to "unlock" a program in order to make an archival copy, and
4. to add features to the program so long as it is not sold or given away without the author's permission.

"Shrink-wrap" Licenses — This is the license that the user is supposed to agree to, based on opening the clear plastic packaging (shrink-wrap) of the software program. Current case law and legal theory now hold that the terms stated on the license in the package are a "contract of adhesion" and are greatly limited in their applicability in infringement suits.[9] Other case law has indicated that contracts which enlarge a copyright owner's rights in disregard of the copyright law, such as stating that an archival copy may not be made or that the program may not be transferred to another machine, are not binding.[10] The scope of protection for computer programs continually evolves.[11]

The Rights of the Producer

The exclusive rights of the producer of the program are:

1. **Reproduction of copies** (excluding fair use portions and archival copies) — According to the Working Group on Intellectual Property Rights (1995, September), a copy would also be:

- when a work is placed into a computer, whether on a disk, diskette, ROM, or other storage device in RAM *for more than a very brief period* [italics added];
- when a printed work is "scanned" into a digital file, a copy — the digital file itself — is made ... [and];
- when other works — including photographs, motion pictures, or sound recordings — are digitized, copies are made.[12]

The phrase, "for more than a very brief period," is the subject of much scrutiny and has led to a heated debate over the situation where a listserv member downloads messages and discovers that one of them contains copyrighted material which has been used illegally. It is likely that "a very brief period" might be the time it takes to download these messages, find out what they are, and then discard them. However, this issue will need to be resolved in the near future through case law or Congress.

2. **Production of derivative works** — Includes annotating, editing, translating, or significantly changing the contents of a file. A derivative work can be one that transforms an audiovisual work into an interactive one.[13]

3. **Distribution of copies for sale or leasing** — This can be online licensing/ sales, distribution in other countries, through franchises, etc. Owners of copyrights in computer programs and sound recordings have the right to control post-first-sale rentals of copies of their works; owners of copyrights in other works do not.[14]

4. **Performance of the work publicly** — If audiovisual, such as a video game, a digital movie, or other work with moving images.[15] A distinction is made between downloading such a work and viewing a performance of or a "rendering" of such a work. The Working Group on Intellectual Property Rights (1995) defines this distinction as follows:

> When a copy is transmitted ... in digital form....[such as]a file comprising the digitized version of a motion picture might be transferred from a copyright owner to an end user via the Internet without the public performance right being implicated. When, however, the motion picture is "rendered" — by showing images in sequence — so that users with the requisite hardware and software might watch it *with or without copying the performance,* then, under the currant law, a "performance" has occurred.[16]

5. **Display of a work publicly**— If graphic, includes "...either directly or by means of a film, slide, television image, or any other device or process...."[17] The Report goes on to say that:

> when any NII user visually "browses" through copies of works in any medium ... a public display of at least a portion of the browsed work occurs ... [and] would appear to fall within the law's current comprehension of "public display." Whether such acts would be an infringement would be determined by separate infringement analyses.[18]

Downloading and browsing were considered infringement in the *Playboy* case,[19] in which at least 50 copyrighted images from *Playboy* were illegally uploaded into a listserv and then downloaded by subscribers for browsing and viewing. Frena, the online service provider (OSP), claimed that he did not know of this infringement, but the court held him liable as contributory infringer. Under P.L. 105-304, the liability of OSPs is limited and, depending on the circumstances of the case, the ISP might not be liable. This would also be a different situation than one in which a subscriber to a listserv unwittingly downloads infringing materials, opens up a file to see its contents, and then discards the material. The law now makes a distinction between the two.

Licensing Considerations

Only one archival copy may be made unless the producer allows more in the license.[20] This is the producer's right.[21] In practice, some producers state on the license that more than one copy may be made of a program, such as Broderbund, Sunburst, and others. Software licensing contracts, terms, and conditions are extremely important in today's marketplace. Software producers have become much more sophisticated in this area.[22]

Public Domain and Shareware

A "**public domain**" program or "freeware," typically available from user groups, such as the Berkeley Macintosh Users Group, is a program which is not copyrighted. It may be copied and used freely. Public domain programs can be adapted, compiled, abridged, or translated into another language, for example. If the new work is sufficiently original, the copyright applies only to the new adaptation, compilation, etc.[23]

A "**shareware**" program is not usually public domain. Shareware is a means of distribution and is often copyrighted. Typically when the program is booted up, if it is copyrighted, then a notice will be displayed. The introductory screen will state that it costs a fee to purchase the program or obtain a manual and/or a fee to "register" the program for updates.

Caveat: Not All Producers Know Copyright Law

Software licenses vary. Some are well-written and some are not. Some are too restrictive and some are not. Large companies that produce a great deal of off-the-shelf software usually have the greatest lenience in their licenses.[24] Some companies' licenses state producers' rights that are more strict than the Copyright Act allows. For example, a license may state that no archival copy may be made. The Computer Software Amendment states that the user may "make or have made" an archival copy for the purpose of protection against human or mechanical failure,[25] yet several licenses have the statement that no archival copy may be made.[26]

The First Sale Doctrine and Software

Under the "first sale doctrine" [Section 109][27] the copyright holder may market copies of the work by methods other than an outright sale, and the copyright holder may, by contract, place restrictions on future disposition of a sold copy. The doctrine states that the privileges described as pertaining to the owner of a copy of the work do not extend to a person who has acquired possession of the copy by rental, lease, or loan. The *Legislative Report*[28] (*H.R. 94-1476*) acknowledges that the copyright owner's cause of action is not for copyright infringement but for breach of contract.[29] The validity of that contract depends on whether or not the contract enlarges the scope of the copyright owner's rights beyond the Copyright Act. If it does, then it is doubtful if it is enforceable.[30]

Obligations and Restrictions of Publishers Beyond the Initial Sale

The producer has an obligation to ensure that the product is in working order and that all manuals, documentation, etc., are present and usable. Most software producers lease their programs rather than sell them. By virtue of licensing a program rather than selling it outright producers retain greater control of the program.

Computer Software — Usage Examples

1. I have some programs that can be multiply booted (loaded into more than one machine). Is it legal to do this? *No, not unless your site license allows it. Some companies allow one copy to be placed on the owner's machine at work and one on a home computer, as long as the two copies are not used simultaneously by the owner. Some companies and certain programs will state on the license that one copy can be booted on one or more (usually no more than three) computers. However, multiple booting of a program is considered to be the same as making multiple copies.

2. I have a compact disc encyclopedia that requires a 3-megabyte setup to be installed on a computer. Since I keep 3 computers set aside for this encyclopedia, would it be legal to boot the setup program onto these 3 computers? I can only use one computer at a time. *Yes, you may, if the encyclopedia is used when resident in the computer. (You cannot copy the program to the hard drive.) In this way it is used on only one computer at a time.

3. I purchased a program that is copy protected, and a backup was not supplied. May I use a "nibble copier" or "locksmith" program to make a backup? *Yes, you may. The law states that the purchaser of a program may make or authorize the making of an archival copy to guard against human or mechanical damage. The language of the law, however, is unclear as to who is responsible for supplying the back-up — the producer or the purchaser. If the disk is not copy protected, meaning it was designed so copies could not be made through normal copying procedures, then it is your legal right to make one archival copy. A backup copy is not to be used as a *second* copy of the original; it is only to be used in the event of damage to the original.

4. Should I request an archival copy (backup) when purchasing school software? *Yes. These magnetic media are fragile. Power surges, human misuse, disk drive problems, etc., can ruin a disk. An archival copy can be used in place of the original until a new disk is received. Many producers will send a replacement disk for a small fee if the original is returned.

Can Do

You may:

1. Make an archival copy of a program even if the "shrinkwrap" says you can't.

2. Use a "locksmith" program to make an archival copy of a program, although purchasing one at a nominal cost is best.

3. Install a CD-ROM setup on more than one computer, so long as it is only used on one machine at a time.

4. Make a copy of licensed software in the process of authorized computer maintenance and repair.

Cannot Do

You may not:

1. Load a program on more than one machine (even if one is at home and one is at work) without checking the license.

2. Assume that because you buy a program, you own it. You only lease it in nearly all cases.

3. Assume that because something is shareware it is not copyrighted.

Tried and True

1. Read the software license. Each one is different. Some larger software companies allow greater use of their software than others.

2. Ask if a software site license is by building/district or by number of copies. Companies offer different types of site licenses, and the cost and use vary.

3. When ordering large quantities of software, remember to negotiate for the price and license.

Beware

1. Set a good example for students. The Software Publishers Association has a hotline that is used extensively to report illegal software use. Disgruntled school, library, and business employees or ex-employees are frequent callers. They also send out investigators, write letters asking for information on pirates, and offer rewards.

2. As with video and music vendors, software vendors report illegal uses that they see when visiting institutions to their employers.

Tips

1. An excellent booklet with K–12 teaching ideas for the ethical use of software is:

> Sivin, J., and Bialo, E. *Ethical Use of Information Technologies in Education: Important Issues for America's Schools.* Washington, D.C.: National Institute of Justice, 1992.

2. The Software Publishers Association has materials available from its offices by phoning 1-800-388-7478. A representative can be requested to speak at your institution, if you are near its offices.

7

Electronic Publishing

Electronic Databases

While controversial, electronic databases have generally been considered copyrightable as compilations.[1] Databases are defined in the *House Report* as "literary works."[2] Section 101 defines a compilation as:

> formed by the collection and assembling of pre-existing materials or of data that are selected, coordinated, or arranged in such a way that the resulting work as a whole constitutes an original work of authorship.

Because of the *Feist* decision a compilation or database must have sufficient creativity and independent creation to be protectable, and much of this may depend on the nature of the database itself.[3] This is because the Supreme Court held that telephone book white pages were not copyrightable because no creativity was required to compile them. The old "sweat of the brow" dictum that courts previously used in compiling databases, when entries were checked by hand, has changed to automated compilation. There must be a minimal amount of creativity.

Downloading

"Downloading" involves the transmission of data from a remote or host computer to the user's on-site storage device for later searching, manipulation, or storage.[4] With the increased use of computers for online searching, e-mail, the wide availability of electronic journals, software, decreasing costs of Internet service providers, and the increasing number and range of programs and services available through subscription, such as America Online, downloading is fast becoming the basis for much computer communication.[5]

Fair Use

Judicial doctrine increasingly supports the principle that:

> copyright protection for compilations of factual material cannot be reconciled with the general principles of the copyright laws ... such works should be conducive to fair use. Authors of compilations, therefore, must be held to grant broader license for subsequent use than persons whose work is truly creative.[6]

Legal opinion generally agrees that databases and compilations allow fair use to a greater degree than other literary works.[7] Fair use is very limited where the intent is for commercial use.[8] However, "copyright may adhere, under appropriate circumstances, in the selection and arrangement of unprotected components."[9] Moreover, "the overall structure, sequence and arrangement of screens, text, and artwork (i.e., the audiovisual displays in general) are protected under the copyright laws.[10]

Downloading under authorized means (such as under a downloading license agreement, for example) of small portions of databases to be temporarily retained for the purposes of teaching, research, scholarship, or criticism is fair use. Downloading to prepare a concordance of a work or to perform a syntactical analysis of a work, with the records discarded after use, would be considered fair.[11] However, keeping archival copies of downloaded works, absent a downloading license agreement, would require the copyright owner's permission.[12] Downloading a small portion of a database into temporary storage for a delayed search for scholarly or nonprofit purposes (without intent for resale), after which the records were immediately discarded, could be considered fair use.[13]

Electronic Publishing

Electronic publishing exists in many forms: journals are published on compact discs, computer disks, and the World Wide Web, either in first publication form or in condensed Web versions accessed through archives accessed through file transfer protocol (ftp). As more electronic journals start up and electronic versions of print journals develop, case law will follow.

Rights of the Electronic Publisher

The bundle of exclusive rights which applies to electronic publishers includes:

1. **Reproduction** — The right to make copies (electronic, paper). This is actually the right not to allow copies to be made, and includes:

> placing all or a substantial part of a work in its original form on magnetic media used directly in computers ... reproducing all or a substantial part of a work in its original form in an electronic database.[14]

This includes text, images, and sounds. While viewing a file or an image, or listening to a sound is not an infringement, uploading or reproducing these text files, images, and sounds for any use other than personal or educational, such as reproducing them on a personal Web site, is an infringement without permission or licensing.

Digital versions of files — text, images, and/or sound — have the same protections as print ones. Only the owner may distribute, adapt, perform, or display them. For example, downloading a single copy of a file for personal use is likely a fair use. Making copies of a file for classroom use requires one to follow the same fair use guidelines as with print materials.

2. **Distribution** — The right to initially sell or distribute copies, whether online, compact disc, hard copy formats, etc., through "sale, or other transfer of ownership, or by rental, lease, or lending" [Section 106 (3)].[15] Writers unions have begun to negotiate for rights in the further distribution of their works in other formats. For example, a writer does a piece for the New York Times and then the work is placed into an online database, perhaps placed on the Web or into a compact disc version. In the past the writer was not compensated for the further use of this work. Writers are now asking for new contracts that bring remuneration for these uses.[16]

Online Copying. The Working Group on Intellectual Property (1995) considered these examples to be copies:

- whenever a digitized file is "uploaded" from a user's computer to a bulletin board system (BBS) or other server...;
- whenever a digitized file is "downloaded" from a BBS or other server...;
- when a file is transferred from one computer network user to another, multiple copies generally are made...;
- when an end-user's computer is employed as a "dumb" terminal to access a file resident on another computer such as a BBS or Internet host, a copy of at least the portion viewed is made in the user's computer. Without such copying into the RAM or buffer of the user's computer, no screen display would be possible.[17]

Digital transmission and use is still in the formative stages. Enhanced encryption techniques will handle many copying problems in the future.

3. **Adaptations** — To change one format to another and to make a derivative work based on that work. Making another version of a work, such as a Web version of an online or print journal, would be an adaptation. (Distributing it would be another right, see above.) If someone downloads an article, then adds new annotations, notes, and graphics or significantly changes the work, then such a work would be an adaptation or derivative work. To make such a work would require the author's permission or licensing, particularly if that derivative work were distributed over the Internet, for example.[18]

4. **Performance** — To perform (if audiovisual) for the public. A performance online would be a live television show, radio show, a rock concert, etc. Downloading is not considered to be a performance. It is a transmission. A "digital transmission" is a transmission in whole or in part in a digital or other non-analog format [Section 101]. To perform a work means to "show its images in any sequence or to make the sounds accompanying it audible" [Section 101].[19] So, if a rock concert can be seen with the human eye, it is a performance. If it is being transmitted from computer to computer — downloaded — it is not.

5. **Display** (still images) — Can be the showing of an image on a computer terminal in a place which is open to the general public (not just a family or social acquaintance). A display of a work pertains to graphic, sculptural, and pictorial works. It is a public display when a graphic is shown on America Online, for example. This means that works which are placed into computer systems are protected like books in a book store or library.

> Placing a digitized version of a photograph in a file online that users can download and view on their computers is not a public display — it is simply making a copy available to individual members of the public. But if the same photo automatically appears on the user's computer screen when he or she logged on to an online service, it would be a public display.[20]

In the case of **sound recordings — digital audio transmissions** — a performance of a sound recording through digital audio transmission, over the Internet for example, is a right reserved to the copyright owner, as well [Section 106(6)].[21]

In the case of **compilations**, it should be remembered that hard work or "sweat of the brow" is no longer rewarded by copyright; only creativity is awarded copyright status.[22]

Electronic Publishing — Usage Examples

For a middle-school research project students have been downloading both copyrighted and public domain images from the Internet and then altering them inside their PowerPoint presentations. Is this legal? *Yes. According to the "Fair Use Guidelines for Educational Multimedia," it is legal if credit is given on a credits page for all photos (not just the ones with a copyright mark) or on the image screen itself, and the projects are either erased at the end of the lesson or unit, stored in the media center for two years and then erased, or are kept in student portfolios. Since the Berne Treaty in 1989, the copyright mark is no longer required, so many of these photos may be copyrighted even if they are not marked.

Can Do

You may:

1. Negotiate and license separately for each of the five basic rights in electronic format.

2. Negotiate electronic distribution rights separately for sections of the U.S., countries, and sections of the world.

3. Download small portions of a database temporarily for teaching, research, scholarship, and criticism.

4. Display graphics in a compact disc, online, or in Web works which are public domain. All other graphics require permission/licensing unless otherwise stated on the license.

Cannot Do

You may not:

1. Make a Web version of a print or online journal without permission/licensing. To make any version of a work is the author's right.

2. Display logos of other companies or firms in electronic publishing without permission. Logos are trademarked. There is no "fair use."

3. Display graphics in electronic publishing for which you do not have permission. There is no fair use of a graphic if the rights holder does not grant permission/licensing.

Tried and True

1. Whether the format is digital or print, the fair use guidelines still apply.

2. Digital versions of works — text, images, sound — have the same protections as print ones.

3. Read each database license agreement. They vary widely. Negotiate terms that are good for your institution.

4. See Principles for Licensing Electronic Resources, Appendix C, for licensing works. It has good ideas and information.

Beware

1. When a file is transferred from one computer network to another, multiple copies are made.

2. When making multiple copies the tests of brevity, spontaneity, and cumulative effect become important.

3. Just because you can copy something doesn't mean you should.

8

Multimedia and the Fair Use Guidelines for Educational Multimedia

Many Examples, No Definition

The term "multimedia" can be applied to an Adobe Premiere–based national cooperative electronic journal publishing venture with high-resolution photographs and charts[1]; a law school moot court case presentation with animations, graphics, or video segments offered as evidence in a state-of-the-art moot courtroom unveiled at the College of William and Mary[2]; a third grade HyperStudio project; or a high school technology preparation class robotics module assessment. One fact is apparent. Educators spend increasing amounts on these materials. United States K–12 educators spent 842 billion dollars in 1998 on electronic instructional materials. The amount was 1 billion in 1999.[3]

Fair use depends on its application in each medium.[4] The use of multimedia is now highly diverse in the field of education. K–12 teachers today have computer-based information storage and retrieval of books, journals, multimedia programs, and indexes available in the classroom, from the library catalog via a local network, and from the Internet. Students use this information, digitize video and still images from multimedia programs, Internet, online information services (such as CompuServe and America Online) and music compact discs to create multimedia projects.[5]

These projects are then placed into both student-produced and teacher-produced print and electronic portfolios for assessment purposes. Portfolio assessment is required in an increasing number of school districts for students and teachers and by national accrediting bodies and professional associations for university education faculty. Popular teaching theories, such as integrated thematic instruction[6] and thematic immersion,[7] emphasize teacher/student developed curricula that rely heavily on research projects, cooperative learning, critical thinking, and the development of life skills.

University faculty are teaching self-paced classes with multimedia authoring systems, developing college multimedia databases,[8] and developing multi-institutional image database collections housed on the World Wide Web.[9] An art faculty member teaches a class on finding, downloading, and using images from the Internet to use for projects.[10] This is why so many higher education groups are vitally interested in the uses of copyrighted materials in networked environments.[11]

Classroom Fair Use: Instructor's Choice

Fair use for classroom purposes of various materials, as long as the work stays in the classroom and is erased, requires that the excerpts be brief. This does not mean that a use should always end mid-sentence or mid-phrase for musical excerpt length. It means that the use should be reasonable. Occasionally, students will need to use a little more than the fair use limits to make a point. This is acceptable. Repetitive uses that are lengthy are not fair use, encourage plagiarism, and decrease the student's imagination and critical thinking skills.

Instructors have a choice in nonprofit educational institutions. They can see if the fair use guidelines for print and music suit their needs or if the Multimedia Guidelines are more suitable for the way the material is used. Either way, instructors are free to choose the interpretation that best suits instructional needs and student outcomes.

The Fair Use Guidelines for Educational Multimedia

Educators need help in the ethical and responsible creation and use of multimedia. The "Fair Use Guidelines for Educational Multimedia" (1996, see Appendix B) provide help to teachers and students in nonprofit educational institutions developing increasingly sophisticated curricula and projects. The Guidelines do not conflict with nor alter the conclusions of either of the *Working Reports* (September 1994, July 1995) of the Working Group on Intellectual Property.[12] See the appropriate charts on the Guidelines for K–12 in Appendix A.

Multimedia — Usage Examples

1. A teacher has assigned all of her students to do multimedia projects to illustrate desktop publishing concepts. She would like to show these projects

on the computers of the lab during School Open House. She would also like to have a multimedia project that she did to illustrate the goals and outcomes of the desktop publishing class to show parents the kinds of learning that have occurred during the year. All of the projects were made according to the Guidelines (portion limits, attribution, opening screen "fair use" statement, and credits). Is this OK? *Yes. While Open House was not specifically mentioned in the Guidelines, such use is to support instructional purposes.

2. A teacher would like to retain examples of student multimedia projects to use in face-to-face instruction to show students in other classes the best work of previous ones. Can this be done according to the Guidelines? *Yes, but for a limited period of time. Under the Guidelines one copy of each project could be kept by the teacher for teaching purposes, and one copy could be kept on reserve in the Media Center for two years after the first instructional use. To retain the projects any longer than that would require "permission for each copyrighted portion incorporated in the production." Thereafter, teacher projects may be retained by the teacher in a professional portfolio for tenure review or job interview purposes. Students may retain their own projects for later personal uses, such as job interviews and graduate school interviews.

3. An instructor for a course available over a remote network with technological limitations (PIN) at 23 remote sites throughout the state would like to show student examples of multimedia projects to illustrate performance assessment concepts and criteria. Is this legal? *Yes. If there are technological limitations on the network "such as a password or PIN and provided further that the technology prevents the making of copies of copyrighted material," then they may be used for remote instruction. It should also be noted that "if the institution's [secured-password or PIN] network or technology used to access the educational multimedia project ... cannot prevent duplication of copyrighted material ... [then the projects may be used] for a period of only 15 days after its initial real-time remote use ... or 15 days after its assignment for directed self-study."[13]

4. Can my fourth-grade students create a Quicktime clip from a segment of a videodisc of a popular movie for classroom use? *Yes, subject to a 10 percent or 30-second time clip. K–6 students are not subject to the limits. [A copyright notice and a credits screen/resource list should be added, as well as a fair use statement. For fourth-grade students, it could either be a template made by the teacher or something like "(Kelly) followed fair use."]

5. I want to digitize a short video clip from a television show to use in a HyperCard program I'm developing for student use. Can I keep it in the program? *Yes, but it must not exceed 10 percent or 3 minutes unless K–6 students are doing it. They may exceed the guidelines.

6. My high school Western literature students want to use short segments of popular music from compact discs for their electronic portfolios.

These portfolios can be seen during our school open house. Is this permissible? *Yes. While the public other than parents could come to an open house, it is unlikely, and it is an educational use for which admission is not charged. They are restricted to 10 percent or 30 seconds from one work or several extracts from one work. A "credits" screen should be provided for all print and nonprint materials used. A notice on the opening screen should state that fair use has been made of materials, and that further use is restricted.

7. I want to retain multimedia projects for exemplary use by students in the next semester class. May I take these multimedia projects to professional education conferences to show student progress? *Yes, you may retain copies of students' multimedia projects to show to next semester students, and these can be taken to professional conferences — not to events where the public attends, though. There is a two-year time limit for saving their work. Some schools, however, require that students and their parents give written permission for this. Should you wish to do anything further with their work, remember that students have copyright of their own work, as well. The students may retain their own projects in personal portfolios for job or school interviews.

8. May I take images from a commercial compact disc image collection and insert them into a courseware package that I am writing for my class? *Yes, if the license on the image collection states that the images are royalty-free. Royalty-free image collections are designed for this purpose. Not all image collections allow use beyond personal use. Use beyond the classroom or professional conference usually requires permission and royalties.

9. I've been asked to give a multimedia presentation to a state-wide workshop for university faculty that utilizes a few short video clips and three short segments of popular music. Am I allowed to do this? *Yes, first, because this is a professional conference, you are also allowed to bring a program that you produced for your class. Second, this is also a workshop which is within a system. You would not be allowed to present these without permission at a public function.

10. I'm making a write-once compact disc of various Quicktime movies that I have created from my own original footage on our new compact disc recorder. I own a legal copy of Quicktime. I will use these movies in my classes. Do I need permission to place Movie Player on my CD-ROM? *No, since it is archival for your own purposes, and you own a legal copy. As an aside, if you were to send this material away for replication, you would be required to sign a statement or provide information such that you have legal copies.

11. Our school district would like to copyright its Web site. Is this possible? If so, what do we need to do? *Yes. The school district may copyright its Web site. It can place a copyright mark on its frames and or at the beginning and end of each page of its site. State and county governments may copyright their works. Only the U.S. government, with few exceptions, may not copyright

its work [17 U.S.C. Section 105].[14] Of course, the copyright mark is unnecessary since 1989, because all works fixed in a tangible medium have automatic coverage. Further protection is provided by copyright registration. (See http://www.patents.com/copyright on the Web.)

Students and Teachers Can Do

1. Use small portions of copyrighted works with proper attribution for classroom purposes (author, title, publisher, place and date of publication) and copyright ownership information (year of first publication, name of copyright holder).

2. Show student or teacher-produced multimedia projects at district/institutional/system inservices, professional conferences, for open house or in the classroom for two years.

3. Keep a project in a teacher or student portfolio for personal use for job interviews, graduate school interviews, or for tenure review.

4. Perform or display a multimedia project in teaching, in directed self-study, or in remote instruction on a secure network (PIN or password) for two years.

5. Perform or display a multimedia project in teaching or in self-directed study for 15 days after initial instruction or 15 days after self-directed study assignment.

Students and Teachers Can Use

1. Ten percent or three minutes of motion media.

2. Ten percent or 1,000 words of text material or one 250-word poem or three 250-word poems by one poet or five 250-word poems by different poets or one 250-word excerpt or three 250-word excerpts of one poet or five 250-word excerpts from different poets from one anthology.

3. Five images by an artist or photographer or 10 percent or 15 images from a collective work.

4. Ten percent or 2,500 fields or cell entries from a copyrighted database or data table.

5. Ten percent or 30 seconds of music and lyrics from one work or from several extracts from one work.

Teachers and Students Can Make These Copies

1. Two use copies may be made and used during the two-year period for teaching purposes, and only one may be placed on reserve.

2. One copy may be made "for preservation purposes ... to replace ... a lost, stolen, or damaged" use copy.

3. One copy for personal uses of the teacher or student or, in the case of a jointly created work, for each co-creator.

Teachers and Students Must

1. Credit sources and copyright ownership information either on each screen or on a credits screen.
2. Use multimedia projects for educational purposes (not commercial ones).
3. Destroy multimedia projects after two years after the first use with a class, unless used by teachers for tenure review, job interviews, or personal portfolios, or by students for personal portfolios, job interviews, or graduate school interviews.

Tried and True

1. Allow students to use small amounts of materials from sources for in-class projects. Teach them to give credit where credit is due by including a reference or bibliography list.
2. K–6 students are not expected to rigidly follow the guidelines. Ethics is the purpose, not arbitrary percentages.

Most Important

Instructors may choose to follow fair use guidelines, which are more lenient than the Multimedia Guidelines, for classroom uses which will stay in the classroom and then be erased. For uses which will leave the classroom — as portfolios or for conferences — it is best to use the Multimedia Guidelines.

9

The Internet and World Wide Web

There are Internet subscribers in 191 nations, nearly every jurisdiction on earth, and 200 subnational jurisdictions.[1] The court found in a recent case that harm caused by a Web site in another state gives one the right to sue in the receiving state because of interstate commerce laws.[2] A recent study by Market Data Retrieval found that there are 8,000 new Web sites a day.[3] The average age of the Internet user is 21 and declining.[4] Because of this enormous growth, BMI, the music licensing agency, has announced a "musicbot" that cruises the Internet searching for unlicensed music and the number of times it is played.[5] Students, ever ingenious, are developing new ways to infringe copyrighted materials, too. "[P]eople all over the world e-mail me for my bootlegged tapes."[6] As of this writing, the Internet now has 320 million pages. This does not include password-protected or "search-walled" material.[7]

The Digital Author's Rights

In terms of digitized information (computer generated or displayed), the author's rights include:

1. reproduction (downloading copies),
2. distribution (electronic transmission of that copy to someone else, such as on a listserv),
3. derivative works (altering a copyrighted image, article, or song and then transmitting it to a colleague),
4. performing rights (such as using a copyrighted song, compact disc clip, or video clip in a Quicktime movie and then transmitting it),
5. public display, if still audiovisual (such as copyrighted images or graphics which have been scanned and transmitted), and
6. digital audio transmission of sound recordings.

E-Mail

A copy is made when a work is saved to disc, disk, ROM or RAM "for more than a very brief period."[8] However, it is not clear if a copy of an e-mail message is considered to be the original if the original message is erased, for example. E-mail messages are considered the copyright property of the author, much like a handwritten letter, unless it "was created by an employee within the scope of employment."[9] Sending a copy of someone else's e-mail message without permission is making a copy. While most people would not care if an entire message were forwarded, some do, so asking permission to forward a message is good manners. Paraphrasing an e-mail message is acceptable. Some people also make it clear in the footer or header that it is permissible to use their e-mail.

Changes in Copying Under P.L.105-304 in Networks and the Internet

Certain types of copies are now permissible under P.L. 105-304. Section 1201(f) allows software developers to circumvent protection measures of lawfully owned computer programs for purposes of reverse engineering (interoperability), encryption research and security testing. Also permitted is the manufacture of a circumvention component which is designed to prevent access by minors to objectionable/pornographic material. Section 1201 also permits disabling a "cookie," which collects or disseminates information on the user, under certain conditions [1201(i)].

Nonprofit libraries, archives, and educational institutions may gain access to a commercial copyrighted work in order to make a good faith determination of whether or not to acquire the work [Section 402]. Broadcasters are also allowed to make permitted ephemeral reproductions. Title II of the 1998 act also limits online service provider's liability for copyright infringement in several important situations. Liability for transitory copies — the storing of material at user request, referring users to material at other online locations (such as through links), system caching, in which the online service provider makes a temporary copy of material at the request of the user, and transmission and routing (providing connections for material through the service provider's system and for intermediate and transient storage of material in such activities) have all been exempted if monetary, and injunctive relief has been limited if certain conditions are met.

Copying HTML

While there is some dispute over the specifics, it is generally considered fair use for students to copy html and print it out for purposes of scholarship and research as long as the protectable elements (i.e., content) are not copied.[10]

Copyright Notice and Fines

Since the United States became a Berne signatory, the copyright notice has not been needed on a work for it to be copyrighted.[11] A work on the Web does not need a copyright notice to be protected. However, it is always a good idea to put a copyright notice since it strengthens the protection, and since there are certain remedies that apply only to registered copyrighted works.[12] Such a notice could affect copying. The commercial copyright violation penalties of the law have been raised to a felony when over 10 copies have been made and over $2,500 worth of work has been infringed.[13]

Using/Placing Materials in University Networks

There are four "fair use" criteria — nature of the work, purpose of the use, amount and substantiality of what was used, and the effect on the market. When materials are placed into an institutional network for distribution, for example, then copying would be "institutional, systematic ... [and] archival."[14] Simply put, because a use is for research and scholarship, it is not sufficient for a finding of "fair use" when institutionalized copying is involved.

Because of the use of networks, the parameters of "fair use" in a network context are undergoing a great deal of scrutiny as Internet 2 develops and as groups like the Coalition for Networked Information, and others, create networks for sharing university scholarship. In response, associations move toward journal publication, such as the Association of Research Libraries, as one solution. Other approaches are needed. Kenneth Crewes (1993) states that the "limited and controversial right of fair use that Congress established ... is constantly eroded by opposing interests and by universities that inadequately recognize and protect their own interests."[15]

Resource sharing is a critical issue at a time when university libraries are seeing 12 percent inflation per year, but in many cases are receiving only 6 percent increases in budgets.[16] Journal subscriptions for the sciences can cost up to $24,000 per year per subscription and as low as $20. The subscriptions held in libraries are steadily being reduced in number. This is being made possible because of electronic delivery of articles online. However, it can cost more than the subscription to get a few articles. There are no easy solutions to the problems of academic research and scholarship.

Some universities are placing the full text of dissertations on their Web sites. Since placing the work on the Web means that a copy is made, some universities have students sign permission forms when their theses and dissertations are taken to the publications office to be posted on the Web.[17] Other universities place a statement in their enrollment form that students will abide by the university handbook, which would say that all work done as a requirement of the university is university property or that the student agrees to assign all intellectual property rights to the university.

Online Service Provider Liability

Title II (P.L. 105-304) establishes limitations on the liability for online service providers (OSPs), which are defined in the act as entities that transmit, route, and connects users to online communications or provides online or network services, such as storing digital material, caching or providing location tools (directories, links). Because of this broad definition, libraries and educational institutions are considered OSPs as well as independent service providers. The statute took effect immediately upon enactment and provides "safe harbors" for system storage and information locating tools, system caching, and transmission and routing. It also exempts OSPs from certain liabilities if certain procedures are followed and requirements are met.

Conditions for Liability Limitation

Activities which are covered are transitory digital network communications. OSPs must not place material online, modify content or store it longer than is necessary for it to be considered transitory. Systems must be automatic and passive. In order to qualify an OSP must: 1) designate an agent to receive notices from copyright owners about infringements and send them to affected subscribers, 2) advise the Copyright Office of the agent's name and address and post this information on the OSP's Web site, 3) develop and post a policy, 4) comply with "takedown" provisions for removing offending material and "putback" notice requirements of "counter notice" to copyright owner of dispute and replace material in two weeks unless the matter is taken to court, and 5) make the system able to accommodate industry-standard technical measures used by owners to protect their works from unauthorized access and infringement.

Notice and "Takedown" Provisions

The "counter notice" must have: 1) the subscriber's name, address, phone number and physical or electronic signature, 2) identification and location of the material to be removed, 3) a statement subject to a perjury penalty that the material was removed by mistake or misidentification, and 4) the subscriber must consent to local federal court jurisdiction or the appropriate judicial body overseas.

Procedures

To qualify for limitations on OSP activities certain procedures must be undertaken: 1) material must be placed online by someone rather than the OSP, 2) the OSP may not modify the material, 3) any copy of the material during intermediate storage must be in no longer than is "reasonably necessary" or in transient storage, 4) the OSP must not have "actual knowledge" or any material or activity that is infringing and if/when it does become aware it must then remove or disable access as soon as is practical. In addition, the OSP must not initiate transmissions, not make copies of material during intermediate storage available to other users, must not select recipients of material, or receive financial benefit from the infringing activity. Transmission and routing must be automatic. Rules on refreshing and reloading must be followed when updating material. The OSP may not interfere with copyright protection mechanisms, such as passcodes or fees.

Copyright Owner Obligations

The copyright owner must follow standard data communications protocols when refreshing, reloading, in updating material. The owner's technology must not "significantly" interfere with the OSP's system in intermediate material storage, not take information from the OSP's system or network about someone which it could have acquired through direct access to the person, and comply with notice and takedown procedures.

System Does Not Need Active Monitoring

For an OSP to limit liability it is not necessary to actively monitor use or affirmatively seek out information about material, except as otherwise stated for system maintenance.

Limitation on Liability of
Nonprofit Higher Educational Institutions

Section 512(3)(e) states that when public or other nonprofit institutions of higher education are OSPs, and when a

> faculty member or graduate student who is an employee of such institution is performing a teaching or research function ... such faculty member's or graduate student's knowledge or awareness of his or her infringing activities shall not be attributed to the institution

if certain conditions are met. They are:

1. The faculty member or graduate student's activities do not involve online access, including e-mail, to materials that were "required or recommended" within the preceding three years for a course taught by an employee of the institution.

2. The institutions within the preceding three years have not received more than two notices of "claimed actionable" infringement by the faculty member or graduate student.

3. The institution provides accurate materials to all users of its system or network that describe and promote compliance with copyright law. The institution, if all rules are followed, would qualify for protection from monetary claims and could not be required to terminate a subscriber or block access. However, it would be subject to injunctive remedies, such as evidence preservation. Useful Web sites on OSP liability and limitations are:

Copyright Office Notice on Interim Regulations:
    http://lcweb.loc.gov/copyright/onlinesp

Copyright Office Interim Regulations:
    http://www.aop.org/legis/interim.html

Lutzker and Lutzker Executive Summary with OSP Highlights:
    http://www.ala.org/washoff/osp.html

Jonathan Band, Morrison and Foerster, LLP, Short Analysis of the DMCA:
    http://www.dfc.org/links/links/links.html

EDUCAUSE Statement on Copyright Office Interim Regulations for "Service Providers":
    http://www.educause.edu/netatedu/contents/reports/agentletter981110r.
    html

It must be noted that further rulemaking will occur in the near future. As previously stated, Web site information changes. Consult each location for specific data.

"Works for Hire"— College and University
Internet and Mediated Course Components

For many reasons universities are examining in depth the use and publication of faculty writings for electronic distribution, either over intranets, consortia, or the Internet. With the recent introduction of Internet II the ability of university-sponsored research to be shared will increase in the coming years. While patents have long been a negotiated item at universities, with varying percentages alloted to the faculty member, department, college, and university, universities are developing new approaches to Internet and mediated course components, as well. To illustrate the rapid changes in the use of the Internet and World Wide Web for course and course component delivery, Ken Crewes' book, *Copyright, Fair Use and the Challenge for Universities,* published in 1993, made no mention of this topic. As universities look for ways to capitalize on technology transfer and the management of intellectual property which utilizes the Internet, the conditions under which these materials could be considered "work for hire" could change.[18]

Section 201(b) states that the employer is the author of a work "unless the parties have expressly agreed otherwise in a written instrument...." William Patry, Counsel to the Subcommittee on Intellectual Property and Judicial Administration, Committee on the Judiciary, United States House of Representatives, states that "the United States stands virtually alone in the world" on this aspect of copyright law.[19] This may be an important distinction in a time when international treaties have an increasing effect on U.S. copyright law. Mr. Patry states that while academics receive a "teacher exemption" for academic writings, there is much that is unclear.

"The central question is whether the hiring party has the right to control the manner and means by which the product is accomplished."[20] The key element for answering this question is the extent to which substantial use of university resources was utilized in the creation of a work. Mediated courseware and course components, such as Web-based courses and CD-ROM-based courses with Web or other online components, typically involve a greater degree of institutional support than writings which can be easily done at a home computer.[21] The faculty member is advised to discuss any mediated courseware idea with appropriate parties and to develop an agreement should capitalization be an issue. Large universities typically have committees to hear ideas which may have capitalization potential and to advise on the ownership and legal status so that intellectual creativity is fostered and faculty have procedures and due process.

The Association of University Technology Managers (http://autm.rice. edu/autm) deals with university licensing and technology transfer activities and began after the passage of the Bayh-Dole Act. This act allowed universities and other nonprofit organizations to retain title to and to license inventions made under federally supported projects. Their Web site maintains an active list of copyright policies, legislation, licensing, and other topics of interest to those seeking guidance with technological works.

Most academics sign away their copyright as a precondition to having a work published. Web and consortia-based publishing is different, in that the author publishes in a different medium and copyright is assumed because of being "fixed in a tangible medium of expression." The publishing hierarchy may change in the future. The "ACM interim copyright policy" of the Association for Computing Machinery (http://www.acm.org) has sections dealing with electronic publication, distribution of works from non–ACM servers, digitized copies, electronic reserves and coursepaks. The ACM envisions a world of scientific and technical publishing with literature stored in a digital library and a network of databases offering browsing, searching, extracting, and repackaging; "simple pricing schemes will be used to collect nominal fees from those who have not subscribed to the database services"; works will evolve as they change and be stored on copyright holder servers as a service to readers; and finally, "virtual publications in which individuals assemble readable views of documents from prototype documents containing links" will be created. Universities wish to capitalize on their stake in publications and research in this new scheme.[22]

Message Boards, "Chat" Rooms, Usenet or Discussion Groups

Message boards, both public and private, have become an important forum for public discourse and activity. In 1989 it was estimated that there were 3,500 — 4,000 of them in the United States.[23] Although most are privately run, large commercial boards have grown which offer a vast array of services at an hourly connect rate. Online service providers (OSPs) are those people who set up and maintain the system for others to use. Many message boards contain pirated software, credit card numbers, passwords to systems, and other confidential information.

The *LaMacchia* case, reported to be the "largest single instance of software piracy ever reported,"[24] involved David LaMacchia, who used Massachusetts Institute of Technology workstations for his bulletin board system (BBS). Roughly one million dollars worth of pirated software was placed on the system by users and copied. He did not post any of it, nor did he copy it. However, he was sued for copyright infringement. The government could not prove that he set up the system "for purposes of commercial advantage or private financial gain" [Title 17, Section 506(a)].[25] Because of this the case was dismissed. However, should students or employees set up or take part in such activities for "commercial advantage or private financial gain," then this would be criminal copyright infringement.[26] P.L. 105-304 reduced liability for system operators because of cases like these. If proper rules and procedures are followed then active system monitoring is not required and the OSP is not liable.

Copyright Signs Posted on Computers

Copyright signs should be posted on public use computers, particularly if they are within the library/media/technology center staff control and view. Unsupervised machines pose less legal liability because of the inability of staff to witness wrongdoing. However, if neglect of duty, i.e., "purposely looking the other way," is proved, then staff are more liable than if they were just ignorant of the activity [Section 504(c)].[27]

Hyperlinks: Association for Computing Machinery Interim Copyright Policies

The Association for Computing Machinery (ACM) has developed a useful statement that gives guidance in developing electronic distribution schemes, such as Web pages and other online or Web-based products.[28] P.L. 105-304 also provides a "safe harbor" for online service providers who provide directories, information location tools, and hyperlinks under certain conditions.

These policies have three basic assumptions:

1. Transmitting an ACM copyright work through a computer network is a form of copying.

2. The recipient of an ACM copyright work is not free to copy it and pass it on without permission from the ACM.

3. Links, although used for copy-on-demand, are a form of citation (ACM, 1995).[29]

In brief, the ACM states that:

1. "ACM treats links as citations."

2. "If an author wishes to embed a copyrighted object rather than a link in a new work, that author needs to obtain the copyright holder's permission ... and [the] notice 'included here by permission, by [holder]' should be placed at the location of the object."

3. "If someone creates a work whose pattern of links substantially duplicates a copyrighted work, [then] prior permission from the copyright holder [is required]."[30]

Posting K–12 Student Work to the Web

Increasing numbers of school districts are posting student work to the Web in the form of portfolios or as elements of the school Web site. Copyright issues affect ownership and permission to use student work. Privacy law and common sense dictate the need to ensure that work posted on the Web does not invite "shopping for a victim." The non-majority status (under 18 years of age) of most K–12 students also defines the legal role and responsibility of school personnel. (See Appendix Q, School Sample Permission Forms.)

Searching for Public Domain Materials on the Internet

The Internet has made searching for public domain materials easier. Washington, D.C. is not only the nation's capital, it is the capital of public domain materials.[31] The Government Printing Office Database, the White House, the National Geophysical Data Center, and the Consumer Information Catalog are all public domain Web sites.

The Library of Congress alone holds over 13 million prints and photographs, as well as 200,000 film titles and thousands of drawings, maps, and posters. The National Archives has eight million photographs and 150,000 reels of film; 160,000 sound recordings; and more than 20,000 tapes.[32]

Wertz recommends this site for finding public domain materials:

Images   http://www.PDImages.com

Artwork Sources on the Web

Yahoo! has excellent art sources, selected computer graphics and animations that can be reached by going to Art on the Internet. Geocities has many images, animations, and icons, including 3-D (http://www.geocities.com). The list grows every day. At publication, some sites are:

The ClipArt Connection   http://www.ist.net/clipart/index.html

This site has artwork and links to other locations.

Image Search Tools   http://www.rcls.org/psearch.htm

For finding images on the Web, this site has several of the best tools.

Music Sources on the Web

There are both free and cost music sources on the Web. Of course, the free music is not the same quality as cost music, most of which is downloadable.

Most sites will state if the music is available for further use or not. If it is not, then a link would be advised. CDNow is the world's largest online music store (http://www.cdnow.com). In general, music of high quality is not available on the Internet to be copied. However, there are many sources for midi and .wav files. A good one is The Daily.WAV (http://www.dailywav.com). For music or multimedia courses or other courses for which music is integral to the course material this, and several others, are excellent.

Internet — Usage Examples

1. A professor would like to quote an e-mail in a paper. Does the professor need permission to do this? *Yes. Quoting an e-mail would require permission, unless permission to do so was provided in the e-mail or the footer. The professor may, however, paraphrase and cite the e-mail.

2. May I post e-mail I receive to my discussion group? *No. See number 1 above.

3. A teacher who is adding a class Web page to the school Web site would like to place a copyrighted cartoon on the site. Is this permissible? *No. Cartoons are individually copyrighted, so fair use cannot be made of them on a Web site. Literally millions of people would see it, and the cartoonist could argue that it diminishes the market for that cartoon.

4. See number 3 above, only this time a Disney character would be placed on the Web site. Is this permissible? *No. Disney employs both copyright and trademark.

5. May I upload copyrighted software to a message board for downloading by others? *No. You must have a license or permission.

6. Students in a high school HTML class would like to copy short HTML segments for use in their class. Is this permissible? *Yes. HTML is not copyrighted. The text that it tags is, though. Be careful that students don't use copying the HTML as an excuse for copying the text, images, etc.

7. A teacher would like to publish high school Web site examples of student work in a paper. She will ask for written permission from the parents. Is this appropriate? *Yes. Written permission must be obtained from the parents, if the students are under the age of majority (18).

8. May students in a teacher's middle-school English class copy/paste images and information from the Web and use them in their own class multimedia research projects, including papers and music from the Web? *Yes. Students may copy and paste images, music, and papers to research projects that are *not* posted on the Web, but are used in research projects, such as in Hyper-Studio, PowerPoint, etc.

9. May students copy a Web site or a part of a Web site for a Web site construction class report to be put on a school server? *Yes. Since this is not a Web server, the use will be internal. If a site is copied as an example to study

Web site elements for an HTML or Web site construction course, then this is permissible.

Do Not Post

1. A picture of a student with a name next to the picture so that the child can be identified.

2. Class pictures that have so few students that the identities of the students can be easily determined.

3. Identifying information so that someone could call the student, know the home address, or determine the student's habits.

4. Anyone other than an instructor or other educational personnel to be the contact person for a Web site or page.

5. Personal Web pages for students. While it may be possible to do this for all students, the links might be inappropriate.

6. Student pictures, even if not identifiable with a student's name or other information, without parent permission.

Can Do

You may:

1. Make links to other Web locations on one's own Web site.

2. Copyright a personal Web page.

3. Copyright a school district Web page, provided that all permissions have been acquired.

4. Place a copyright mark on your Web page, even if you do not register it with the Copyright Office.

5. Copy "fair use" sections of HTML for research, scholarship, and criticism.

6. Paraphrase another person's e-mail or listserv message with proper credit given.

Cannot Do

You may not:

1. Make links to other pages in which only the frame(s) shows and not the copyright owner's information. If the links are within frames, so that the frame looks like it is the property of the person who linked to it instead of the copyright owner of the other Web page, you would be liable for copyright infringement.

2. Publish student work on Web pages without parental consent, if under 18, or student permission, if over 18.

3. Quote the entire contents of another person's e-mail or listserv message without asking permission.

Tried and True

1. There is a mix of copyrighted and uncopyrighted works on the Internet.

2. A copyrighted work is not required to have a copyright notice on it.

3. Teach students to keep it short, paraphrase, and give attribution.

4. Put a copyright mark © on all work that you post to the Web that you value. While copyright protection already exists for this work, by placing the © mark on it, you tell others that you wish to be given credit for this work. In addition, if each page or frame has a © mark on it, copy centers are less likely to copy it.

Online Service Providers

Can Do

Online Service Providers (OSPs) may:

1. Be libraries, educational institutions, or other public or private entities because of the broad definition of an OSP.

2. Consider system storage, information location tools, system caching, and transmission and routing as authorized activities.

3. Limit liability by designating an agent to receive copyright notices and send them to subscribers, advise the Copyright Office of the agent's name and address and post it on the OSP Web sites, develop and post a policy, comply with "takedown" and "putback" provisions for "counter notice" in case of disputed material, and make the system able to accommodate industry-standard technical measures used by owners to protect unauthorized access and infringement.

4. Devise procedures to limit liability—not place material online nor modify material, copies must be in transient storage no longer than "reasonably necessary," the OSP must not have "actual knowledge" of infringing material/activity and when OSP does become aware it must remove/disable, nor should OSP initiate transmissions or interfere with passcodes.

Cannot Do

Initiate transmissions, place materials in system for users, or make changes to user material.

Tried and True

1. OSPs must develop systems which are automatic and passive.

2. OSPs are not required to actively monitor system use or seek out offenders, except when under normal system maintenance.

3. Institutions of higher education are not liable for faculty member or graduate student infringements if: 1) the faculty member's or graduate student's activities do not involve online access, including e-mail of "required or recommended" materials within the preceding three years for a course taught by an employee of the institution, 2) the institution has not received more than two notices of "claimed" "actionable" infringement by the faculty member or graduate student within the preceding three years, and 3) the institution provides accurate materials to all users of its system or network. If all rules are followed the institution would be protected from monetary claims and would not be required to terminate a subscriber or block access.

Beware

1. The Software Publishers Association (SPA) has investigators that search the Internet for violations.

2. Broadcast Music Incorporated (BMI) has a "musicbot" that searches the Internet for unlicensed music and can detect the number of times it is played.

3. "Whether you charge money or not, you can still violate someone's copyright."[33]

4. There are ways to find out if someone is stealing graphics on the Internet.[34]

Tips

1. There are several resources on Internet law. Two that are useful:

> Rose, L. *Netlaw: Your Rights in the Online World.* Berkeley: Osborne McGraw-Hill, 1995.

Another that is useful for electronic publishing is:

> Fishman, S. *The Copyright Handbook: How to Protect and Use Written Works.* 3rd ed. Berkeley: Nolo Press, 1996.

2. Montgomery County, Virginia, public school system has an excellent question-and-answer section on student Web publishing and Internet use covering many areas at http://ei.cs.vt.edu/~cs3604/lib/worldcodes/aup.montgomery.html misc.

See Also

Chapter 10 on Distance Learning has information on Internet and World Wide Web courses. Permission forms examples for materials used on the Web can be found for K–12 and college in Appendix Q, School Sample Permission Forms.

10
Distance Learning

Growth of Distance Learning

Distance learning has many forms: satellite, fiber optics, digital video through videoconferencing or audiographics, telephone, Integrated Services Digital Network or ISDN, etc. An increasingly large number of colleges and universities use e-mail; and more than 14 percent of all institutions put class materials, such as syllabi, on the Web.[1] It has grown dramatically in the last ten years. The *Electronic University: A Guide to Distance Learning Programs*[2] lists nearly 100 degree or certificate programs in the United States and Canada and estimates that 300,000 people take these courses. Distance education exists in every state. As of this writing, 27 states already use some form of digital video for instructional purposes. K–12 education has more distance learning students than universities do.[3]

Fair Use

A wide variety of materials are used in distance learning: text, cartoons, slides, photographs, video, Web sites, audiotapes, music, movie clips, e-mail and listserv postings, etc. All add to permissions "headaches" for those who deal with distance education in its many forms.

Some of the issues in distance learning are brought about by the technologies involved. For example, "face-to-face instruction" may be defined in one state as two-way interactive communication. Compressed video would then fall under this definition. Bruwelheide (1994) states that "the old, literal definition, where the teacher and the class shared the same physical location, no longer applies."[4] Transmission is one issue, but another one is copying at the site. Class size, the type of network (secured or unsecured), and other elements all conspire to make distance learning a "minefield" of controversy because of the diversity of available technologies.

Fair use of materials is governed not only by the four fair use criteria (purpose of the use, nature of the work, amount and substantiality of the work taken, and effect on the market) but also by the three tests: spontaneity, brevity, and cumulative effect. Since most distance learning is planned well in advance, one of the tests — spontaneity — is already excluded.

In addition, the cumulative effect would be a problem when the class size is several hundred (or several thousand) if the excerpt, even though brief, is placed on an unsecured network to which the public has access. Then the transmission of a work becomes a public performance, thereby becoming an infringement.

Developing distance learning is also not an easy task because of the constant development and sophistication of the technologies. Luckily, some of the problems have also decreased as time goes on. The development of secured networks through PIN and password protection and other engineering techniques have provided much-needed methods for controlling access, so that classes are private and transmissions are not public.

Distance Education Developments

While CONFU developed initial guidelines for discussion and review, it failed to create distance learning guidelines.[5] Section 403 of the Digital Millennium Copyright Act provided that not later than six months after the Act (April 28, 1999) the Copyright Office would provide a study on how to promote distance education through interactive digital networks while maintaining a balance between owners and users.[6] Eight factors were given that would be studied [403(b)]:

1. the need for an exemption from exclusive rights of copyright owners for distance education through digital networks,

2. the categories of works to be included under any distance education exemption,

3. the extent of appropriate quantitative limitations on the portions of works that may be used under any distance education exemption,

4. the parties who should be designated as eligible recipients of distance education materials under any distance education exemptions,

5. the parties who should be designated as eligible recipients of distance education materials under any distance education exemption,

6. whether and to what types of technological measures can or should be employed to safeguard against unauthorized access to, and use or retention of, copyrighted materials as a condition of eligibility for any distance education exemptions, including ... [those set out in] ... Section 110(2),

7. the extent to which the availability of licenses for the use of copyrighted works ... through interactive digital networks should be considered,

8. such other issues relating to ... interactive digital networks.

The Copyright Office solicited statements by December 7, 1998, and invited written submissions, met with interested parties, and held public meetings in spring 1999. The results of these discussions were that no new legislation was needed. This rapidly growing educational sector will develop and mature with the sophistication of the technology, since many of these use problems will be handled through market developments.

Transmission of Nondramatic Literary or Musical Works

Nondramatic literary or musical works are:

> works, *other than audiovisual works* [italics added], ... such as books, periodicals, manuscripts ... or cards, in which they are embodied [Section 101].

Musical, dramatic, and nondramatic works are not defined in the law. However, films, tapes, and phonorecords are considered nondramatic works in the sense of their physical embodiment. An instructor may hold up a phonorecord to show students in a distance learning class. To play the phonorecord would be a performance of a musical work. An instructor may discuss a novel. When that novel is acted out, it becomes a dramatic work. Section 110(1) specifically allows nondramatic literary or musical works to be transmitted for educational, charitable, or governmental purposes. Copyright owners of sound recordings also have a digital audio transmission right.

Nondramatic Literary or Musical Work Permissible Transmissions

Section 110(2) states that the categories for the transmission of a "nondramatic literary or musical work or display of a work" that may be made without permission or licensing include the "systematic instructional activities of a governmental body or a nonprofit educational institution." For-profit educational institutions would not be included. Permissible groups are:

1. **Teachers and other teaching staff:** "classrooms or similar places" such as institutional library media centers, computing labs, etc.
2. **The disabled:** "persons ... [who] because of their disabilities, or other special circumstances prevent their attendance in classrooms or similar places."
3. **Government personnel:** "officers or employees of governmental bodies as a part of their official duties or employment."

4. **Religious services:** "performance of a nondramatic literary or musical work or a dramatic-musical work of a religious nature, or display of a work, in the course of services at a place of worship or other religious assembly."

5. **Nonprofit educational, religious, or charitable purposes:** "transmission to the public" if "without any purpose of direct or indirect commercial advantage and without payment of any fee or other compensation for the performance to any of its performers, promoters, or organizers" if

    a. "no direct admission charge;"

    b. "the proceeds, after deducting reasonable costs of producing the performance, are used exclusively for educational, religious, or charitable purposes ... except where copyright owner [objects] in writing ... is served at least seven days before the ... performance ... and ... [complies] with requirements of the Register of Copyrights."

6. **Nonprofit governmental body, agricultural, or horticultural fair or exhibition**

7. **A vending establishment:** "open to the public at large without any direct or indirect admission charge, where the sole purpose of the performance is to promote the retail sale of copies or phonorecords ... and performance is not transmitted beyond the ... establishment."

8. **Veterans or nonprofit fraternal organization:** "a social function ... to which the public is not invited ... if the proceeds ... after deducting the reasonable costs of producing the performance are used exclusively for charitable purposes."

Blind and Handicapped Permissible Transmissions

Nondramatic literary or musical works are allowed to be transmitted to:

1. **Blind or handicapped who can't read normal print:** "in the course of a transmission specifically designed for and primarily directed to blind or other handicapped persons who are unable to read normal printed materials as a result of their handicap."

2. **Deaf or handicapped unable to hear aural signals:** "accompanying a transmission of visual signals, if the performance is made without any purpose of direct or indirect commercial advantage [by a] governmental body ... a noncommercial educational broadcast station ... or ... a cable system."

Dramatic performances are allowed to be transmitted: **"on a single occasion** of a dramatic literary work published at least ten years before the date of the performance ... for ... blind or other handicapped persons who are unable to read normal printed material." It must be done without "direct or indirect commercial advantage," and "its transmission is made through a radio sub-carrier."

University Fraternity or Sorority Charity Exception

Transmission is not allowed to a university fraternity or sorority unless the event is "held solely to raise funds for a specific charitable purpose."

Definition of Performance

When a literary work is performed, as in a drama, play, ballet or pantomime, it becomes a dramatic work and is not eligible for the nondramatic exemptions.

> To "perform" a work means to recite, render, play, dance, or act it, either directly or by means of any device or process or, in the case of an audiovisual work, to show its images in any sequence or to make sounds accompanying it audible [Section 101].

Both dramatic works and audiovisual works are performed. Audiovisual works are performed with the aid of devices or machines.

Audiovisual Works

These works are a separate category because they

> consist of a series of related images which are intrinsically intended to be shown by the use of machines or devices such as projectors, viewers, or electronic equipment, together with accompanying sounds [Section 101].

The playing of a videotape is a performance which is acceptable in traditional face-to-face teaching. When a videotape is transmitted through satellite, cable, or methods outside an institution, it becomes important to limit such a performance through PIN or password so that it is not open to the general public. If the general public can view a performance, then permission and licensing are needed.

Videocassette Transmissions and Video Courses

Videos are increasingly being used in video-based courses and as a supplement to mixed media courses. For example, a number of taped lessons by the instructor could be sent to students during a semester course which are supplemented with three in-class meetings and e-mail. In the instance mentioned, commercially made videos could be shown during the in-class meetings.

All commercial videocassettes are leased to the user,[7] and most producers withhold transmission rights.[8] The restriction on the transmission of videocassettes is because they are audiovisual works and are not to be used in uncontrolled environments in which the general public has access. Such a use would then require a theatrical license for showing, not an educational one. When ordering the video, it is best to state what the use will be, such as "for viewing on PIN or password-protected satellite network." In this way such a use is stated in the request, and permission may be granted through the order form.

The key to video transmission in the educational context is to restrict the transmission to students enrolled in the class. Videos that are mailed to remote sites for copying for individual students for a class would need permission.[9] A video transmitted with restrictions that prevent the general public from viewing or copying videos would be a permissible use, such as a two-way interactive fiber optics network, PIN or password-controlled satellite network, or other controlled environment for a course.[10]

Web-Based and Internet-Based Courses

Web-based courses are an increasingly important and cost-effective way of delivering instruction and are offered at the high school,[11] college, and university levels.[12] Web-based courses can combine many formats to present unique opportunities for the student to "tailor" the learning experience to individual needs. For example, Web-based courses can be restricted through a Web-based learning system, such as Learning Space, Top Class, Web-Course-in-a-Box or other commercially available program which is password-restricted, has restricted e-mail functions, and other services. Other Internet courses can be offered via e-mail with supporting materials such as instructor-made videotapes, readings and books mailed to the student upon enrollment. Readings and other sections of the course can be offered on the Internet at the instructor's Web site or on a Web server that is password restricted.

There are many possible technological combinations for such courses. Just as with satellite, fiber optic, and cable technology, the key to providing materials is to restrict access by the general public. Because of the sheer magnitude of the potential audience and the complete inability to control reproduction of works sent unrestricted on the Internet and Web, licensing for certain materials is necessary and in some cases will not be granted for this reason alone. The decision to license or not to license is one of the bundle of rights of the copyright owner. Following are some guidelines for course materials for the Web and Internet.

Quicktime Video Clips

1. *Commercially prepared clips on compact disc:* Check the licensing agreement to see if Internet or Web use is excluded. While image compact discs may state that they are "royalty free," their use may or may not be allowed on the license. Licenses are exclusionary. The rule is that if the license does not restrict such use, then it is permitted.[13]

2. *Clips available on the Web and Internet:* Those clips that are available just by downloading may or may not give permission to copy. If permission is not given, then they can be "hot linked" (automatically linked to through a pointer) or can be cited with a Universal Resource Locator and the student can go to the site and view it. It is possible to find out if someone is linking to your site. Should this person wish to have the link removed, they may do so and the link should be removed. For these reasons any alteration of the link's frames would not be permissible.

Some clips are engineered so that they cannot be copied. There are on-line services by commercial vendors that allow downloading for a fee or are password-protected for downloading purposes. Their licenses may state that their use is restricted to personal use only or a license fee is required for other uses, in which case the owner should be contacted.

Display

Display of a work

> means to show a copy of it, either directly or by means of a film, slide, television image, or any other device or process, or in the case of a motion picture or other audiovisual work, to show individual images nonsequentially [Section 101].

This right, with certain exceptions, is reserved to the copyright owner. There is a wide range of images that can be used for distance learning. Individually copyrighted photographs must have permission or licensing to be displayed. Student artwork may or may not require student or parental permission. A college or university's artwork collection could have works for which the artist owns the copyright or the institution does. In cases where the institution owns the copyright, photographs or slides of the work can be made or images can be digitized from the works owned by the university. Otherwise, "thumbnail images" may be the only option for use in distance learning courses where the university does not own the copyright to the work that is kept in a university collection. A "thumbnail" is

> used in a visual on-line catalog or image browsing display to enable visual identification of records in an educational institution's image collection; is a small-scale, typically low-resolution, digital reproduction which has no intrinsic commercial or reproductive value.[14]

There are many types of works, types of transmissions and course formats, and artwork types to be considered in developing distance learning courses:

1. *Images available on the Web and Internet:* Hotbot, the Amazing Picture Machine, and some other search engines and sites allow a search for an image only.[15]

2. *Digitizing images for use on the Web and Internet:* There are different categories of images:

  a. *Images made by students who are under the age of 18 (K–12):* Such images could be drawings, photographs, etc. A statement on the permission form that the images are the work of the student would be advised, as well as a statement that the student is legally responsible for the image being a lawfully created one (and not plagiarized). Permission for these images would be requested from the parents. This would also make the child and parents feel that their work was appreciated and valuable. Pictures of students themselves are a different matter. See the Internet chapter.

  b. *Images made by students who are over the age of 18 (college and university):* See above. Permission for these images would be requested from the students themselves. While students in this category have reached the age of legal independence, the college or university still functions as the parent ("in loco parentis"), and caution is advised in posting the images of students themselves. See Internet chapter.

  c. *Images from print materials:* Images can be collectively or individually copyrighted. Georgia Harper, General Counsel for the University of Texas system, states on the UT Web site that when digitizing images, "limit access to all images to students in the class and terminate access at the end of the term."[16]

    d. *Images from online materials:* These could include online versions
of periodicals, advertising or images on Web sites. In virtually all
cases it is best to make a link to that visual, since most of this material is copyrighted. In cases where it is not, allowance for Web and
Internet use will be stated. In many cases the image cannot be
taken. In other cases the image is "watermarked," so that its use
can be tracked.[17] While Netscape and Microsoft Explorer have
image capture functions, just because an image can be captured
does not mean it should be. These functions were intended for
personal use.

Company logos and trademarks are a special case. Do not take a logo
from a company to put on a course Web site without permission, unless course
access is restricted or such use is integral to the course (such as a comparison
of logos on the Web, either for business or art purposes, for example). Even
then a link is suggested. Logos are trademarked, not copyrighted. (See also
The Internet and World Wide Web, Chapter 9.)

Student Use of Artwork on Course Web Sites

Students may use web browsers to capture and save images for course
assignments and place these on restricted-access Web servers. Copyrighted
images should not be posted on college- or university-maintained personal
web pages for students.

> Students may download, transmit and print out images for personal study
> and for use in the preparation of academic course assignments and other
> requirements.[18]

Categories of Materials that Require Permission/Licensing

Other than the exceptions noted in the previous section, the categories
of works which fair use will not cover are:

1. entire audiovisual works copied for use or transmitted in courses with
unrestricted access,
2. dramatic literary or musical works copied for use or transmitted in
courses with unrestricted access.

New guidelines or a change in the copyright law would affect the use of the
above works in distance learning courses.

Video Transmission — Usage Examples

1. May an instructor on a two-way video and audio interactive fiber-optic network show a video if the number of students is 30? *Yes. Access is restricted, and the class size is the same as a face-to-face class size. In some states the fact that it is two-way interactive makes it by definition "face-to-face."

2. Same as above question, but may I show it on a password- or PIN-protected satellite network? *Yes. Access is restricted.

3. May I show videotapes created by an institution for a telecourse? *Yes. This would be permissible.

4. May I show a video via closed circuit to an entire class, half of which must view it in another room because of room size constraints in the original classroom? *Yes. It is one section of a course in an emergency situation.

5. If an instructor records a videotape of a two-way interactive class of 18 students that contains copyrighted works, including a videocassette played for educational purposes, and the tape is kept for review purposes for that semester only for students who were absent to view, would this be permissible? *Yes. The purpose is review for students who were absent. Students should not be allowed to make their own copies of the classes, however, and the tapes should be erased at the end of the semester.

6. Same as number 5 but may a tape be made and kept for backup purposes in case of technical difficulties for the rest of the semester only? *Yes. This would be permissible.

7. May a faculty member record a brief segment of a television program on a channel that is free to the public through regular broadcast television stations (ABC, CBS, NBC, Fox, USA) and show it for a PIN- or password-restricted satellite course? *Yes. If it was a brief clip, this should be permissible. If an entire program were copied for the class, then permission would be required. If it was a program on a pay-per-view channel, this would not be permissible. If it was on some subscription/cable/satellite channels (The Learning Channel, The Discovery Channel), it might be permissible. On other subscription/cable/satellite channels (Encore, HBO, Cinemax) it would not be permissible.

8. Same as number 7, but may the clip be included if the course is not PIN- or password-protected? *No. Any time a clip is shown without restrictions, it is by definition open to the public and therefore could be a public performance even if the purpose was educational.

9. Same as number 7, but may I use it in a course that is given on a two-way interactive fiber-optics network? *Yes. Access is restricted and, as mentioned before, is most likely considered as face-to-face instruction.

10. Same as number 7, but may I use it in a course on the school's public

access cable channel? *No. In a large city where many people receive the cable channel, such a use would require permission (ABC, CBS, and so forth).

Artwork Used in Distance Learning — Usage Examples

1. May I copy a logo from another Web site and use it as my own for my Web-based course? *No. This is not permitted. If it were used as an example for a Web-based course, it might be permitted, although the company could request that it be removed and a link added, instead. In a course with restricted access this would be more permissible.

2. May I place a student's artwork in my university Web-based course on a secured, password-protected Web site for this course? *Yes, if the student has granted permission or there is a statement on the enrollment form that the student will abide by the student handbook and or the form/handbook states that work produced by the student for course assignments is the intellectual property of the university. Requesting student permission for artwork is recommended.

3. May I digitize photographs from a copyrighted art book and place them in a video I will make for students enrolled in a videotape version of the course? *No, not without permission or licensing. Photographs are usually individually copyrighted.

4. May I digitize drawings that the university has in its art collection for use in my Web-based art course? *Maybe. If the university owns the copyright to these drawings, then this is permissible. If the university only owns the drawing but the artist retains the copyright, then a "thumbnail" or miniature, postage-stamp-size image is allowed.

Useful Web Sites for Distance Learning Issues

Regents Guide to Understanding Copyright and Fair Use.
　　http://www.peachnet.edu/admin/legal/copyright/copy.html
　　This excellent site covers many types of distance learning and has a large question-and-answer section.

USPTO Web Site.
　　http://www.uspto.gov/
　　This site has information, news, reports, etc., on intellectual property. The CONFU reports on multimedia, distance learning, and digital images are on this site.
　　Again, Web site information or addresses can change. Check each address for specific communication.

Harper, G., General Counsel, University of Texas System. UT Rules of Thumb.
    http://www.utsystem.edu/OGC/IntellectualProperty/
    This excellent site has much copyright information for distance learning
at the university level. The "rules of thumb" provide guidance in a short form
on several topics (i.e., work made for hire, telecourse, software policy).

Can Do

You may:

1. Transmit a nondramatic literary or musical work.
2. Transmit a dramatic work to the blind or handicapped on a one-time
only basis of a work that is at least ten years old.
3. Show a photograph, chart, table, or still from a motion picture in a
televised telecourse which has restricted access (PIN- or password-protected).
4. Use public domain material—artwork, Quicktime clips, text, or
music—in a distance course, whether it has restricted or unrestricted access.
5. Use "thumbnails" of artwork, when the institution does not own the
copyright for instructional purposes.

Cannot Do

You may not:

1. Copy a copyrighted video for a course.
2. Transmit a copyrighted video in a course with unrestricted access
without permission.
3. Create a videotape of clips of other videotapes and broadcast it without permission.
4. Use music from a popular CD to accompany a presentation in an unrestricted course.

Tried and True

1. Use small amounts of other people's copyrighted work in restricted-
access courses.
2. Limit access to course materials.
3. Terminate student access to course materials at the end of the term.
4. Get permission for works that are used repeatedly.
5. Remember that course use and fair use may not be the same.

Beware

1. Others can find out if you have used their artwork or music on your
course Web site.
2. Others can find out if you have linked to their Web sites.

Policy Suggestions

Bruwelheide (1994) provides several recommendations on policy.[19] Following are a few of them:

1. Develop a copyright policy and have it adopted by a governing body.

2. Provide training in the policy and consider having employees sign a statement (or clause in their contract) that they will abide by it.

3. When in doubt, ask for permission. In the long run, it's cheaper than controversy or a lawsuit.

4. "[T]here is a great deal of educational copying which is legitimate."

5. Give credit on all legally made copies and uses of materials.

6. Develop a form letter for permissions. (The author suggests a phone call during which a contact person is identified, with a fax and e-mail address for quick followup.)

7. Retain a paper trail of permissions.

8. Develop procedures for monitoring use.

Part IV
Library Use of
Copyrighted Materials

11

Library
Reproduction Rights

Section 108: Library Reproduction Rights

"Library reproduction rights" is an important, and highly contested, part of the copyright law and its amendments, including the two revisions in 1998 (the Digital Millennium Copyright Act and the Copyright Term Extension Act). In part because of that, Section 108 is "(1) lengthy, (2) complex, (3) sometimes ambiguous, and (4) heavily embellished by legislative history."[1] The five-year study [Section 108(i)] conducted after the law's enactment stated that the Copyright Office found the library provision to be a "workable structural framework for obtaining a balance between creators' rights and users' needs."[2] However, the American Library Association not only raised objection to the belief of the Register that a balance had been struck, it raised objection to the premise of the *Report* itself.[3] The five-year report requirement in the law was later repealed in 1992. Because of the continuing controversy and the lengthy and sometimes conflicting legislative history of this section, noted legal authorities Alan Latman and Robert Gorman observed that "it is no wonder that some libraries, preferring to avoid the minefield described above, are removing themselves from photocopying activities."[4] Even with the controversies, most compliance with Section 108 provisions has proceeded for nonprofit libraries at an orderly pace.[5] However, there are many definitional ambiguities that remain for the tests of time and technology to resolve.[6]

While the *House Report* specifically states that a library or archive need not be nonprofit nor generally open to the public, it must be open to those doing research.[7] Libraries in for-profit institutions have changed their copying practices greatly since the historic *American Geophysical Union v. Texaco, Inc.*, case.[8] A commercial purpose was found in Texaco library's photocopying since it was done to "improve Texaco's commercial performance" and since copies were made for the company employee files rather than to directly aid a specific study being done.[9] Because of this case, document delivery companies and systems sprang up almost overnight to accompany the need for payment mechanisms for copying in for-profit companies, as the distinction between copying in nonprofit and profit companies was further defined through the combined decisions on this case.[10]

Reproduction of Works in Last 20 Years of Protection

The Copyright Term Extension Act of 1998 provides that libraries, archives and nonprofit educational institutions may treat works in their last 20 years of protection (the life of the author + 70 years) as if they are in public domain for noncommercial purposes, provided that 1) the work is "not subject to normal commercial exploitation" and 2) use of the work stops if the copyright owner provides notice to the contrary — even if the work had never been commercially exploited (P.L. 105-278).

General Provisions of Section 108:
Reproduction by Libraries and Archives[11]

Section 108 Copying Eligibility Conditions

For a library or archive to be eligible for Section 108 copying of a work or phonorecord, certain conditions must be met:

1. *Noncommercial purpose* — the copy must be reproduced without any purpose of "direct or indirect commercial advantage" [Section 108(a)(1)].

2. *Collection accessibility* — the collection must be available for use by others "doing research in a specialized field" [Section 108(a)(2)].

3. *Copyright legend* — the work must include a "notice of copyright" [Section 108(a)(3)] or a legend stating that the work may be protected by copyright if no copyright notice can be found.

4. *Isolated and unrelated copying* — the reproduction and distribution of works or phonorecords must be "isolated and unrelated" [Section 108(g)].

5. *The copy becomes "the property of the user"* — [Section 108(d)(1)].

6. *The copy's purpose is educational* — "private study, scholarship, or research" [Section 108(d)(1)].

7. *A copyright warning is prominently displayed at order desk* — "a warning of copyright in accordance with the requirements that the Register of Copyrights shall prescribe by regulation" [Section 108(d)(2)].

In addition, the library, archive, or its employee must also:

8. *Be unaware of related or concerted copying* — there must be no "substantial reason to believe" that multiple copies are being made, either "on one occasion or over a period of time" [Section 108(g)(1)].

9. *Not engage in systematic copying* — no "systematic reproduction or distribution of single or multiple copies" [Section 108(g)(2)].

10. *Not engage in interlibrary arrangements in which the receiving library's purpose is to substitute for subscription or purchase of a work* — there must be no "purpose or effect that the library or archives receiving such copies or phonorecords for distribution does so in such aggregate quantities as to substitute for a subscription to or purchase of a work" [Section 108(g)(2)].

"**Reproduction**" was not defined in the Copyright Act. However, with the Digital Millennium Copyright Act some of the restrictions on digital materials and preservation have been relaxed. The scope and use of this section has grown in direct proportion to newer technologies that allow for analog and digital reproduction, such as facsimile and computers (P.L. 105-304). Section 108 includes articles, individual and collective works, illustrations, diagrams or similar works, and audiovisual news programs [Section 108(h)].

Section 404 has been amended to allow "three copies or phonorecords if the copy or phonorecord reproduced is currently in the collections of the library or archives" (P.L. 105-304) Conditions must be met:

1. "solely for purposes of preservation and security";

2. "for deposit for research use in another [not-for-profit] library or archives";

3. Section 108(c): "solely for the purpose of replacement of a copy or phonorecord that is damaged, deteriorating, lost or stolen, 1) if the library or archives has, after a reasonable effort, determined that an unused replacement cannot be obtained at a fair price; and 2) any such copy or phonorecord that is reproduced in digital format is not made available to the public in that format outside the premises of the library or archives in lawful possession of such copy."

4. "for purposes of this subsection, a format shall be considered obsolete if the machine or device necessary to render perceptible a work stored in that format is no longer manufactured or is no longer reasonably available in the commercial marketplace."

If the above conditions are met, the categories of works that the library or archive may copy in whole or in part are:

1. **Unpublished works** — a copy or phonorecord of an unpublished work "solely for purposes of preservation and security" or for deposit or research use in another library which also meets the copying provisions. [Section 108(b)]

2. **Published works** — a copy or phonorecord of a published work "solely

for the purpose of replacement of a copy or phonorecord that is damaged, deteriorating, lost, or stolen, if ... an unused replacement cannot be obtained at a fair price" [Section 108(c)].

3. **Interlibrary loan copies** —where the user makes a request from another library or archive of "no more than one article or other contribution to a copyrighted collection or periodical issues, or to a copy or phonorecord of a small part of any other copyrighted work" [Section 108(d)]. Two conditions must be met: 1) it must be the "property of the user" [Section 108(d)(1)], and 2) a copyright warning is displayed "prominently" according to the requirements of the Register of Copyrights [Section 108(d)(2)].

4. **Interlibrary loan copies of works unavailable at a fair price** —based on a "reasonable investigation ... [that a work] ... cannot be obtained at a fair price [Section 108(e)]. Two conditions must be met: 1) it must be the "property of the user" [Section 108(e)(1)], and 2) a copyright warning is displayed "prominently" according to the requirements of the Register of Copyrights [Section 108(e)(2)].

5. **Audiovisual news program copies** —A library is allowed to reproduce and distribute by lending "a limited number of copies and excerpts by a library or archives of an audiovisual news program" [Section 108(f)(3)]. Two conditions must be met: 1) it must be the "property of the user" [Section 108(f)(2)], and 2) a copyright warning is displayed "prominently" according to the requirements of the Register of Copyrights [Section 108(f)(2)]. The library or archive must meet the eligibility provisions, as well.

Excluded Works

Section 108 excludes musical works, pictorial, graphic, or sculptural works, and motion pictures or other audiovisual works other than news programs set forth in Section 108(b).

Definitions of "Reasonable Investigation" and "Reasonable Price" [as amended by P.L. 105-304]

Based on some available definitions of these two terms from various sources, the test would be for an impartial observer, after reviewing the circumstances, to come to the conclusion that the decision was equitable. The tests themselves seem to rely on independent decision-making made by cost comparisons under normal purchasing conditions and in accordance with standard library purchasing policies.

> **"Reasonable investigation"** has been defined by the *House Report (94-1476)* as: [Varying] ... according to the circumstances of a particular situation... It will always require recourse to commonly known trade sources in the

United States and in the normal situation also to the publisher or other copyright owner (if such owner can be located using the address listed in the copyright registration), or an authorized reproduction service.

"Reasonable price" has been defined by:

1. Bruwelheide (1995) as[12]:

> [T]he price close as possible to manufacturing costs plus royalty payments.... If the original format was multivolume and single volumes are not available, it could be argued that the full set price is not a fair price for a single volume.

2. Reed (1987) as[13]:

> *Original format —* ...the latest suggested retail price of an unused copy. *Reproduction —* the price as close as possible to manufacturing costs plus royalty payments. The copy should be available within 30 days. If the original format was multivolume and single volumes are not available, it could be argued that the full set price is not a fair price for a single volume.

3. The Association of American Publishers and the Authors League of America as[14]:

> the fair price of a work is defined as: a) the suggested retail price if available from the publisher; b) if not so available, the prevailing retail price; or c) if an authorized reproducing service is used, the normal price charged by that service.

Library Liabilities for Certain Types of Copying

The library or archives or its employees will be held liable for cases in which

1. *there is awareness or a "substantial reason to believe"* that related or concerted reproduction or distribution of multiple copies or phonorecords of the same material, whether made on one occasion or over a period of time, and whether intended for aggregate use by one or more individuals or for separate use by the individual members of a group [Section 108(g)(1)].

2. *systematic reproduction or distribution* in such a way "as to substitute for a subscription to or purchase of such work" [Section 108(g)(2)].

Prohibitions on Circumvention of Protection Technologies

While Title I of the Act deals with prohibitions on circumvention of protection technologies and prevents the sale of certain kinds of video recorders for two years and 18 months, respectively, the Librarian of Congress is to conduct rulemaking to determine if the "anti-circumvention" prohibitions will "adversely affect" individuals and institutions' "ability to make noninfringing uses" of copyrighted works (texts, maps, software). In addition the librarian must issue a three-year waiver from anti-circumvention prohibition if it adversely or is likely to adversely affect fair use. Nonprofit libraries, archives and educational institutions are exempted from criminal penalties if it can be demonstrated that they were unaware the such actions violated the law. Title II expressly states that many valuable activities based on the Fair Use Doctrine will not constitute illegal "anti-circumvention."

Copyright Notice Stipulations for Libraries

The copyright legend stipulated in Section 108(a)(3) as amended by P.L. 105-304 and succeeding subsections and the copyright warning that is stipulated in Section 108(d)(2) and succeeding subsections are not specified in terms of type size, wording, and so forth. The American Library Association has exemplary notices, and there are many notice types in copyright licensing books and journals.

Sample Warning Concerning Copyright Restrictions

The copyright law of the United States (Title 17, United States Code) governs the making of photocopies or other reproduction of copyrighted material. Under certain conditions specified in the law, libraries and archives are authorized to furnish a photocopy or other reproduction. One of these specified conditions is that the photocopy or reproduction is not to be "used for any purpose other than private study, scholarship, or research." If a user makes a request for, or later uses, a photocopy or reproduction for purposes in excess of "fair use," that user may be liable for copyright infringement. This institution reserves the right to refuse to accept a copying order if, in its judgment, fulfillment of the order would involve violation of copyright law.[15]

Interlibrary Loan (ILL)

While P.L. 105-304 allows interlibrary loan of digital copies to other libraries and archives [Section 404], interlibrary loan questions date back to the Commission on New Technological Uses of Copyright Works.[16] The CONTU suggested that the borrowing library adhere to the "rule of five"— five articles per periodical for the past five calendar years.[17] The lending library must now include a copyright legend on all copies and check to see if the requirements for the notice of compliance with the guidelines have been filled.

If the request does not comply, the American Library Association recommends that the request be denied.[18] However, some lending libraries either fill the request with a warning or call the borrowing library and ask for this information.[19]

The law permits libraries and archives to reproduce and distribute materials for interlibrary loan provided there is no substantial aggregate use by one or more individuals, and there is no systematic distribution of multiple copies. Obviously, conditions such as these require institutional discretion according to subscription policies and usage, yet, since the law has gone into effect, few interlibrary loans have gone beyond the five-copy limit on photocopied journals.[20]

The terms "related and concerted" and "systematic" reproduction or distribution of interlibrary loan materials have been a source of disagreement for librarians and their counsel due to the apparent inability of legislators to define them.[21]

The Register of Copyrights enumerated the guidelines [Subsection 208(g)(2)] in a different manner to draw attention to the major points of the House guidelines[22]:

1. The guidelines of the *House Report* were intended to cover "the most frequently encountered interlibrary case"—obtaining photocopies of articles published within five years prior to the request.

2. The meaning of the (g)(2) provision for older works will be left open to later interpretation.

3. "The guidelines don't apply to entities that exist to make and distribute photocopies from a central source."

4. The "aggregate substitution quantity" is "six or more copies of one or more articles from a given title during a calendar year."

5. No more than five copies from a work can be made during a calendar year for other materials.

6. If the library has a subscription to a periodical or a copy of other materials, but the works are not available, then the copying is considered "local" rather than ILL.

7. A photocopy can only be requested instead of an ILL if the requesting library could have supplied the copy from its own collection, but the work was unavailable for copying.

8. Only requests accompanied by representations that the requesting library is complying with interlibrary loans can be filled.

9. Requesting libraries must maintain records on the disposition of all requests governed by the guidelines "until the third calendar year after the year in which the request was made."[23]

The "rule of five" does not apply to ILL requests made by libraries which have entered subscriptions to the works of which a patron desires a copy.[24]

Records should be kept until December 31 of the third calendar year from which the request was made. For example, if a request was made January 23, 2000, the records should be kept until December 31, 2005. The requests must be kept in the same order in which the loan was made until that third calendar year. Information contained in the record should be summarized before it is destroyed.[25]

Unsupervised Photocopying Equipment

The library is not responsible for illegal photocopying when warnings on the danger of copyright infringement are displayed. These signs can be purchased. If the librarian is requested to make a copy, or to loan it out, the request can be refused. It is sufficient that a staff member has reason to believe that a request for a copy from reserve is to be used illegally. The librarian does not have to ask how the material is to be used. Comments of the patron are enough. In addition, copying machines in the library should also have a notice like this one:

> NOTICE: PHOTOCOPYING RESTRICTIONS
> The copyright law of the United States (Title 17, United States Code) governs the making of photocopies or other reproductions of copyrighted materials. The person using this equipment is liable for copyright infringement.[26]

The library is not liable for illegal photocopying of reserve or other material made on unsupervised copiers. The meaning of "unsupervised" has not been clearly defined, but if a copier is in another room, or out of the view of the librarian, the librarian is not liable. There are different types of notices, but the notice should indicate that the institution is not liable for the copyright infringement of the patron on an unsupervised copier, and that the patron is responsible for violations of copyright law in that instance.

Reserve Room Photocopying

The legislative history of the 1976 act indicates that the issue of library reserve photocopying "did not receive great attention during revision" and was not addressed in Section 108 of the act.[27] The Register's *Report*, the ALA, and the American Association of Law Libraries (AALL) agree that, unlike other library photocopying practices which are restricted, library photocopying of materials for reserve room use falls within the fair use provisions of Section 107 under the concept of the "library-as-agent."[28] "Reserve copying is legal only if authorized by the copyright owner or by Section 107."[29] The only specific recommendation made by the Register's *Report* was that permission should be obtained for multiple-term retention of multiple reserve copies.[30] However, some libraries allow multiple-term retention, believing that "the guidelines forbid repeated *copying*, but nowhere forbid the repeated *use* of material."[31] Other legal commentators concur that reserve room services are an extension of classroom copying guidelines, yet few definite answers to the number of copies which can be placed on reserve can be provided.[32] With regard to the special needs of higher education, the Section 107 guidelines state that "there may be instances in which copying which does not fall within the guidelines stated below may nonetheless be permitted under the criteria of fair use."[33] It was also noted in the *Report* that both the Association of American University Professors and the Association of American Law Schools strongly criticized the Section 107 guidelines as "too restrictive."[34] The *Report* noted that "the Committee believes the guidelines are a reasonable interpretation of the *minimum* standards of fair use."[35]

When placing multiple copies of fair use materials on reserve, it has been recommended that the photocopies be identified as belonging to that faculty member and should include full bibliographic information and should bear a notice of copyright.[36] The ALA and the AALL believe that a reasonable number of copies in most instances will be six.[37] Other factors which permit more copies in the library reserve room situation are:

1. The amount of material should be reasonable in relation to the total amount of material assigned for one term of a course, taking into account the nature of the course, its subject matter, and level [Section 107(1) and (3)].

2. The number of copies should be reasonable in light of the number of students enrolled, the difficulty and timing of assignments, and the number of other courses which may assign the same materials [Section 107(1) and (3)].

3. The material should contain a notice of copyright [Section 401].

4. The effect of photocopying the material should not be detrimental to the market for the work. (The library should own at least one copy of the work.)[38] [Section 107(4)].

Library Networks

The Register of Copyrights believes that library networks may not make use of Section 108, and doubts the applicability of Section 107.[39] However, the American Association of Law Libraries (AALL) believes that "the simple fact that libraries become members of networks does not necessarily preclude them from replication rights provided by Sections 107 and 108."[40] Because of the formative stages of such large networks, the controversy and opinion that surrounds ILL in library networks will quite possibly change.

Libraries may not agree among themselves to purchase subscriptions to journals that other libraries have agreed not to purchase in a cooperative arrangement. That is because, according to Section 108(g)(2), the "purpose or effect ... [is to] substitute for a subscription to or purchase of such a work." Copies may be obtained from the Copyright Clearance Center (CCC) by fax, phone, online, or from other authorized providers.

Newsletters

While fair use applies to copying small sections of newsletters (such as the table of contents), the *House Report* had these special comments:

> It is argued that newsletters, as distinguished from house organs and publicity or advertising publications, be given separate treatment. It is argued that newsletters are particularly vulnerable to mass photocopying, and that most newsletters have fairly modest circulations. Whether the copying of portions of a newsletter is an act of infringement or a fair use will necessarily turn on the facts of the individual case. However, as a general principle, it seems clear that *the scope of the fair use doctrine should be considerably narrower in the case of newsletters than in that of either mass-circulation periodicals or scientific journals....* Copying by a profit-making user of even a small portion of a newsletter may have a significant impact on the commercial market for the work.[41]

Pasha Publications, Inc. v. Enmark Gas Corporation[42] (1992) held that copying and faxing an entire newsletter for commercial purposes was not fair use. The other case was *American Geophysical Union v. Texaco, Inc.*, which was about copying.[43]

House Report 94-1476 states that:

> As a general principle, it seems clear that the scope of the fair use doctrine should be considerably narrower in the case of newsletters than in that of either mass circulation periodicals or scientific journals.[44]

In summary, photocopying the table of contents or subscribing to reprints of the summary part of a subscription would be an option.[45] Libraries qualifying under Section 108 copying should follow fair use guidelines closely. For-profit libraries, except in isolated instances of photocopying, should monitor newsletter copying for the need for subscriptions or licensed use.

Selective Dissemination of Information (SDI)

Routing tables of contents and selected articles for patrons as a library service is covered by this section. It is clear that photocopying of tables of contents as a regular service to patrons would be within fair use. Routing of selected articles to patrons through SDI service would be permissible so long as the service was requested by the patron, and one subscription to a journal was not ordered and routed systematically to take the place of ordering several.

Libraries are not permitted to purchase one subscription to a journal and then route a large number of copies of an article to interested employees (a CCC license should be obtained for this purpose).[46] Some in-house copying at user request is within fair use. However, neither the act nor the legislative history provides numerical guidelines on what constitutes copying in such large quantities as to be systematic copying. Careful record keeping of patron SDI requests will aid in determining if copying is within Fair Use [Section 107] and Library Photocopying Guidelines [Section 108].

Commercial Publishing of U.S. Government Works

Commercial publishing of uncopyrighted government works is an acceptable practice for certain publishers because of the limited exposure and printing of certain documents which have importance for selected populations. In most cases the commercial prices are at least twice as high as the prices the Government Printing Office (GPO) charges for the same documents.[47] The advantage of purchasing from a commercial publisher is the improved typesetting and paper quality more suitable for library or institutional use.

Should one not desire these features and, instead, prefer purchasing the original document, it is advisable to check authorship. If it is a government publication, it will be so noted. Since some government works are contracted, and thus eligible for copyright, the lack of a copyright mark will indicate that the work is a government work and has been previously published by the GPO.

Electronic Copies

P.L. 105-304 codifies the right of libraries, archives, and a nonprofit educational institution that "functions as such" to make a "facsimile or digital form" of a work for preservation purposes. Libraries can make electronic copies of works. A deciding factor in the handling of these works, however, is the handling of the work that is transmitted and the disposal of the initial library copy once the user copy has been received. Electronic copies are still copies. Section 108, as amended, makes it now permissible for libraries "to reproduce no more than three copies or phonorecord of a work." This would include, for example, the copy that was faxed to another site. The originating copy would be discarded. The copy that arrived at the site would be the one copy that was sent. To keep or use the originating copy would be to make two copies. Accurate records are essential for making any electronic copies.

It should be noted on the topic of digital copies that the Working Group (1995), in response to Section 108 not covering digital reproduction, stated that "it is important to expand the exemption so that digital copying by libraries and archives is permitted under certain circumstances."[48] It recommended that Section 108 be amended to allow libraries and archives to 1) prepare three copies of a work in digital form as long as only one copy is in use, 2) not to require copyright notice, and 3) to authorize the making of digital copies for preservation. All of the recommendations were added by P.L. 105-304.

Electronic Reserves

A draft version of the electronic reserve guidelines was developed in 1996 but never reached fruition.[49] However, discussions have been continued by the American Council of Research Libraries (ACRL) Electronic Discussion Group.[50] Because of access afforded by new technologies, a corresponding narrowing in what constitutes fair use in college, university, and special libraries has developed, as well.[51] A growing number of universities are implementing electronic reserves in restricted environments. Access is limited by IP address and a name-proxy server, with password identification, in most instances. When access cannot be restricted, then public domain material — lecture notes (as long as copyrighted articles are not part of them), past exams, problem sets, keys, notes, assignments — are allowed. Libraries that are accepting electronic reserves take into account access, number of students, the type of material, and other considerations, depending on the nature of the work to be placed on reserve. Permissions are required for some works subject to the nature, scope, or extent of copying.

In the spring of 1994 the National Science Foundation, Advanced Research Projects Agency (ARPA), and NASA developed a Digital Libraries Initiative which was responded to internationally. Beginning in 1994 the Digital Libraries Research Conference began with 30 projects. Progress continues to be made in this effort.[52]

Library Reproduction — Usage Examples

1. We have some old unpublished photographs, phonorecords, and manuscripts in our American history collection that are deteriorating, and we would like to preserve them by making a copy of them. May we do this? *Yes. Unpublished works and phonorecordings that the library owns may be copied for preservation and security purposes, including digital copies.

2. Same as question 1, but we would like to copy microfilm and microfiche. May we do this? *Yes. These are "similar adjuncts" and are used to make copies. Up to three copies may be made for preservation and security purposes [Section 108(h)].

3. Same as question 1, but we would like to copy a published book for preservation and security purposes. May we do this? *Yes. The library must have first made "reasonable investigation" to locate an unused replacement copy and have determined that one cannot be purchased at a "reasonable price."

4. Same as question 3, but what does "reasonable investigation" and "reasonable price" mean? How do we go about it? *Answer: "Reasonable investigation" generally means that the library should go through the normal routine that is used in other purchases: contact trade sources, the publisher (if listed on the copyright registration), or an authorized duplicating service. "Reasonable price" means that if it is in the original format, then the latest retail price of an unused copy. If the original format was single volume and the fair price is for a multivolume set, then the price of a full set could possibly be considered too high. An impartial observer should be able to understand and agree with the decision made by the librarian.

5. We would like to lend phonorecords in our collection, but the phonorecords we have now are deteriorating. May we copy phonorecords to loan to patrons? *Yes, but see questions 3 and 4 for the conditions under which this can be done. In addition, the lending copy must become the property of the user, and the librarian must have no indication that the work will be used for anything other than research or scholarship.

6. May we make a copy of a copyrighted videotape in beta format for preservation and security purposes? Our beta-videotape machine is not repairable. *Yes. See question 4. A copy or copies may be made when the equipment is no longer commercially available.

7. May we make a copy of a copyrighted videotape for lending purposes? *Yes, but *only* if it is not "subject to normal commercial exploitation" or if it can be "obtained at a reasonable price" [Section 404] and it is for "preservation, scholarship or research" [Section 404]. For example, the original could be deteriorating or on obsolete equipment (beta). See question 6.

8. We would like to begin having electronic reserves for a faculty member with a Web-based course that is password-protected and averages 20 students per semester. May we copy her lecture notes, past exams, and other material, which the professor created for this purpose? *Yes. These are uncopyrighted works.

9. Same as question 8, but the professor would like to add articles and excerpts from books. May we do this? *Yes, provided that they are taken off at the end of each semester and are not used repeatedly. The student number is within fair use and access to the system is restricted.

10. Same as question 9, but the number of students is 300. May we place

materials on electronic reserve? *No. The size of this class, even with restricted access, is sufficiently high to warrant permission or licensing.

    11. Since the Copyright Term Extension Act (P.L. 105-278) has extended copyright terms, may I copy a work that went into public domain in 1922? *Yes. Assuming the work was renewed for another 28 years, it went into the public domain January 1, 1998. This will not happen again until January 1, 2019.

Can Do

Libraries and archives may:

1. Make up to three copies of a work or phonorecord if:
    a. noncommercial purpose;
    b. collection is accessible to those doing research in a specialized field;
    c. work has a copyright notice, or if a legend states that the work may be protected by copyright if no copyright notice can be found;
    d. the copying is unrelated and isolated;
    e. the copy becomes the property of the user;
    f. the copy's purpose is educational;
    g. a copyright warning is displayed prominently at the desk;
    h. it is in the last 20 years of its copyright term provided that the work is not commercially exploited (unless the copyright owner objects).

    To qualify, the library must also:
    i. be unaware of related or concerted copying;
    j. not engage in systematic copying;
    k. not engage in interlibrary arrangements in which the receiving library's purpose is to substitute for subscription or purchase.

2. Make a copy of a work in its collection and distribute it if:
    a. it is done for preservation or security;
    b. it is for deposit for research use in another nonprofit library or archives;
    c. it is to replace a work or phonorecord that is damaged, deteriorating, lost, stolen, or is commercially exploited if, after reasonable effort, a replacement cannot be obtained at a reasonable price.
    d. the equipment on which it is to be used is no longer commercially available.

3. Make:
    a. digital or other copies of unpublished works for preservation or security;

    b. digital or other copies of published works for replacement of lost, stolen, or deteriorating works which can't be obtained at a reasonable price;

    c. interlibrary loan copies of one article or other contribution to a copyrighted collection or small part of a phonorecord;

    d. interlibrary loan copies of works unavailable at a reasonable price;

    e. audiovisual news program copies.
See number 1 above for conditions.

    4. A "reasonable price" test would be for an impartial observer to see the decision as equitable based on standard library acquisition procedures.

    5. A "reasonable investigation" would be to use common trade sources or an authorized reproduction service.

    6. Treat reserve room copies as an extension of classroom copying guidelines.

    7. Place multiple copies on reserve when:

    a. the amount of material is reasonable in relation to the total amount;
    b. the number of copies is reasonable;
    c. material contains copyright notice;
    d. photocopying is not detrimental to the market for the work.

    8. Library systems may make use of Section 108.

    9. Copy the table of contents of a newsletter if first requested by employees.

    10. Purchase a journal subscription and then route the journal to employees.

    11. Make electronic copies to fax for interlibrary loan.

    12. Place copies of works on electronic reserve when access is restricted through password or other means.

    13. Make up to three copies of a work in a format for which the equipment is no longer commercially available.

Libraries Must

    1. Display a copyright warning prominently at the desk.

    2. Display a copyright warning on unsupervised photocopying equipment and other equipment capable of copying.

    3. Digital copies made for preservation replacements of published works must not be "made available to the public in that format outside the premises of the library or archives."

    4. Display a copyright legend on all copies of works.

Cannot Do

Libraries may not:

1. Copy musical works; pictorial, graphic, or sculptural works; and motion pictures.

2. Reproduce or distribute copies of works when there is a "substantial reason to believe" that the copying is related or concerted.

3. Reproduce or distribute in order to substitute for a subscription individually or in the aggregate.

4. Library networks may not make use of Section 108.

5. Copy to the same extent with newsletters as with other periodicals.

Tried and True

There is no better short-form information for libraries of all types than the Rules of Thumb on the University of Texas Web site maintained by Georgia Harper, Office of General Counsel, at http://www.utsystem.edu/OGC/IntellectualProperty/.

Works, even in their renewal term, published through 1922 came into public domain January 1, 1998. This will not happen again until January 1, 2019. Call the Copyright Office and ask one of their information specialists for public domain information on specific materials.

12

Library Video Use

Motion Picture and Video Exhibition

Libraries that lend legally acquired videos or films for patron use are within the copyright law, even if a nominal fee or a deposit is required for their use.[1] The Motion Picture Association of America (MPAA) has stated that "libraries which circulate cassettes for use at home do not infringe the Copyright Act."[2] However, should a borrower state that the tape will be used for exhibition at a public place, such as a civic group's presentation to the general public, then the lender has the duty to inform the borrower that such a use may violate copyright law. The librarians and or the institution could be held as contributory infringers. A contributory infringer is one who "must either actively operate or supervise the operation of the place wherein the performances occur, or control the content of the infringing program, and expect commercial gain ... and either direct or indirect benefit from the infringing performance."[3] The same situation would hold true if the borrower stated the intention to make a copy. School librarians have both Sections 107 and 108 for classroom and library use of videotapes.[4] Sinofsky states this position succinctly:

> My title, library media teacher, instead of school librarian, reflects the fact that under the latest revision of the California Education Code, school librarians are credentialed teachers. As a teacher, the library is my classroom.[5]

The ALA recommends the following for loan and duplication[6]:

Loan.

1. Videotapes labeled "For Home Use Only" may be loaned to patrons for their personal use. They should not knowingly be loaned to groups for public performances.

2. Copyright notice as it appears on the label of a videotape should not be obscured.

3. Nominal user fees may be charged.

4. If a patron inquires about a planned performance of a videotape, he or she should be informed that only private uses of it are lawful.

5. Video recorders may be loaned to a patron without fear of liability even if the patron uses the recorder to infringe a copyright. However, it might be a good idea to post notices on equipment which may be used for copying (even if an additional machine would be required) to assist copyright owners in preventing unauthorized reproduction.

Duplication (After the Digital Millennium Copyright Act [P.L. 105-304]). Under limited circumstances libraries may make up to three copies of a videotape or a part thereof for preservation purposes and loan them, but the rules of Section 108 of the amended P.L. 105-304 apply to this reproduction. (See Library Reproduction Rights, Chapter 11.)

Prohibitions on Circumvention of Protection Technologies. While Title I of the act deals with prohibitions on circumvention of protection technologies and prevents the sale of certain kinds of video recorders for two years and 18 months, respectively, the Librarian of Congress is to conduct rule-making to determine if the "anti-circumvention" prohibitions will "adversely affect" individuals and institutions' "ability to make noninfringing uses" of copyright works (texts, maps, software). In addition the librarian must issue a three-year waiver from anti-circumvention prohibition if it adversely or is likely to adversely affect fair use. Nonprofit libraries, archives, and educational institutions are exempted from criminal penalties if it can be demonstrated that they were unaware such action violated the law. Title II expressly states that many valuable activities based on the Fair Use Doctrine will not constitute illegal "anti-circumvention."

Public Libraries. The American Library Association takes this position on in-library uses[7]:

1. Most performances of a videotape in a public room as part of an entertainment or cultural program, whether a fee is charged or not, would be infringing, and a performance license is required from the copyright owner.

2. To the extent a videotape is used in an educational program conducted in a library's public room, the performance will not be infringing if the requirements for classroom use are met.

3. Libraries which allow groups to use or rent their public meeting rooms should, as part of their rental agreement, require the group to warrant that it will secure all necessary performance licenses and indemnify the library for any failure on their part to do so.

4. If patrons are allowed to view videotapes on library-owned equipment, they should be limited to private performances; i.e., one person, or no more than one family, at a time.

5. User charges for private viewings should be nominal and directly related to the cost of maintenance of the videotape.

6. Even if a videotape is labeled "For Home Use Only," private viewing in the library should be considered to be authorized by the vendor's sale to the library with imputed knowledge of the library's intended use of the video-tape.

7. Notices may be posted on video recorders or players used in the library to educate and warn patrons about the existence of the copyright laws, such as: MANY VIDEOTAPED MATERIALS ARE PROTECTED BY COPY-RIGHT. 17 U.S.C. SECTION 101. UNAUTHORIZED COPYING MAY BE PROHIB-ITED BY LAW.

The entertainment corporation MGM/UA commenced a licensing system for library exhibition based on the number of card holders a library has for a mutually agreed upon number of scheduled exhibitions plus unlimited unscheduled showings, with rights and formulas varying by institution.[8] The wide acceptance of videos may indicate that such licensing for public performance (categories number 1 and number 4 of the ALA statement, above) is a direction that motion picture distributors would like to see taken. However, the categories outlined by the ALA statement indicate that a broad-based licensing scheme for all in-library exhibition is unacceptable.[9]

Public libraries may not show videotapes "for home use only" in a public space without public performance rights licensing.[10] This would include videos intended for any public viewing: garden clubs, genealogy groups, and so forth. Disney and other videos shown for Children's Department services would be included in this group, as well.

School Libraries. School librarians regularly purchase videos, set up viewing schedules for teachers, and tape programs for classroom use at the request of instructors according to the "Guidelines" (see Appendix A). All these activities are legally permissible. Quite often, however, there is confusion about labels on videos which state that a use is "For Home Use Only." This is a cautionary label for those who would tape programs for resale and who would tape illegally. These labels are not applicable to most school library situations. A school library that lends or shows a video it has purchased, in the course of "systematic teaching activities," is not infringing copyright law.

However, should the librarian lend a tape to a teacher or student with knowledge that the video will be duplicated for resale or public exhibition (an infringement), then that librarian could be considered a contributory infringer, just as for photocopies or computer software.

Media Distribution Systems

Media distribution systems come in several types. They can be a network of monitors linked to a central unit holding a master video unit, a network of monitors linked to a central wall system with one or several videocassette players, a network in which only one video at a time can go out to all points or selected points, or other variations. The purpose is to send videos to classrooms, study rooms, patient rooms, or other rooms instead of pushing a cart to that room, thereby eliminating transportation time, employee time in distributing them, and increasing efficiency. While such services are useful, they often present copyright problems when tapes are requested to be used on the system.

As explained in Library Reproduction Rights, Chapter 11, librarians have few rights when handling many user's requests. While the individual teacher may bring in a home-use tape to show in class, the librarian must be sure that it is a legal copy before taking the responsibility of showing it to others, let alone cataloging it and placing it in the collection. Solutions include:

1. having faculty sign at the desk that the video to be shown is a legal copy;

2. showing only copies for which a distributor's or producer's name and label are shown;

3. acquiring rights to videos which the instructor wishes to show and keep afterward in the library collection. There are several books for this purpose, such as *The Video Locator* and the *Video Source Book*. One of the best is *Videohound's Golden Movie Retriever*. This is updated yearly and contains information about movies on videocassette, laser disc, and CD-ROM. It also has a Web site guide and alternate format and category indexes. It is published in Detroit by Visible Ink.

Teachers want to teach students. They have a fair use exemption to copy a print or nonprint work and show it spontaneously to capture the "teachable moment" (*H.R. 94-1476*). For this reason they may wish to tape something off-air themselves and show it the next day. This becomes a problem, however, when it is repeated 100 times throughout the building or district. In some districts this use is prohibited. In others the teacher may wheel a cart to show this type of thing. It is a district or institutional administrative decision which has the force of administrative law if the board or other governing body makes a formal policy and votes on it.

In some cases librarians are asked to accept video material that is obviously a copy or has been copied without permission or licensing. In cases for which no administrative support for acquiring legally obtained copies is given, the librarian may choose to limit his or her liability for such use (particularly if a video or other vendor is aware of this situation) by informing a supervisor of one's awareness of such practices and one's belief that such uses are copyright infringement. An oral discussion could be documented by a note including names, date, and a synopsis of the discussion; or if witnessed by others, with their names jotted down on a piece of paper. A copy of a written letter sent to the administrator could be kept in one's files.

Videos — Usage Examples

1. A librarian is requested to copy a short segment of a commercial television program for classroom teachers for instructional purposes on rare and timely issues, such as child abuse or teenage alcoholism. Is this permitted? *Yes. Should an instructor wish that the segment be kept in the library for use in later classes, permission or licensing is necessary.

2. Can a media center director/librarian send around a list of possible programs that a teacher might like to request for off-air taping? *No. Off-air taping should only be done at the request of the individual teacher.

The following seven examples are from the ALA[11]:

3. A book discussion group meets in a classroom at the high school. May they watch a videotape of *The Grapes of Wrath*? *No. The discussion group is not made up of class members enrolled in a nonprofit institution, nor is it engaged in instructional activities; therefore the classroom exception would not apply. Any such performance would be an infringing public performance, because it is a place where a group of persons larger than a family and its social acquaintances are gathered. Permission of the copyright owner should be sought.

4. A patron asks if he can charge his friend admission to watch videotapes at his home. *Answer: The library's duty in this situation is merely to state that the videotape is subject to the copyright laws. In fact, as long as the patron shows the videotape at home to family or social acquaintances, the performance would not be a public one, and therefore not infringing even if they share the cost of the videotape rental.

5. A patron asks if he can charge admission to the general public and show the videotape at a public place. *No, this is an infringement; however, the librarian's duty is the same as in the previous situation.

6. A librarian learns that a patron is borrowing videotapes and using them for public performances. Should the librarian continue to lend? *No, there is a duty to notify the patron that the material is subject to the copyright laws. There is room for a variety of approaches to this situation, but there is no legal reason to treat videotapes differently from any other copyrighted materials which are capable of performance. While there is no clear duty to refuse to lend, there is a point at which a library's continued lending with actual knowledge of infringement could possibly result in liability for contributory infringement.

7. I have been asked to add pirated videos to the school's collection. If I accepted them, would I be legally responsible? *Yes, you would. Do not accept pirated copies of any media into the school's collection. This also includes any copies made under the off-air guidelines which were not subsequently licensed. While it is possible to keep a small segment of a program for fair use purposes,

"librarying" of complete unlicensed programs is prohibited. If the teacher or library media specialist is aware that an item is illegally made, then he or she, as a responsible party to the act, could be legally liable. In the event that a program was accepted (regardless of the medium) without the receiver's believing or having reason to believe an item was illegally made, then that person would have to accept the "burden of proof" that he or she did not know the program was illegal. In such a case there would be no fine. This is called the "innocent infringer" provision.

8. I have been asked to accept a home-use videotape made by a teacher to be used on the media distribution system. Should I show it? *It depends. If it was taped off-air the night before, then licensing can be obtained, and the video can be shown for 10 days and retained for 45 days. (See Appendix A, Chart 3, and Appendix F.) If the video was made several years ago, then tell the teacher that he or she needs to acquire a license, and that you will be happy to use money in his or her (and or your) budget to acquire it by the time it needs to be shown. You may also ask that a policy be developed to handle just such uses and be adopted by the Board of Education.

9. We have in our collection some 16 mm films. We can no longer show the films due to obsolete equipment, since 16 mm projectors are no longer made and ours are in poor working condition. We have tried to contact the copyright owners of these films. In some cases they have transferred the film to tape, in others they have not, or are out of business. May we transfer the later category of films to tape? *Yes, provided that you have documented your attempts and they would be considered to be a "reasonable" attempt. Since these films are no longer commercially exploited then it should be fine to do so.

Can Do

You may:

1. Purchase and use videotapes that say "For Home Use Only" in schools and libraries.

2. Loan videotapes to patrons and students.

3. Show a videotape in a public library if the requirements for classroom use are met.

4. Lend videotapes intended for home use only to patrons and students for personal use.

5. Make up to three copies of audiovisual works for preservation purposes to be used inside the school for checkout and library use.

6. Make up to three copies of works which are not for sale any longer and are in obsolete formats and use them inside the school/library for checkout purposes.

Cannot Do

You may not:

1. Obstruct the copyright notice on a videotape.
2. Knowingly lend a videotape to a group for a public performance.
3. Show a videotape to the public in a public space or in a group room without permission or licensing.

Tried and True

When ordering videos for closed circuit use, put this information on the purchase order. It's usually accepted.

Beware

1. Media distribution systems in schools place more liability on librarians for video use. If a librarian knows or has reason to believe that someone has brought in an illegally acquired or produced video, then the librarian can be held liable as a contributory infringer.
2. Video sales representatives will report unauthorized uses of videos that they see in schools, colleges, and other institutions to the company.
3. Neither video rental store personnel nor video catalog salespersons have specialized copyright knowledge concerning school use.

13

Library Software and Internet Use

As with unsupervised photocopying [Section 108], the librarian can reduce liability for illegal copying of disks and the Internet if a sign is displayed near the computer stating that the making of a copy of copyrighted materials is illegal. If the librarian has reason to believe that illegal copying is intended, then it is the duty of that person to withhold the disk for lending purposes [Section 108(g)]. If such an illegal use is made with the full knowledge of the librarian, then he or she becomes liable, because another's infringing was furthered.[1] If willful infringement is proved, then in addition to actual (based on profits made from the infringement) or statutory (court-imposed) damages, court costs and attorney's fees could fall to the losing party.

Software Loan. The ALA recommends these steps when loaning software:

1. Copyright notice placed on a software label should not be obscured.
2. License terms, if any, should be circulated with the software package.
3. An additional notice my be added by the library to assist copyright owners in preventing theft. It might read: SOFTWARE PROTECTED BY COPYRIGHT, 17 U.S.C., SECTION 101. UNAUTHORIZED COPYING IS PROHIBITED BY LAW.
4. Libraries generally will not be liable for infringement committed by borrowers.

School Library Software Use and Loan. Computers are used for instruction, teacher checkout of popular classroom programs, student checkout of tutorial disks and other programs, Internet searching, multimedia research projects, and a host of other uses that have ethical and legal implications. While court cases on the illegal use of software, individually or in networks, have been rare, the Software Publishers Association often sends out letters of warning (called "cease and desist" letters) about illegal use. Such letters usually state what the institution must do to remedy the situation, and the institution or library takes those steps. In any such case the district, its officers, and individual employees would be named. The school library media specialist, as director of a central repository and charged with the control of software dissemination, could very likely be included in such a suit as a "contributory infringer" if he or she had knowledge that the software was used for illegal copying.[2]

Just as with the Motion Picture Association of America and the American Publishing Association, the Software Publishers Association and others send out investigators when reports of illegal copying are made.[3] There are a variety of ways to deal with the problem of potential infringement. Some school districts require teachers who use school equipment to sign statements that they will comply with copyright laws, educate students about the legal and ethical problems caused by illegal use of software, purchase or lease software through a person authorized to sign software license agreements, be responsible for enforcing the district's policy and terms of licensing agreements, and take steps to prevent unauthorized copying or the use of unauthorized copies on school equipment. Other districts make the International Council on Computers in Education (ICCE) statement a clause in the district contract that "the legal or insurance protection of the District will not be extended to employees who violate copyright laws."[4] While both the teacher and the district will likely be sued together, this clause means that if a teacher is sued for copyright infringement, the district will not pay for that person's legal fees.

The benefits of this or other such policies signed by all concerned would be to create better relations with producers when the district decides to preview or purchase software.[5] In the case of a district that had adopted such a policy, it could also be noted on the form the terms and conditions of the district policy on copyright and copying by personnel. The use of such a form is a gesture of commitment, one which could aid in negotiating previews or multiple copy discounts.

The International Society for Technology in Education (ISTE), the Software Publishers Association, and other groups have position statements on software policies.[6] In addition, the Office of Technology Assessment published two studies which assessed the effects of new information and communications technologies on United States law and practices regarding intellectual property.[7]

School Library Internet Use. School use of the Internet increases daily. Traffic on the Internet doubles every 100 days.[8] The educational market for electronic materials is such that K–12 education in the United States spent nearly $842 million on software, videocassettes, and online subscription materials in 1997. In 1998 the figure was nearly one billion.[9] Just as with other materials, school library media specialists are liable for illegal uses by students and teachers when they are aware of the reason for the use and could be considered contributory infringers.[10]

Acceptable use policies, having students take home an Internet permission sheet to be signed by parents about legal and ethical uses of the Internet, and other measures such as monitoring students as closely as possible, are necessary. However, library media specialists frequently have one or more general computer-use labs in or near the library media center that must be staffed by the library media specialist or an assistant. Copyright warning signs should be posted on computers, scanners, and other equipment that can be used for downloading, scanning, or copying materials.

Students and faculty should be made aware that there is a mix of copyrighted and uncopyrighted materials on the Internet. Just because someone can download something does not mean that she or he should. Some information sites are:

1. The C/net site (http://www.news.com) is an excellent site that can be used for teacher and student information purposes. It has a quiz called "Tell It to the Judge" by Jane Black that is useful for faculty in-service and student information and other useful copyright news and information.

2. The "Ten Big Myths About Copyright Explained" site by Brad Templeton is also an informative location (http://www.templetons.com/brad/copymyths.html).

3. The Software Publishers Association site has information for schools and will send posters, a video, self-audit kit, model district policy statements, and other materials for use in schools (http://www.spa.org).

4. The U.S. Copyright Office site will send Circular 92 (the Copyright Act) and Circular 21 ("Reproduction of Copyrighted Work by Educators and Librarians"), as well as Circular 1 (General Copyright Information) and other circulars as requested (http://lcweb.loc.gov/copyright).

Policies should be in place about faculty and student: 1) downloading of materials to hard drives and networks, 2) downloading and copying to disk, 3) scanner use with the Internet, and 4) what kinds and levels of punishment should be exercised when materials are downloaded and or used illegally. A board policy should be in place for these kinds of uses. In addition, downloading and distributing pornographic materials from the Internet may be a criminal offense in certain instances. Revoking Internet privileges may be the only deterrent in some cases.

It is not necessary for a policy to cover all the possibilities and exceptions. Should the committee that writes the policy and the board choose to limit the uses, then it may do so according to administrative law. Just as with other materials use, if the board has a policy that is narrower than the copyright law and it has been formally adopted, then faculty and students must follow it.

Public Library Internet Use. Internet services in public libraries are fairly commonplace. Section 109, The "First Sale Doctrine," permits the owner of a lawfully made copy to dispose of it by lending or other means. This doctrine allows the public library system to lend materials. It does not, however, allow one to make more copies. Copies of Internet materials are governed by Sections 107 (Fair Use) and Section 108 (Library Reproduction Rights). Copies may be made for patrons (research and reserve copies) and for other libraries' patrons (interlibrary loan).

The important distinction for Internet use is that in order to distribute a copy, a copy must be made and that "the First Sale Doctrine does not apply to electronic works."[11] Libraries do have the right to distribute digital copies of any work according to Section 108 requirements (see Library Reproduction Rights, Chapter 11). However, they do not have the right to digitize works in their collections without permission.[12]

Just as with photocopying on unsupervised photocopiers, it is permissible to allow a patron to download an article from an unsupervised computer with an Internet connection, provided that a copyright warning sign is posted; it is for research purposes or personal use; it is the property of the user; and the librarian has no reason to believe, or any indication from the patron, that it will be used otherwise. These are the same stipulations that exist for other copies made in the library.

If a work is downloaded and faxed for interlibrary loan purposes at the request of the user, then written records should be kept and the first copy should be disposed of so that two copies do not exist. Policies should be in place about patron copying to print and disk. Some libraries charge a minimal fee for Internet use and require that patrons sign an Internet user's agreement which includes library policies and the conditions for terminating the agreement.

Library Online Service Provider Liability Limitations

Institutional libraries, schools, and others which maintain networks to be "online service providers," according to Title II of P.L. 105-304, and are exempted from copyright liability based solely on the content of a transmission made by a user of a library computer system. One of the problems with the Internet has been that musical CDs and movies have been posted on sites for downloading with a fee. Because it is difficult to trace these sites, copyright owners have sued the online service providers.

Libraries and educational institutions also provide software to link users to sites, store information on servers and facilitate displays and performance by users. These are all acts that, until the present update, P.L. 105-304, were illegal. See The Internet and World Wide Web, Chapter 9, for a detailed evaluation.

College and University Library Fair Use Sites

Following are some of the excellent sites that have information for university libraries on all topics:

1. Stanford University Libraries site (http://fairuse.stanford.edu).
2. Consortium for Educational Technology in University Systems (CETUS): Fair use of copyrighted works (http://www.cetus.org/fairindex.html).
3. University of Texas System, Office of General Counsel (http://www.utsystem.edu/OGC/IntellectualProperty).
4. North Carolina State University Libraries site (http://www.lib.ncsu.edu/).

Library Software — Usage Examples

1. Does a media center director have extra legal responsibilities? *Yes. Section 108 of the Copyright Act, which has to do with library photocopying, also has implications for software copying in a microcomputer lab or media center where one or more computers are housed. Legal liability can be reduced if a copyright sign is posted, similar to the one posted over the photocopier, stating that it is illegal to copy copyrighted materials.

> NOTICE
> It is illegal to copy or otherwise make duplicates of commercially produced software. Copying of such software will result in immediate disciplinary action and possible legal action by the publisher.

While younger children could not read this sign, the library media specialist or teacher could tell them about and demonstrate proper use.

If the librarian has reason to believe that someone is copying a program illegally, then it is the librarian's duty to withhold the disk from circulation. If the librarian knows about and allows the illegal duplication of a copyrighted disk, then the librarian might share in the legal liability.

2. A school library media specialist would like to make software available to lend to students. Can software be lent in such a way as to minimize illegal copying? *Some library media centers have adopted policies specifically for this purpose. Students who want to borrow software must take home a permission slip that they and their parents must sign. This form states that the student is responsible for ethical use of the software and promises not to make illegal copies. The parents also sign this statement and acknowledge their responsibility for their child's behavior. Not only is this policy a good way to inform unwitting parents of their children's responsibilities, but it also might reduce the school's liability.

If you would like to pursue checkout of copyrighted programs, a form should be made which would include: information on the legal use of copyrighted programs, a district policy statement on such use, a statement concerning any charges should a disk be returned damaged, and a statement that both the student and his or her parents will abide by copyright regulations and assume full responsibility for student checkout and use of such programs. This form should be signed by the parents and returned in order to commence software checkout.

Software checkout is being successfully implemented in both public and school libraries. Another simple way to set up a software-lending program for students is to compile a library of public domain software. Public domain software offers many opportunities, because such programs generally are easy to copy and because a wide array is available.

3. A teacher requested the librarian to place on reserve pirated copies of software programs. Could the librarian be held liable for placing them on reserve? *Yes. The librarian could be held for contributory infringement, and the institution could also be held liable for infringement.[13]

4. I have a computer located in our library media center for student and teacher use. Lately I have noticed students bringing in disks and trying to make copies. What should I do? *Answer: There are several possible solutions. Four comparatively simple steps to take first are to explain the need for ethical behavior, give examples of both ethical and unethical behavior when classes visit through the year, and make it clear that there will be suspension of privileges should unethical behavior occur. Also, post a copyright or similar notice near the computers concerning illegal copying. Such a notice relieves the library media specialist of legal liability to some extent when he or she is unable to monitor its use all the time (just as with unsupervised photocopiers; see number 1 above). The librarian should refuse to let students use the computer until a permission slip has been signed by their parents stating that their child will not be doing illegal copying. Prepare sign-up sheets so that use can be better controlled.

Sometimes Internet privileges have to be revoked. It is wise to have a procedure, such as whether or not warnings should be issued. If so, how many? What privileges will be suspended? If and when a letter to the parents is sent? Have a policy in place, and let students and their parents know what it is about.

The following six examples are from the ALA:

5. A math teacher puts a copy of HyperStudio on reserve in the school library. The disk bears no copyright notice. May the library circulate it? *Perhaps, if it is a legal copy. The lack of copyright notice may put the library on notice that this is a copy rather than the original program. If the original is retained by the teacher as an archival copy (i.e., not used), then it should be shown to the librarian. If it is not a legally owned copy, then its use would

violate the copyright laws and most license agreements. It would be wise to establish a policy for placing materials on reserve which prevents this.

6. May the library make an archival copy of a program on its reserve shelf? *Yes. Section 117 permits the owner of the software to make or authorize the making of one archival copy. If the teacher who put the program on reserve has not made one, she or he may permit the library to do so. Remember, most license agreements and the copyright laws permit the making of one archival copy.

7. Same as number 6, except the reserve copy is damaged. May the library make another copy (assuming it has the archival copy) for circulation? *Yes, the purpose of an archival copy is for use as a backup in case of damage or destruction. The library may then make another archival copy to store while circulating the original.

8. Same as number 7, except the reserve copy is stolen. May the library make another copy for circulation? *Yes, if the original copy is a legal one in the library's or instructor's possession, and the reserve copy is the archival copy. See number 6 above.

9. When the teacher retrieves his or her copy of the program, may the library retain the archival copy? *No. When possession of the original ceases, the archival copy must be transferred with the original or destroyed. If it is returned with the original, the teacher would not be permitted to make additional copies — he or she would have an original and the archival copy. Most license agreements contain similar provisions.

10. Why should we adopt a copyright policy? Maybe we should just wait until matters become clearer. *I wouldn't advise waiting. All things being equal, should a producer have to decide, the district without a policy would be at a disadvantage. This is presumably because those districts which do not have a copyright policy indicate their unwillingness to address the issue and thereby treat the problem. Much of the information which decides whether an investigator will be sent in is anecdotal, that is, either witnessed by a representative or by informed sources. The old adage that it is "better to be safe than sorry" still rings true.

License Agreements

The understandable dilemma for software producers is to encourage sales and discourage piracy. "The rule of thumb in the software industry is that at least one unauthorized copy exists for every authorized one."[14]

Producers are relying increasingly on trade secret protection; patent protection; and hardware/software protection devices, such as access locks, game cartridges, key diskettes, dangles, hardware locks, registration, and tracking serial numbers because of the failure of standard copyright protection. Software patents have been issued, though with controversy and mixed success.[15]

Online access to software through the Internet, America Online, and other companies has proved to be a useful and workable avenue as well, though not used extensively as yet.

While software producers should write licenses that protect their products to the furthest degree, this protection doesn't extend to user's forfeiture of rights reserved or granted to them in Sections 107 (Fair Use) to 118 of the Copyright Act.[16] As a result, if the license is for a standard mass-marketed program with a shrink-wrap license, then the following prohibitions are invalid, even if stated in the license agreement: 1) not being able to make an archival copy, 2) not being able to loan the program as part of a library service, 3) not being able to make adaptations necessary for running the program, and 4) not allowing borrowers to make adaptations in order to run the programs. However, in libraries where it was the case of not allowing borrowers to make adaptations, it would be wise to make a new loan copy each time it was lent in order to ensure that the program was free of these adaptations that could interfere with the next person using it.

Typical Questions and Answers for Software Use in Libraries

Q. Can a library make an archival copy of a program if it has a "lock" on it?

A. **Yes**, the librarian may make an archival copy of any program that it possesses using a commercial copy program even if the copyright owner has a "lock" on it.

Q. What responsibility does the library staff have to enforce the provisions of these license agreements in the case of books with computer disks or compact discs?

A. Some license agreements are unclear for various reasons, but in most instances it is because the producer could not imagine all the usage possibilities that could exist, particularly within libraries. Quint (1989)[17] gives an example of a license whose first provision was that the buyer was authorized to "use the software specified below only on a microcomputer located within the facilities." She questioned the extent to which "facilities" could be applied:

Q. Within the library?

A. **Yes**.

Q. Can it be used within the college or university?

A. **Unlikely**. The main issue is if it could be easily duplicated, placed on a network, or used as more than one copy and deprive the owner of profit. If the answer is "no" to the foregoing, then it would be fine.

Q. Does it mean one machine at a time or one machine only?

A. It means one machine at a time.

Q. Can the machine be connected to a local network that supports more than one user?

A. A network license is needed.

Computer Software Rental

Software rental is regulated in much the same way that the rental of sound recordings is handled in record stores.[18] But there are exemptions. For example, if nonprofit libraries and educational institutions are renting, leasing, and lending computer software for a nominal fee, this use is exempt. The transfer of possession from one nonprofit educational institution to another is exempt. Software lent by nonprofit libraries must bear a notice of copyright, warning borrowers that unauthorized copying may violate copyright law. Libraries are required to have a warning fixed to the package of any circulating software.[19]

Internet — Usage Examples

1. A teacher has requested that I forward an e-mail by another teacher who has some interesting ideas and materials that she wants to buy. May I forward this e-mail? *No. E-mail is the intellectual property of another person. It can't be forwarded to someone else without permission.[20] Revealing facts from e-mail is not an infringement, though.[21]

2. Library patrons have brought in pictures with copyright marks on them and asked to use the scanner so that they could be saved to disk. Should we let them? *No. If they ask to do this and you are aware that the pictures are copyrighted, then you should point to the copyright warning sign and tell them that this is an infringement. You can not be sure of each use of unsupervised scanners. However, if someone comes to you and tells you that she or he will make an infringing copy, then you must refuse use.

3. A library patron wishes to post an image on a disk to the Usenet. Should the library allow her or him to do it? *No. Unless the picture is from a royalty-free graphics library that is identified as a lawful copy, it is difficult to tell if the picture is copyrighted or not. Uploading something to the Internet creates a copy. This is something best done at home by the patron.

4. A faculty member would like to digitize 30 seconds of a song with a computer in the library and place it on the Web site that a class is making. She says it is for classroom use. Should I let her? *No. Using 30 seconds of a

song for a multimedia project is acceptable. Posting a copyrighted song to the Web is inviting trouble. ASCAP and other agencies regularly search the Internet for illegal uses of music.

5. A student would like to post a graphic from the Internet to the school Web site. Our school board policy does not allow the copying of graphics to the school Web site. All graphics must be original. The student says that since it is in the public domain, it should be allowed. Do we have to let her? *No. Board policy can be narrower than the copyright law. Administrative law must be followed, and you may tell her that she can not.

6. Our public library maintains a Web site with location tools, directories, and hyperlinks to other Web sites. Are we within the law? *Yes, but according to P.L. 105-304 your library is an "online service provider" and must follow the regulations of Title II, as well. The American Library Association has a guide for this purpose. See also The Internet and World Wide Web, Chapter 9.

Can Do

You may:

1. Make board policy narrower than the copyright law for Internet and software use.

2. Copy digital works to preserve them or for security reasons according to Section 108 and Section 107.

3. Allow patrons to download and print materials from the Internet for their own personal and research uses.

4. Provide a library Web site.

Cannot Do

You may not:

1. Digitize works that are in analog form (videos, slides) without permission or licensing.

2. Allow a patron to use the computers, scanner, or other digitizing or computer equipment for illegal reasons without telling him or her that it is against copyright law. If you allow it, then you could be a contributory infringer.

3. Fail to follow Title II of P.L. 105-304 if your library maintains a Web site.

Tried and True

1. Require students and patrons to sign an Internet user agreement or have parents sign it in the case of a minor. Terms and conditions of use, as

well as the termination of Internet privileges, should also be made clear. You
may have to terminate privileges.

2. Many things are copyrighted on the Internet. Just because a student
or patron can take something off the Internet doesn't mean that she or he should.

3. Posting or forwarding someone else's e-mail is technically a violation
of copyright law, but it is acceptable to state information received in an e-mail
to another person.

4. Copyright in digital formats changes rapidly. Subscribe to the American Library Association's Washington Office listserv for fast-breaking news
and updates, and visit its Web site at http://www.ala.org/washoff/ctguide.html.

Beware

1. A student or patron that frequently posts or downloads materials to
bulletin board systems, Usenet groups, or other systems should be checked
out. Illegal activities, such as credit card scams, pornographic materials, copying copyrighted materials, are common activities for some groups.

2. Libraries and archives which host Web sites are considered "online service providers" (OSPs) and are subject to the same rules, regulations, and procedures of independent OSPs. See Chapter 9 for Title I and Title II information
in P.L. 105-304.

Tip

On most PCs you can check the history of Internet use to see where the
student or patron has been. If you suspect illegal activity (or pornographic
materials use), learn how to use this feature.

Tip for Library OSPs

1. See Appendix O for the American Library Association's Guides to the
Digital Millenium Copyright Act (DMCA) (P.L. 105-304).

2. Maintain a passive network. You may include locational tools, directories, and hyperlinks. When in doubt, add the hyperlink and not the material itself.

Tip for Interlibrary Loan Copyright Notices

The DMCA changes in Section 108 state that a work sent through interlibrary loan must have a copyright notice or, if there is no notice, a "legend"
stating that the work may be protected by copyright. This applies to all copying, whether it is a book, a journal article, or a chapter of a book.

Part V
Permissions and
Policy Development

14

Permissions

Why Do I Need Permission?

Because of the nature of fair use, there will be times when the line between "fair" and "unfair" will be unclear. In those situations, the questions to be asked are: Is the material important? Is the time needed to get permission reasonable? Could the use bring about a lawsuit? If the answer is "yes" to one or more of these questions, then obtaining permission would be in the best interest of all concerned. An efficient policy will save time, trouble, and duplicated effort. Permissions are easier to obtain now with the use of the fax, since a phone call and a fax follow-up are often all that is needed.

Even with the "broad insulation" intended for the educator and nonprofit user by the new "innocent infringer" provision, there will be times when an infringement case could be raised.[1] If one is brought up, there are several possible results:

1. The user could win and pay nothing.
2. The user could win and still pay court costs and attorney's fees.
3. The user could lose, pay a minimum $200 fine, court costs and attorney's fees.
4. The user could lose, pay a $200 fine, court costs, and attorney's fees for both parties.
5. The user could pay up to $100,000 fine for one or more violations in criminal infringement, court costs, attorney's fees for him or herself, and possibly for the other party.[2]

As is evident, even if the instructor or the institution were innocent, he or she and it *could* pay.

Once it has been decided to seek permission, there are procedures that can simplify the process. Certain types of permissions are generally granted without a fee. They are:

1. Requests for quotations from scholarly books where the use may be more extensive than what is normally considered fair.

2. Transcripts for the blind.

3. Requests for reproduction of portions of material to be used one time, in an experimental situation, or in a curriculum development program.

4. Requests for selections of a book or its illustrations for reviews or articles concerning the book.[3]

Douglas (audiovisuals) and Mucklow (print) found variations in the granting of permissions and the fees for usage.[4] Situations can be unique. Douglas gave examples of permissions from her own experience. One publisher allowed the making of 500 copies of a short story for a $12 fee and a credit line. Another publisher allowed reproduction of a series of tests (prohibited from fair use under the guidelines). The last publisher would not grant permission because inexpensive reprints (50 cents each) were available. Mucklow found that text and illustrations generally did not require a fee for educational use. Photographs and poems ran from no charge to $50 each. The responses vary according to the publisher or author, the circumstances of the use, and the type of material being reproduced.

Permissions and the Publisher

Unless the author retains copyright, it is the publisher and not the author who answers permissions requests. Unpublished materials would, of course, be directed to the person who wrote it. Publishers examine requests carefully. The more exact the information in the request the more efficiently the permission is handled. The American Association of Publishers (AAP) and the Authors League of America say in their pamphlet on uses and permissions that "one of the most frequent reasons cited by permissions departments for delays in answering requests of this nature is incomplete or inaccurate information contained in the request."[5]

Granting a request involves a check on the status of copyright, obtaining and determining exactly what the material is for which the permission is requested (it could be in the warehouse), and calculating and assigning royalty fees to the author, if they are needed.

There are four questions a publisher must answer to fulfill a request:

1. Is the permission consistent with any agreement with the author?

2. Is the material used the author's own, or is it something for which he or she had (or has) to get permission?

3. What is the amount requested, and how will it be used?

4. Should there be quantitative limits (number of copies), time limits (one-time or repeated usage), or geographic limits (institutional or off-campus)?

The Request Format for Print Materials

The address and phone number of the publisher, if not on the work, can be obtained from *Literary Market Place* or *Publishers' Trade List Annual* for books, the *Videohound* or the *Video Locator* for videotapes, *Writer's Market* for books and periodicals, *Computer Books and Serials in Print* for computer-oriented materials, and *Ulrich's International Periodicals Directory*. An initial phone call or other communication can facilitate the request greatly; discussing in advance the intended use, charges, and the information needed by the publisher to grant the request can save time. In a few cases, a single phone call will do, as a fee may not be required.

Whether or not a fee is likely, a follow-up fax, e-mail, or letter is necessary. It should name the contact and the date the call was made. Form letters have mixed success. In some large institutions where a usage is questionable, but not far from a clearly fair use, a form letter might be all that is necessary. But if a use is important, or if it is clearly more than fair use, the request should warrant an individually typed letter. See example on page 144.

The format should include:

1. The title, author, editor or compiler, and the edition used.
2. The exact amount of material to be used, page numbers, and a photocopy of the material requested, if possible.
3. A reference to the contact person by name in the letter if the initial contact was made by phone.
4. The nature of the use, including how many times the material will be used, whether on- or off-campus, and whether in classrooms or in promotional mailings, and so forth.
5. The number of copies to be made.
6. How the material will be reproduced (ditto, off-set, photocopy).

The AAP and AL also suggest that one request all permissions for specific projects at the same time, and that one not ask for blanket permission — which cannot, in most cases, be granted.[6]

The Request Format for Videos

The address and phone number of the producer, if not known, can be obtained from the *Video Source Book* or the *Video Locator*. If possible, an initial phone call is recommended, as programs are often negotiable, depending on the intended use. In requesting to make a videotape copy or in requesting to retain a copy made according to the "Guidelines for Off-Air Recording," much the same information should be requested as for print materials. See page 145 for an example. The format should include:

Sample Print Permissions Letter

Date

Permissions Department
School Book Company
Wichita, KS 67217

Dear Director:

I would like permission for one of our instructors, Deta Baker, to duplicate the following for classroom use next semester (beginning date):

Author:	Linda Halvin
Title:	*Studies in Modern Sociology*, 3rd ed., 1979 (out of print).
Copyright:	1975, 1979.
Material to be duplicated:	pages 23–33 of Chapter 2 — "Quantitative Methods" (photocopies enclosed).
Number of copies:	33
Form of distribution:	supplied to students gratis for classroom use in fall semester only.
Type of reprint:	photocopy

The page above will be used as a supplementary reading for the class
"Advanced Quantitative Methods in Sociological Research."

Enclosed is a self-addressed, stamped envelope to send back the signed
permission form.

Sincerely,

June Sanger, Director
Rossmore Media Center
Maricopa Community Center
Los Angeles, CA 90020

Sample Permission Form Letter

Phone #_____   Fax # _____

Contact person _____

Date:

Dear   :

   Per our telephone conversation, I would like permission to use the following material in my book (title) to be published (date) by (company):

Author:

Title:

Copyright Date:

Volume/Number/Pages:

# of Pages to be Duplicated:

I would like this information by (date), if possible.

Please sign below if you are willing to give permission for this material and fax to:

(Name, Title)

(Institution)

(Fax #)

(Phone #)

_____ Yes, I give permission for this material to be duplicated in the book.

_____
Signature

Thank You!!

1. Title.
2. Type of reproduction (½", ¾").
3. If only a portion of the tape is required, then name section and minutes of portion.
4. Number of copies.
5. Nature of use, specific class and class size, if possible, and nature of transmission, whether closed circuit (CCTV) or instructional fixed service (ITFS).
6. If initial contact was made by phone, refer to contact name in letter.

Computer Software License Requests

While standard lab packs can be acquired (five packs, ten packs) for application software, network software, and building site licenses, district use (often based on annual daily attendance — ADA) must be negotiated individually with the copyright owner. This license can be based on one or more programs that the producer, distributor, or jobber, such as *MacWarehouse, PC Connection*, or *Educational Resources* may have in inventory. For example, three programs could be negotiated for as a package, just as it could be done for one, or discounts are given for larger orders. If possible, it is best to negotiate based on class size rather than the size of the school.

In preparing to request licensing for software, various directories providing names, addresses, and phone numbers can be used. However, not all companies publish information on special volume discounts or on-site licensing. This information can often only be obtained by a phone call, if possible, or a letter. *Technology & Learning* publishes an annual directory and awards list. Other periodicals have program evaluation lists and annual awards. Software reviewing tools, such as *TESS (The Educational Software Selector)* available from the International Society for Technology in Education (ISTE) and other outlets, are also available. Acquiring software licensing is based on the variables of school district, or consortium size, number of computers, and the proclivity of the individual producer or jobber, and prices vary.

Handling Permissions

In requesting permission, whether for royalty purposes or not, there are seven steps to be followed:

1. Call first, then fax your request.
2. Refer to the contact by name in the permission letter.
3. Use a format. Use letterhead paper, if possible.

4. Specify a date when you would like an answer. Do this for your own follow-up purposes. Most permissions people have backlogs.

5. Make a file folder for each negotiation, including all pertinent information: name, address, phone number of publisher, the name of the contact (if any), and a copy of the work from which permission is requested.

6. When negotiation has been completed, forward a copy of the signed agreement to the user and keep one copy in the folder.

7. If you have a Web site, then enter a list of permissions groups (see sampling of Permissions Web Sites below) and put in links for quick information checks.

In any institution in which permissions are necessary, an administrator should be responsible for these kinds of uses. He or she could serve as a copyright clearinghouse for faculty members. This ensures that the procedures are simple, efficient, and legal. By having one person responsible, the institution could be better protected from lawsuits and replication of effort.

This practice would help in other ways, as well. The administrator could advise faculty on photocopying questions.[7] He or she could oversee a centralized duplicating center to make sure that the law is followed. Since cumulative uses are something individual teachers cannot be aware of, but for which institutions are responsible, this person would be in a position to view total faculty usage. Lastly, and most important, the faculty would be relieved of some of the burden of requests and other paperwork, and would be free to teach.

Permissions Web Sites

All Formats
U.S. Copyright Office
   http://lcweb.loc.gov
University of Texas Permissions Web Site
   http://iron.utsystem.edu/home/OGC/IntellectualProperty/permissn.htm

Periodicals
Copyright Clearance Center
   http://www.copyright.com
Uncover
   http://www.uncover.com

Images
Kodak Picture Exchange (fee-based)
   http://kodak.com
Academic Press Image Directory
   http://academicpress.com

Artists Rights Foundation
  http://artistrights.org
American Society of Media Photographers
  http://ASMP.org
Visual Resources Association
  http://www.oberlin.edu/~art/var/vra.html

Music
NMPA/Harry Fox Agency
  http://www.nmpa.org
ASCAP
  http://www.ascap.com/
BMI
  http://bmi.com
SESAC, Inc.
  http://sesac.com
Kohn on Music Licensing
  http://www.kohnmusic.com
All Music Guide
  http://musicguide.org

Public Domain Images
Library of Congress American Memory Project
  http://lcweb.loc.gov

Print Permissions Information
Copyright Permissions Web Site, Professional Center Library for Law and
  Management at Wake Forest University
  http://www.wfu.edu/library/copyright

Model Policies for Colleges and Universities
http://www.library.yale.edu:80/~okerson/copyproj.html

Can Do

You may:

1. Negotiate. It doesn't hurt to try if you are pleasant and courteous.
2. If the copyright holder has gone out of business, then document this
and use the material.

Cannot Do

You may not:
Use a copyrighted material because you think the price is too high. You
have to abide by what the copyright owner wishes, even if the price is exor-
bitant.

Tips

1. Make a Web site of links or a list of names, addresses, phone numbers, and fax numbers for quick checks. Beda Johnson (1993) has the following suggestions[8]:

2. "Document all contacts — by date, person with whom you spoke, station, producer, and their phone numbers. If you must leave a message, leave your name, school, phone number, and title of program you are researching. Saves time."

3. Give as much information as you can about a use.

4. Tell the contact you need documentation for your files. This information is vital.

5. If a permission fee is involved, you can try to negotiate.

6. If not, then ask if the program is for sale or rent.

7. If so, ask for information about contacting the distributor.

8. Explain when asking for rights for retention about the type of use — closed circuit, ITFS — then document your request and the name and title of the person who gave it. Ask for written approval.

9. Express appreciation for the support of your educational program.

10. If a program is not available, then note this for your file. You want to be able to explain why you don't have the material.

Note: See "Getting Permission" on the University of Texas site. It is an excellent resource with many pertinent links for different types of materials. (http://www.utsystem.edu/home/OGC/IntellectualProperty/permissn.htm)

15

Policy Development

Why Have a Policy?

All institutions should have a written and approved copyright policy. Without a policy, institutions are open to illegal uses of materials, embarrassment, and litigation.[1] If policies are in place for budget development, student discipline, and dress codes, it is reasonable to assure that materials use and development will also have uniform procedures. Since P.L. 105-304, policies for nonprofit educational institutions, libraries, and archives are necessary because these entities are now considered to be "online service providers" if they maintain online systems. (See Chapter 9.)

There are four major purposes for developing a copyright policy, according to the late Charles Vlcek, author of *Copyright Policy Development* and *Adoptable Copyright Policy*[2]:

1. A policy protects the institution's staff, faculty, administrators and governing board from potential litigation. If employees have been informed and provided with necessary information to make usage decisions, then such a policy transfers the infringing responsibility from the institution to the infringer.[3]

2. It provides direction to employees by informing them of what the institution considers to be legal and approved uses of copyrighted materials.

3. It provides employees with policy authority to refuse to accept potentially infringing materials requests. A written basis is provided with which to explain why a request cannot be filled or must be changed in order to comply with the law.

4. The last and most important purpose is to avoid costly litigation. While most alleged copyright violations rarely go beyond a "cease and desist" letter sent by the attorneys of copyright holders, few cases are publicized because of the embarrassment to the institution.

The Software Publishers Association, representing 1,150 members, stated that in 1994 it received 30 phone calls a day on its anti-piracy hotline. Based on these calls the SPA took action against 447 organizations which resulted in 197 audits and lawsuits, 95 percent of which were against corporations. This was a 23 percent decrease from 1993. In addition, 250 "cease and desist" letters were sent out.[4] The SPA has placed investigators on the Internet to track down violators. Audiovisual and computer vendors also report back to their offices any potential infringements for further investigation, as well. ASCAP and BMI have field investigators, as does the Motion Picture Association of America.

The Association for Information, Media, and Equipment (AIME) offers membership services, such as copyright violation reports, a copyright information packet, reward labels, an AIME newsletter, a copyright law video, speakers on copyright, and a copyright hotline service. On average, over 200 calls a month were logged in 1994 on the Copyright Hotline, with representation from all 50 states, including Ontario, Canada. The purpose of the Hotline is to provide membership information, request copyright information, and to give individuals an opportunity to report violations anonymously.

Policy Elements

1. A statement that the board or governing entity intends to abide by the copyright law and expects its employees to comply with stated policy.

2. A statement prohibiting copying not specifically allowed by the copyright law, fair use guidelines [Section 107],[5] any other applicable exemptions in the law, such as library guidelines [Section 108],[6] copying for the blind, license agreements, or with the proprietor's permission.

3. A statement placing the liability for willful infringement upon the person making the request. In this way the responsibility is transferred from the institution to the violator. "The statement should make it clear that no legal assistance to the infringing employee will be provided for alleged copyright infringements not covered within the permissive uses stated within the policy or without prior written permission from the institution's legal counsel."[7]

4. A statement that creates a position of copyright officer for the institution. This person should be one of the officers of the institution who is in authority to develop, implement, and answer questions. License and permission agreements should be centralized in this office. This person should also be the liaison with the institution's legal counsel.

5. A statement mandating the development of a copyright manual detailing what uses of copyright materials may or may not be done by the institution's employees. Employees cannot be held responsible for illegal uses or copying as specified in the policy unless they know what constitutes legal and illegal uses of copyrighted materials. A manual must be developed to explain the law and its exemptions. This manual should be disseminated to all employees

who use copyrighted materials. It should also be updated as needed to reflect changes in the law.

    6. A statement mandating placement of appropriate copyright warning notices to be placed on or near all equipment capable of making copies. Section 108 mandates that copyright warning notices be placed on or near equipment capable of duplicating materials in libraries, including self-service and attendant copy centers.[8] While copyright warning notices are mandated by law, the language is not. Suggested ways of handling this are to:

    a. Require employees to sign releases stating they will not make illegal copies of institutional software.

    b. Place signs on counters that state the conditions under which tapes and computer programs will be copied (must have label that identifies material as a legal copy for computer programs, videos, and so forth).

    c. Place copyright warning signs on institutional equipment such as video recorders, compact disc recorders and videodisc players,

    7. A statement mandating the development and retention of appropriate copyright records. To simplify permissions, a single centralized location in the college, school, or institution should be established for the storage and easy retrieval of all copyright records.

    It is wise to remember that a "test case," i.e., a case to test a certain part of the copyright law or a new technology, is most powerful against those institutions which do not have a policy.

    Janice Bruwelheide recommends these sites for policy development[9]:

1. Copyright Management Center, Indiana University — Purdue University at Indianapolis
   http://www.iupui.edu/it/copyinfo
2. Copyright Management Center, University of Texas System
   http://www.utsystem.edu/OGC/IntellectualProperty/
3. Copyright Office, Washington University
   http://publications.urel.wsu.edu/Copyright/Copyright.html
4. Stanford University Libraries Copyright and Fair Use Site
   http://fairuse.stanford.edu

Other sites for university policy examples include:
1. Learning the Ropes: Intellectual Property at UCLA
   http://www.research.ucla.edu/guide/ROPESa.htm
2. The Association of University Technology Managers
   http://autm.rice.edu/autm/index.html

16

Alternatives and
Scenarios for
Media Center Directors

Serving employees' materials needs is also a human relations issue:

> ... media directors need to be familiar with the nuances of the copyright law, especially if they will be the resource that faculty turn to for guidance and support.[1]

A study done by Wertz[2] and replicated in 1993 by Chase[3] found that college and university media directors' knowledge of the copyright law was lacking (only 15 percent of the 144 respondents of the 1984 study could reach or exceed a 75 percent proficiency in the law). This is all the more reason for an adopted policy that all employees are familiar with.

In the instances when the answer is "no," a suitable alternative can be provided. One "rule of thumb" is to try to provide another way for an employee to fulfill instructional or usage aim. For example, if a tape cannot be copied, then have the information available as to where a legal copy can be obtained or how long it typically takes UPS or Federal Express to get a legal copy from a distributor. Purchase materials that answer various copyright questions, such as the *Video Source Book*. Adequate support information supports the "no" with up-to-date published articles, legal advice, and sources of other materials.

Above all, remember that other employees look to the service provider as the media professional. They may know about their disciplines, but they cannot be aware of all the selection tools available, or even of all the different royalty-free music, compact discs, computer programs, and other materials that are available to someone in this capacity. In those instances where a "judgment call" is necessary, the following are some scenarios with answers for difficult questions that might help in dealing with patrons.

Scenario 1: Copying an illegal tape.

An employee brings in a tape that has no producer identification on the container and asks for the copy to be made. He or she states that it was copied off-air, or perhaps that a "friend" provided it. You ask if it was taped off-air in the last 45 days. The answer is "sometime last semester and now I would like to have a copy made for myself." When you explain that permission or a license to purchase it must be obtained first, the employee then asks, "Why won't you make a copy of this tape for me? It's for an educational purpose."

According to the off-air taping guidelines (see Appendix A, Chart 3), that copy should have been erased in 45 days if taped at a school. For-profit institutions do not have this exemption. If taped for home use, then it is not the media center's responsibility to house or copy it. If you wish to have it copied ,then written permission to copy it is necessary. If you like, I would be happy to find the producer in the Videohound's Golden Movie Retriever *and find out the cost of this tape and the fastest way to get it here. You might also want to consider (if in a nonprofit educational institution) off-air taping a substitute before your class, since you do have 45 days for this purpose. I would be happy to do this for you.*

Alternative answers could be:

- I'll look up the producer and give you information on how to get permission.
- From looking at the *Video Source Book*, it costs $125 and will take 14 days to get it here or two days Federal Express. We can also rent it for $25, but it will take longer to get here.
- It would be illegal for me to copy that program a) not knowing when it was taped, and b) without permission.
- You may be unaware that asking me to copy that tape is asking me to break the law (and possibly the institution's written policy). I'm sure you wouldn't want that. Let's examine some alternatives.
- Here are some other materials we could order for your class, or I can check on interlibrary loan for you. You might like to read our institution's policy, too.

Scenario 2: Making an illegal copy of a legally made tape, or "where are the copyright police?"

A faculty member brings you a legally made video acquired from a friend, another department, or agency. He or she asks you to make a copy for "classroom purposes." You refuse, explaining that the tape must be purchased, just as this one was (see Scenario 1). The question is then asked, "Why can't you copy this tape for me? Besides, how is anybody going to find out if it's illegal, anyway? There aren't any 'copyright police,' are there?"

Actually, while there are no "copyright police," vendors have ways of finding out. Two common ways that vendors find out are either from a disgruntled (usually former) employee that you and I know or by one of the vendor representatives.

I have the Videohound's Golden Movie Retriever, *which has information on the video you want to use. Would you like me to see how much it would cost to purchase it and how soon we can get it?*

In addition, organizations such as the Software Publishers Association maintain a copyright hotline where violations can be reported anonymously. Audiovisual, music, and motion picture associations use either staff or contracted investigators to check out suspicious copyright activities. Breaking copyright law could involve both the media center and the individual in a possible lawsuit.

The author on several visits and speaking engagements has been told by various people of visits by vendors to copy centers, media centers, schools, and businesses, and has been informed that people have personally reported violators (their employers) for copyright violations.

Scenario 3: Adding a copied computer program to the collection.

An employee asks the media center director to catalog a computer program copied off-air by a friend and add it to the collection. When you refuse, the employee states, "If copyright violations are such a problem, then you should be able to name some lawsuits."

As a matter of fact, I can. Here is a list of violations from the Software Publishers Association that I think you should look over. This list includes violations from schools, universities, businesses, and other institutions. Included are the results of the situation, including fines, actions requested (such as program erasures and seizures), and so forth. By the way, the Software Publishers Association regularly sends me notices of lawsuits, settlements, and other violations.

In most cases, violations are settled out of court, so there won't be a public record unless information is passed along by word-of-mouth or made available by such organizations. The author knows of "cease and desist" letters sent to three major universities in her home state. All three were sent to business departments over the use of computer software.

Scenario 4: Putting illegally made computer programs on reserve in the media center.

An employee presents ten illegally made copies of a purchased computer program and asks to have them placed on reserve for students to use. He or she states that since it isn't part of the permanent collection and they are the property of the employee, it should be fine, since they are only to be there for one month. When the media center director refuses because each copy must be either legally purchased, made with a site license, or permission to make copies must be stated in the warranty or in the documentation, the employee asks, "Why can't you keep them here? I'm not asking you to catalog them or add them to the collection. I just want you to keep them for me. What's wrong about that?"

Plenty. I'm legally responsible for any media housed in the media center, whether it's officially or temporarily a part of the collection. If I know that material stored here is illegal, then I am legally liable for being a contributory infringer. It's clear that these are not purchased or licensed. How soon do you need them for your class? I can check on the price of a lab pack and phone in an order if you can get authorization. Most jobbers will ship within 48 hours for a little extra delivery charge.

Other responses might be:
- Here's a supplier of public domain programs you might want to use. They are much less expensive.
- We could work with your class so that students could use the legally made programs on a self-study basis in the lab or by arrangement.
- Let's use one purchased program on the file server so only one student can use it at a time until we buy more copies.

Scenario 5: Making an archival copy of a computer program.

"Can I make an archival copy of this computer program? The producer did not provide a backup."

Yes. I would be happy to copy it for you. Just remember that this copy is not to be used as a second copy on another machine you own.

Vault Corp. v. Quaid Software Ltd. has helped to better define the area of computer software use.[4] The use of a copy program in order to unlock a program to produce an archival copy is legal and permissible even if the producer states in the license that one may not be made. Such a use is also not considered to be a breach of the licensing agreement. This means that while software producers should write licenses that protect their software, this protection does not extend to forfeiture of user rights reserved for them in the Copyright Act.

In addition, the Computer Software Rental Amendments Act of 1990 grants owners of copyright in computer programs an exclusive right to control public distribution of the program.[5] P.L. 105-304 allows up to three copies to be made for preservation purposes if kept in-house. An exemption in the law allows nonprofit educational institutions and libraries to lend, rent, or lease them without permission from the copyright owner.

Scenario 6: Student bulletin board system (BBS) operators and the Internet.

A faculty member in charge of a computer club asks, "Can my students be system operators for our computer club bulletin board system in the media center? They will also be posting information gained from the Internet for us. You'll be there, and they won't need any real supervision."

They will need supervision. All kinds of things are possible on a BBS connected to the Internet. In fact, if anything illegal happens, both you and I could be contributory infringers for it as well as accessories if negligence could be proved in a criminal case. Here's part of an article I'd like you to read on the problems with students using electronic bulletin boards.

It is estimated that there are 3,500 to 4,000 electronic bulletin board systems in the U.S.[6] Although most are privately run, large commercial boards have grown, offering many services at an hourly connect rate. The private BBSs contain, in addition to pirated software, credit card numbers, passwords to the system, and other confidential information. If the system operator knowingly placed pirated software on the system for "commercial advantage or private financial gain" [Section 506, Title 17(a)],[7] then he/she is liable for criminal copyright infringement.[8] Otherwise, the system operator is not held liable, according to P.L. 105-304, if Title II rules and procedures are followed. (See Chapter 9.)

You could be liable for a student who engages in illegal activities in your media center if the student was supposed to be supervised to any extent. These liabilities should be carefully considered and discussed with the teacher/sponsor. Just as with supervised copiers of any kind, the media center director is legally liable for that student's supervision if negligence can be shown involving a copyright infringement. All student-use computers should have copyright warning signs posted on all computers, particularly those used for BBSs. Student use must be monitored regularly. If you are prepared to do this, I will be happy to help.

Scenario 7: Receiving a "cease and desist" letter for illegal copying.

You have been notified in writing that you must "cease and desist" from certain activities, or your institution will be sued by XYZ video/computer/compact disc company. Legal counsel is now looking the matter over and is engaged in dialog with the alleged infringed company. You ask: "Who can be sued?"

Any and likely one of each level of the chain of command. The Copyright Remedy Clarification Act makes it possible for copyright owners to sue public institutions.[9] However, the time-honored "deep pockets" theory is that the person most directly responsible, along with each level up to the top will be named, so that department heads, principals, the governing board, and the like will be held liable.

Scenario 8: Student productions and copyright penalties.

A student or faculty member asks the media specialist to edit copyrighted music, graphics, or video for a student production to be shown to a civic group or other public exhibition. When you refuse, they ask, "What's the worst that can happen if anybody finds out?"

There isn't just one "worst thing" that can happen. Here are a couple: 1) you could use it in your entry to a national competition to which the public is invited and have the producer stand up and tell you that permission for the music wasn't granted and request that the sound be turned off; 2) the presentation could be made and a member of the audience who was not happy with the presenter or the institutions or the teacher could call one of the copyright hotlines to report this use. Then we would both have some explaining to do, at the least, to our supervisors, the dean, the principal, or whoever else was notified. Here are some sources for free, uncopyrighted music available on compact discs. Let's see if you can use any of these. I have information here on the Discovery Toolkit. One is issued each month during the school year on a different topic, such as ecology and holidays. A site license is part of the package, and it contains text, graphics, clip art, and music that can be put together for student projects (Pierian Spring Software Web Site). I also have a jobber and specialty catalogs for royalty-free music and image compact discs, and there are several Web sites with public domain materials that you can find in a search of Yahoo!

Anyone who uses graphics, images, music, and text for productions should be careful of where and when these materials are obtained, and they should be used only within the classroom or in similar situations (such as a closed, free-of-charge professional workshop for educators within a system). Should a production be presented at a convention or other venue open to the general public, then permission and licenses must be obtained. The best avenue is to use public-domain music and image programs or to make original graphics or take pictures (with proper releases from subjects). P.L. 105-304 exempts nonprofit educational institutions of higher education from faculty or graduate student employee infringement under certain conditions. (See Chapter 9, page 81.)

Remember, the job of service providers is to do more than say "no." The aim is to help other employees reach professional goals. Providing reasonable alternatives that help in reaching these goals helps everyone.

Part VI
Notes and Resources

Notes

Chapter 1. A Copyright Primer

1. Henry, N. (1975). *Copyright-information technology: Public policy* (2 vols.). New York: Marcel Dekker.
2. Ibid.
3. Nimmer, M. (1970). Does copyright abridge the first amendment guarantees of free speech and press? *UCLA Law Review* 17: 1180–1204.
4. Negroponte, N. (1995). *Being digital*. New York: Alfred A. Knopf.
5. Patterson, L. (1968). *Copyright in a historical perspective*. Nashville: Vanderbilt University Press.
6. White, H. (ed.) (1978). *The copyright dilemma*. Chicago: American Library Association.
7. Reitz, N. (1973). Williams and Wilkins: The impact of technology on copyright. *Los Angeles Bar Bulletin*, 445–472.
8. Library of Congress, United States Copyright Office (1996). *Circular R92*. Washington, DC: U.S. Government Printing Office.
9. Lee, R. (1997). *A copyright guide for authors*. Stanford, CT: Kent.
10. Kozak, E. (1996). *Every writer's guide to copyright and publishing law* (2nd ed.). New York: Henry Holt.
11. Lee, R. (1997). op cit.
12. Melton, M. (1997). International cyberspace licensing perils. *Understanding the intellectual property license* (Co-chairs: L. Pirkey, S. Progoff, B. Weiss, and S. Snowman). New York: Practicing Law Institute.
13. Marke, J. (1967). *Copyright and intellectual property*. New York: Fund for the Advancement of Education.
14. U.S. Congress, House, Judiciary Committee. *Report No. 94-1476. Report together with additional views (to accompany S. 22)* (94th Congress, 2nd session). Washington DC: U.S. Government Printing Office, September 3, 1976, 130–133.
15. *H. R. 94-1476*, 53–56.
16. *H. R. 94-1476*, 53.
17. 17 U.S. Code 13 (1998).
18. Douglas, J. (1974, December). Copyright as it affects instructional development. *Audiovisual Instruction*, 37–38.
19. *H. R. 94-1476*, 57.
20. Section 104 was amended by the Act of October 31, 1988, Public Law

100-568, 102 Stat. 2853, 2855, which allows for the restoration of copyright for works published in Mexico or Canada between January 1, 1978, and March 1, 1989. Moreover, it had to have lost its protection because of failure to include the required copyright notice on the published copies. There are other stipulations, but the number of works subject to this exception are limited. Potential owners had until January 1, 1995, to register.

21. U.S. Dept. of Commerce, Patent and Trademark Office (1996). *Basic facts about trademarks*. Washington, DC: U.S. Government Printing Office.

22. *H. R. 94-1476*, 60.

23. *H. R. 94-1476*, 120.

24. *H. R. 94-1476*, 61–65.

25. See *Community for Creative Non-Violence v. Reid*, 490 U.S. 730 (1989), for further enumeration of factors. See also *Aymes v. Bonelli*, 980 F. 2d 857 (2d Cir. 1992), for an analysis of the factors of the Community for Creative Non-Violence opinion which also examines the totality of parties' relationship.

26. Patry, W. (1994, annual update). *Copyright law and practice.* (3 vols.). Washington, DC: Bureau of National Affairs.

27. Polking, K., and L. Meramus (1981). *Law and the Writer.* Cincinnati: Writer's Digest Books. Also: Lutzker, A. (1997). *Copyrights and trademarks for media professionals.* Newton, MA: Butterworth-Heinemann.

28. Ossola, C. (1995). Copyright ownership and transfer. *Advanced seminar on copyright law 1995* (Co-chairs: R. Dannay and K. Spelman). New York: Practicing Law Institute.

29. Wincor, R. (1982). *Rights contracts in the communications media.* New York: Law & Business.

30. *H. R. 94-1476*, 52.

31. See Chapter 9 for further discussion. See also Rose, L. (1995). *Netlaw: Your rights in the online world.* Berkeley: Osborne McGraw-Hill, for legal information on Internet topics; and Denning, D., and H. Lin (1994). *Rights and responsibilities of participants in networked communities.* Washington, DC: National Academy Press. Discussion groups on the Internet are debating the extent to which an item unknowingly downloaded from the Internet from a listserv and then discarded constitutes a copy, which involves a combination of legal and computer expertise in order to know how messages are loaded, saved, and transmitted. See also the American Library Association (1996, January 24). *Access to electronic information, services, and networks: An interpretation of the "Library Bill of Rights."*

32. Information Infrastructure Task Force, Working Group on Intellectual Property Rights (1995, September). *Intellectual property and the National Information Infrastructure.* Washington, DC: U.S. Patent and Trademark Office.

33. *H. R. 94-1476*, 53, or Working Group on Intellectual Property Rights. (1995, September).

34. Section 511, as amended November 15, 1990, P.L. 101-553, 104 Stat. 2749.

35. DuBoff, L. (1995). *The law (in plain English) for writers* (2nd ed.). New York: John Wiley and Sons.

36. As amended by the Act of October 31, 1988, P.L. 100-568, 102 Stat. 2853, 2860.

37. Latman, A., R. Gorman, and J. Ginsburg (1985). *Copyright for the eighties* (2nd ed.). Charlottesville, VA: Michie Bobbs-Merrill, 514.

38. *Feist Publications, Inc. v. Rural Tel. Serv. Co.*, 499 U.S. 340. (1991).
39. Osterberg, R. (1995). Litigating a copyright infringement case. In *Advanced seminar on copyright law 1995*. New York: Practicing Law Institute. See also Hartnick (1983). Summary judgment in copyrights from Cole Porter to Superman. *Cardoza Arts & Entertainment*, L.J. 53; *Street v. J. C. Bradford and Co.*, 886 F. 2d 1472 (6th Circuit 1989), which states that substantive law governing the case will determine what issues of fact are material; and *Williams v. Crichton*, 1994 Copyright L. Dec. 27, 293 (S.D.N.Y. 1994), which granted summary judgment.

Chapter 2. Exceptions to Author's Rights: Section 107, "Fair Use"

1. *Folsom v. Marsh*, 9 F. Cas. 342 (C.C.D. Mass. 1841) (No. 4, 901).
2. See Chafee, Z., Jr. (1945). *Reflections on the law of copyright*. Columbia L. Review 503, 511; and Latman, A. (1960). *Fair use of copyrighted works*. Copyright Law Revision Study No. 14. The late Dr. Jerome Miller also provided information and published monographs on copyright, such as *The copyright directory* and *Using copyrighted videocassettes in classrooms and libraries* for education and library audiences, which are still available in libraries and contain useful information.
3. Cohen, S. (1955). Fair use in the law of copyright. *American Society of Composers and Publishers Copyright Law Symposium*, 43, 38–49.
4. *Farmer v. Calvert Lithographic Co.*, 8 Fed. Cas. 1022, No. 4, 651 at 1026 (C.C.E.D. Mich. 1872); *Macmillan Co. v. King*, 223 F. 862 (1914); *Henry Holt and Co. v. Liggett and Meyers Tobacco Co.*, 23 F. Supp. 302 (E.D. Pa. 1938); *Rosemont Enterprises, Inc. v. Random House*, 366 F. 2d 303 (2d Cir., 1966), cert. denied, 385 U.S. 1009, 17 Ed. 2d 546, 87 Sup. Ct. 714 (1967); *Williams and Wilkins v. the United States*, 172 U.S.P.Q. 670 (Comm'r C. Cl. 1972), rev. 487 F. 2d 1345 (Ct. Cl. 1973), affirmed by an equally divided court, 420 U.S. 376 (1975); *Wihtol v. Crow*, 309 F. 2d 777 (8th Cir. 1963); *Dallas Cowboy Cheerleaders, Inc. v. Scoreboard Posters, Inc.*, 600 F. 2d 1184 (1979); *Universal City Studios, Inc. v. Sony Corporation of America*, 480 F. Supp. 429, 203 U.S.P.Q. 656 (C.D. Cal. 1979), rev. in part, affirmed in part, 659 F. 2d 963, 211 U.S.P.Q. 761, 551 PTCH D-1 (9th Cir. 1981), rev. 52 U.S.L.W. 4090 (1984). See also Copyright fair use: Case law and legislation. (1969). *Duke Law Journal*, 73–109; and Lawrence, M. (1982). Fair use: Evidence of change in a traditional doctrine (27 *ASCAP Copyright Law Symposium 71*). While the above cases were ruled in favor of either private parties or educational defendants, two other cases ruled against educational defendants: *Wihtol v. Crow*, 199 F. Supp. 682, 132 U.S.P.Q. 392 (S.D. Iowa 1961), rev. 309 F. 2d 777, 135 U.S.P.Q. 385 (8th Cir. 1962), in which a church choir director incorporated a copyrighted hymn in a new arrangement which was publicly performed; and *Encyclopedia Britannica Educational Corporation v. Crooks*, 447 F. Supp. 243 (W.D.N.Y 1978), in which defendants videotaped a number of copyrighted educational films without permission and distributed them to member school districts via catalog. However, case law and the 1976 act have granted broad application to the fair use doctrine. See Patry, W. (1995). *The fair use privilege in copyright law* (2nd ed.). Washington, DC: Bureau of National Affairs, for the most comprehensive study of fair use to date, including all pertinent case law. See also Patry, W. (1997, cumulative supplement). *Copyright law and practice*. Washington, DC: Bureau of National Affairs.

5. *Sony Corporation of America v. Universal City Studios, Inc.,* 464 U.S. 417 (1984); *Harper and Row Publishers, Inc. v. Nation Enterprises,* 471 U.S. 539 (1985); *Stewart v. Abend,* 495 U.S. 207 (1990); and *Campbell v. Acuff-Rose Music, Inc.,* No. 92-1292, cert. granted, 61 U.S.L.M. 3667 (March 29, 1993).

6. See Patterson, L. R. (1991). *The nature of copyright: A law of user's rights*; and Crews, K. (1993). *Copyright, fair use and the challenge for universities,* for further discussion of this issue.

7. Sinofsky, E. (1995, November-December). The water's not safe yet! *Tech Trends,* 12–14.

8. U.S. Constitution. Art. I, sec. 8, cl. 8. See also *Fogarty v. Fantasy, Inc.* 510 U.S. 517 (1994). This decision emphasizes that the purpose of copyright protection is "enriching the general public through access."

9. I. Stat. 124.

10. For discussions of the purpose of fair use in the public interest see *Rosemont Enterprises, Inc. v. Random House, Inc.* and *Time, Inc. v. Bernard Geis Assoc.,* 293 F. Supp. 130 (S.D.N.Y. 1968). Latman, Gorman, and Ginsburg (1985). *Copyright in the eighties* (2nd ed.) Charlottesville, VA: Michie Bobbs-Merrill, includes a discussion of the First Amendment issues raised most recently in copyright and fair use considerations. Other discussions on this topic are Nimmer, M. Does copyright abridge the First Amendment guarantees of free speech and press? *UCLA Law Review* 17, 1180-1204; and T*riangle Publications, Inc. v. Knight-Ridder Newspapers, Inc.,* 626 F. 2d 1171 (5th Cir. 1980), which held that the defense of fair use and the First Amendment are separate. See also Rosenfield, The Constitutional dimension of "fair use" in copyright law, *The Notre Dame Lawyer* 50, 790–807; and *Harper and Row Publishers, Inc. v. Nation Enterprises,* 557 F. Supp. 1067 (S.D.N.Y. 1983), rev. 753 F. 2d 195 (2d Cir. 1983), cert. granted (U.S. 1984), in which the Copyright Act, the court declared, "was not intended to provide such a private monopoly of act at the expense of the public's need to be informed." See also *Fogarty v. Fantasy, Inc.* (1994) in number 8 above; and Patterson, L. (1992, Spring). *Understanding fair use law and contemporary problems* 55(2), 249–266.

11. *H. R. 94-1476.*

12. Seltzer, L. (1978). *Exemptions and fair use in copyright: The rights tensions in the 1976 copyright act* (p. 36). Cambridge, MA: Harvard University Press. See also Photocopying and fair use: An examination of the economic factors in fair use. (1977). *Emory Law Journal* 26, 849–884.

13. *Henry Holt and Co. v. Liggett and Meyers Tobacco Co.* involved the use of three sentences for a commercial advertisement. *Karll v. Curtis Publishing Co.,* 39 F. Supp. 836, 51 U.S.P.Q. (E.D. Wis. 1941) turned upon the "purpose for which the letters were included in the book" as well as the other fair use factors. See Georgia Harper's discussion of the four fair use factors in light of the *Texaco* decision on her Office of General Counsel for the University of Texas System Web site, Professional fair use after *Texaco* [online] at http://www.utsystem/OGC/IntellectualProperty/tex2.html.

14. Talab, R. (1986). *Commonsense copyright: A guide to the new technologies.* Jefferson, NC: McFarland.

15. Patry, W. (1994, annual update). *Copyright law and practice.* (3 vols.) Washington, D.C.: Bureau of National Affairs. See this work for the most complete coverage of the codified doctrine.

16. See note number 10. M. Nimmer notes that the "statute gives no guidance

as to the relative weight of the factors..." Nimmer, M. (1979). *Nimmer on copyright: A treatise of the law of literary, musical, and artistic works* (2nd ed., Vol. 3, Section 13.05[A]). St. Paul, MN: West Publishing. See also note number 12 for Seltzer's (1978) discussion of the importance of the economic aspect. See also Patry, W. (1995). *The fair use privilege in copyright law* (2nd ed.). Washington, DC: Bureau of National Affairs.

17. For discussions of the fair use factors, see Cohen, note number 3, for a definitive analysis. Carnahan, in note number 6, Chapter 3, explores eight aspects of these factors. R. Needham outlined 16 factors affecting fair use determinations in: Tape recording, photocopying, and fair use. (1959). *American Society of Composers, Authors, and Publishers Copyright Law Symposium* 10, 75–103. See also D. Brooks' discussion of fair use factors in Appendix A: Helm, V. (1984). *Software quality and copyright: Issues in computer assisted instruction* (pp. 116–121). Washington, DC: Association for Educational Communications and Technology. The amount of independent research in preparing a work has also been a criterion for determining fair use. When much independent research has been done, fair use has been accepted. See: *Hartford Printing Co. v. Hartford Directory and Publishing Co.*, 196 F. 332 (C.C.D. Conn. 1906); *Toksvig v. Bruce Publishing Co.*, 181 F. 2d 664 (7th Cir. 1950); and *Oxford Book Co. v. College Entrance Book Co.*, 98 F. 2d 688, 691 (2d Cir. 1938). See also the two reports from the Working Group on Intellectual Property. The 1994 *Report*, known as the "Green Paper," and the 1995 *Report*, known as the "White Paper," take different positions on fair use and how each factor is calculated. Working Group on Intellectual Property (1994). *Intellectual property and the National Information Infrastructure*. Washington, DC: U.S. Patent and Trademark Office; and Working Group on Intellectual Property (1995). *Final report of the Working Group on Intellectual Property and the National Information Infrastructure*. Washington, DC: U.S. Patent and Trademark Office. Much has been written about how systematic aggregate use affects the weight of the factors. See also Georgia Harper, Office of General Counsel for the University of Texas System, "Rules of Thumb," and "Professional fair use after *Texaco*." The location is www.utsystem/OGC/IntellectualProperty, for the Web site. Applicable case law is *Princeton University Press v. Michigan Document Services, Inc.*, 855 F. Supp. 905, E. D. Mich. 1994; *Basic Books Inc. v. Kinko's Graphics Corp.*, 758 F. Supp. 1522, S.D.N.Y. 1991; and *American Geophysical Union v. Texaco*, 37 F. 3d 881 (2d Cir.), rehearing denied, 1994 U.S. App. Lexis 36735 (2d Cir., December 23, 1994), replaced with revised opinion, 60 F. 3d 913 (2d Cir.), cert. dismissed, 116 S. Ct. 592 (1995). See also *Campbell v. Acuff-Rose Music, Inc.*, 510 U.S. 569 (1994). The court stated that "nor may the four statutory factors be treated in isolation, one from another."

18. See *Thompson v. Gernsback*, 94 F. Supp. 453, 87 U.S.P.Q. 238 (1950), which affirmed that "scientific, legal, medical, and similar books or articles of learning" are granted greater use of copyrighted materials because of the purpose of their use and the intent for which it is made. A more recent case emphasizing this factor was *Triangle Publications, Inc. v. Knight-Ridder Newspapers, Inc.* in which it was noted that the purpose of the use was the first factor to be considered. *Meeropol v. Nizer*, 560 F. 2d 1061, 195 U.S.P.Q. 273 (2d Cir. 1977), cert. denied, 434 U.S. 1013 (1978), found that the purpose for which a use was made of copyrighted letters was of most importance in finding the use to be fair. *Henry Holt and Co. v. Liggett and Meyers Tobacco Co.*, found that the use of three sentences for a commercial venture (a pamphlet promoting cigarettes quoted from a book

by Holt written for voice teachers) is afforded significantly less latitude than an educational or scholarly use. See also *Dr. Pepper Co. v. Sambo's Restaurants*, 517 F. Supp. 1202 (N.D. Tex. 1981), "any commercial use tends to cut against a fair use doctrine." The nature of the use does not have to be commercial for the use to be an infringement. See *Texaco* (1994); *Kinko's* (1991); and *Michigan Document Services* (1994) cases in number 17 above for discussion. See also *Campbell v. Acuff-Rose* (1994).

19. D. Hayes found that the second factor is the least used factor in determining fair use in: Classroom "fair use": A re-evaluation (1978). *Bulletin of the Copyright Society of the U.S.A.* 26, 101–129. Analyses of copyright decisions involving educational or scholarly uses of materials show that the number of cases involving this type of work are relatively rare when compared with cases involving entertainment works, loosely categorized as popular fiction, music, film, etc. *Rosemont Enterprises, Inc. v. Random House, Inc.* discussed this criterion to some extent. *Henry Holt and Co. v. Liggett and Meyers Tobacco Co.* involved the use of scholarly work on voice to enhance a pamphlet designed to sell cigarettes. The use of the work "has cast reflections upon the term 'commercialist' … which has contributed to negate and deter the sale of his [Feldmerman's] book." The nature of the work and the profit motive of the use made of it amounted to infringement. See also *Harper and Row Pub., Inc. v. Nation Enterprises* and *Eckes v. Card Prices Update*, 736 F. 2d 85 (2d Cir. 1985). For a comprehensive discussion of the second factor, along with supporting cases, see Perry, W. (1985). The fair use privilege. In M. Goldberg (ed.), *Copyright law 1985* (pp. 621–626). New York: Practicing Law Institute. *Feist Publications, Inc. v. Rural Telephone Co.*, 499 U.S. 390 (1991) was historic for several reasons. The court overruled seventy years of precedent to say that telephone book white pages didn't have sufficient originality to be protected by copyright. "Outside of unpublished works, this factor typically receives little attention … the courts weigh the second factor in the defendant's favor when an informational work is at issue, and in the owner's favor when an entertainment work is involved." Patry, W. (1994, annual update). *Copyright law and practice.* (3 vols.) Washington, DC: Bureau of National Affairs. See also Leval, P. (1990). Toward a fair use standard. *Harvard Law Review* 103, 1105, 1116.

20. The criterion of "substantial taking" has been applied often. See *Ager v. Peninsular and Oriental Steam Navigation Company*, 26 C.D. 637 (1884), in which multiple copies were reproduced. *Addison Wesley Publishing Co. v. Brown*, 223 F. Supp. 219, 139 U.S.P.Q. 47 (1963), found "substantial" copying of another work. *Marcus v. Rowley*, 695 F. 2d 1171, CCH Cop. L. Rep. Section 25, 486 (9th Cir. 1983), found substantial copying, even with attribution, in a textbook for a cake decorating course in a nonprofit educational institution to be an infringement. See *Leon v. Pacific Telephone and Telegraph Company*, 91 F. 2d 484, 34 U.S.P.Q. 237 (9th Cir. 1937), in which the amount copied was seen as "wholesale copying and publication." *Macmillan Co. v. King*, 223 F. 862 (D. Mass. 1914), held that King, a tutor, made memoranda sheets which "were intended to outline all subject matter." See *Southwestern Bell Tel. Co. v. Nationwide Independent Directory Serv., Inc.*, 371 F. Supp. 900 (W.D. Ark. 1974), and *Wainwright Securities, Inc. v. Wall Street Transcript Corp.* 418 F. Supp. 620 (S.D.N.Y. 1976), affirmed 558 F. 2d 91 (2d Cir. 1977), cert. denied, 434 U.S. 1014 (1978). Parody is given wider latitude under the fair use doctrine. *Elsmere Music, Inc. v. NBC*, 482 F. Supp. 741 (S.D.N.Y.), affirmed 623 F. 2d 252 (2d Cir. 1980) held that copying parts of "I Love New York" as well as two of the four-word lyrics was a fair use because the parody "I Love Sodom"

is afforded greater leeway. However, parody is not always a successful defense in an infringement suit. See *Loew's, Inc. v. Columbia Broadcasting System, Inc.*, 131 F. Supp. 165, 105 U.S.P.Q. 302 (S.D. Cal. 1955), affirmed sub nom, *Benny v. Loew's, Inc.*, 239 F. 2d 532, 112 U.S.P.Q. 11 (9th Cir. 1959), affirmed per curiam by an equally divided court, 356 U.S. 43, 116 U.S.P.Q. 479 (1958). See also *Kepner-Trego, Inc. v. Leadership Software, Inc.*, 22 U.S.P.Q. 1788 (S.D. Texas 1992). The fair use defense was rejected when the defendant took "heart and soul" of the plaintiff's copyrighted work on executive computer training.

21. In music, particularly, the qualitative aspect is most often found, although it has been applied to other mediums, as well. See *Elsmere Music, Inc., v. NBC*, 482 F. Supp. 741 (S.D.N.Y.), affirmed 623 F. 2d 252 (2d Cir. 1980), in which copying the "heart" of a song ("I Love New York" used for a parody titled "I Love Sodom") was seen as fair use because of the greater leeway afforded parody. See also *Warner Bros. v. ABC*, 720 F. 2d 231 (2d Cir. 1983), 654 F. 2d 204 (2d. Cir. 1982). The Supreme Court stated that while the amount taken was insubstantial, it amounted to "the heart of the book" in *Harper and Row, Publishers, Inc. v. Nation Enterprises*, 471 U.S. 539 (1985). See also *Allen-Myland, Inc. v. IBM Corp.*, 746 F. Supp. 520, 534–35 (E.D. Pa. 1990), 770 F. Supp. 1004 (E.D. Pa. 1991), 770 F. Supp. 1014 (E.D. Pa. 1991) in which only a portion was copied, but it was a "key or essential part of a copyrighted computer program."

22. Seltzer (1978). See also *Hill v. Whalen and Martell*, 220 F. 359, 18 Copy. Dec. 224 (S.D.N.Y. 1914), and *Flosom v. Marsh;* both found that infringement can be found when such a large amount is used that the value of the original could be lessened. As indicated by Seltzer (1978) and Cohen (1955), the effect of the use on the potential market is most often determined by balancing all of the factors. M. Nimmer (1979) described a "functional test" in which if a copy serves the function of the original, fair use might not be used as a defense. The effect of the copies being made afforded potential damage to the market of the originals in the *Universal City Studios, Inc. v. Sony Corporation of America*, 480 F. Supp. 429, 203 U.S.P.Q. 656 (C.D. Cal. 1979), rev. in part, affirmed in part, 659 F. 2d 963, 211 U.S.P.Q. 761, 551 PTCH D-1 (9th Cir. 1981), rev., 52 U.S.L.W. 4090 (1984). The *F.E.L. Publications, Ltd. v. Catholic Bishop of Chicago* (N.D. Ill. 1984) jury awarded a composer-publisher of religious music $3 million in actual damages and $1 million in punitive damages for unlawful copying by the Chicago Archdiocese to compensate for business lost. Plaintiff was heard to exclaim "Thank God!" *Meeropol v. Nizer* also found that the future market value of a copyrighted work is an aspect of the potential market. Indeed, "[a]ll publications presumably are operated for profit." *Koussevitzky v. Allen, Towne & Heath*, 188 Misc. 479, 483, 68 N.Y.S. 2d 779, 783, affirmed 272 App. Div. 759, 69 N.Y.S. 2d 432 (1st Dept. 1947) (cited in *Rosemont*). However, *Williams and Wilkins Company v. United States* held that while there was merit to the effect on the market of the use, the advancement of medical science and the public interest outweighed these considerations. *Williams and Wilkins* is viewed as having a narrow scope (see Latman, Gorman, and Ginsburg). See also the *Texaco* (1994) decision because of the effect of systematic copying which, though in small amounts, affected the market for the periodicals copied. The coursepak cases, *Kinko's* (1991) and *Michigan Document Services* (1994), both affirmed that aggregate copying, even without commercial intent, harmed the market for the works. See *Lewis Galoob Toys, Inc. v. Nintendo of America, Inc.*, 964 F. 2d 965 (9th Cir. 1992) cert. denied, 113 S. Ct. 1582 (1993) in which

there was insufficient proof of harm to the market for derivative works. See also Patry, W. (1994). *Copyright law and practice*, pp. 771–784, for a discussion of determinations of the fourth factor on.

23. *Fisher v. Dees*, 794 F.2d 432, 436 (9th Cir. 1986) cited in Kroft, S. (1993). Copyright litigation overview. *Understanding basic copyright law 1994*, Co-chairs: Spelman, K., R. Newbury, I. Koenigsberg. New York: Practicing Law Institute. See also *Sega Enterprises*, 977 F.2d at 1523-1527, in which "public interest" and "equitable basis" were discussed as being important in the final determination.

24. *H. R. 94-1476*, 68–69.

25. Ibid.

26. *H. R. 94-1476*, 69.

27. Ibid.

28. American Library Association (1995). *Fair Use Statement*.

29. *Princeton University Press v. Michigan Document Services, Inc.*, 855 F. Supp. 905, E.D. Mich. 1994; and *Basic Books, Inc. v. Kinko's Graphic Corp.*, 758 F. Supp. 1522, S.D.N.Y. 1991.

30. *American Geophysical Union v. Texaco, Inc.*, 37 F. 3d 881 (2d Cir.), rehearing denied, 1994 U.S. App. Lexis 36735 (2d Cir., Dec. 23, 1994), replaced with revised opinion, 60 F. 3d 913 (2d Cir.), cert. dismissed, 116 S. Ct. 592 (1995).

31. Botterbusch, H. (1996). *Copyright in the age of new technology*. Bloomington, IN: Phi Delta Kappa Foundation.

Chapter 3. Print Materials

1. *H. R. 94-1476*, 68–70.

2. Patterson, L., and S. Lindberg (1991). *The nature of copyright: A law of user's rights*. Athens, GA: University of Georgia Press.

3. While many publishers did sign the agreement, the American Association of University Professors (AAUP), the American Association of Law Schools (AALS) and the American Council of Education (ACE) expressed concern over the guidelines as being too restrictive in a letter to the Ad Hoc Committee. The Committee replied that "there is potentially a great deal of educational photocopying beyond that set forth in the guidelines that will clearly be lawful in the future as it has been in the past" (letter, *Chronicle of Higher Education*, October 28, 1978, 13).

4. *Act of October 24, 1992, Publ. L. 102-492*, 106 Stat. 3145.

5. Finkelstein, H. Copyright problems on campus. *The College Counsel* 6(1), 203–219.

6. Two discussions on faculty-produced works are (1) Carnahan, W. (1972). Copyright in our realm of learning. *The College Counsel* 71(1), 421–477, including work-for-hire aspects; and (2) Zirkel, P. (1975). Copyright law in higher education: Individuals, institutions, and innovations. *Journal of College and University Law* 2, 342–354, which discusses various aspects of authorship and use in higher education under the 1976 Copyright Act. See *Community for Creative Non-Violence v. Reid*, 490 U.S. at 751–752 (footnotes omitted). The Court applied the factors in a work-for-hire and concluded that Reid was not an employee of the Community for Creative Non-Violence.

7. See DuBoff, L. (1996). *The law (in plain English) for writers* (2nd ed.). New York: John Wiley and Sons; Fishman, S. (1996, April). *The copyright handbook: How to protect and use written works.* Berkeley, CA: Nolo Press; and Brinson, J., and M. Radcliffe (1994). *Multimedia law handbook: A practical guide for developers and publishers.* Menlo Park, CA: Ladera.

8. See *Sherill v. Grieves,* 57 Washington Law Rep. 286, 290 Sup. Ct. D.C. (1929); and *Williams v. Weisser,* 163 U.S.P.Q. 42 (Cal. Ct. App., June 5, 1969).

9. *H. R. 94-1476,* 85.

10. *H. R. 94-1476,* 86.

11. Ibid.

12. See note 2, Chapter 3.

13. *H. R. 94-1476,* 46. See also Sturdevant (Talab), R. (1980). *Print materials in higher education: Selected issues, resulting changes, and "fair use" in the 1976 Copyright Act,* unpublished doctoral dissertation, University of Southern California, for a discussion of materials use in higher education.

14. Letter, *Chronicle of Higher Education,* 13.

15. *H. R. 94-1476,* 68.

16. *H. R. 94-1476,* 67.

17. *H. R. 94-1476,* 69.

Chapter 4. Music

1. Gorder, D. (1992, Fall). *Berklee Today,* 17–19.

2. Melton, M. (1997). International cyberspace licensing perils. *Understanding the intellectual property license* (Co-chairs: L. Pirkey, S. Progoff, B. Weiss, and S. Snowman). New York: Practicing Law Institute.

3. Goldstein, J. (1979). *The performance of copyrighted music: Questions and answers.* New York: Broadcast Music. See also: Erickson, J., E. Hearm, and M. Halloran. (1983). *Musician's guide to copyright* (Rev. ed.). New York: Charles Scribner's Sons.

4. Goldstein, 3.

5. *H. R. 94-1476,* 71.

6. Taubman, J. (1980). *In tune with the music business* (p. 134). New York: Law-Arts Publishers.

7. Magarrell, J. (1978, March 19). Harvard University sued for copyright infringement. *The Chronicle of Higher Education,* 3.

8. *F.E.L. Publications, Ltd. v. Catholic Bishop of Chicago.*

9. *Campbell v. Acuff-Rose Music, Inc.,* 510 U.S. 569, 1994.

10. *Frank Music Corp. v. CompuServe, Inc.,* No. 93 Civ. 8153, S.D.N.Y., 1993.

11. Scott, M. (1995). *Multimedia: Law & practice.* Englewood Cliffs, NJ: Aspen Law and Business. See also Scott, M. (looseleaf, annual update). *Scott on multimedia law: Development, protection, and distribution* (2nd ed.). New York: Aspen Law and Business.

12. Sinofsky, E. (1994). *A copyright primer for educational and industrial producers* (2nd ed.). Washington, DC: Association for Educational Communications and Technology.

13. Knave, B. (1996, March). Everything you wanted to know about releasing your own album. *Electronic Musician,* 32–34.

Chapter 5. Audiovisual Materials

1. Section 101.

2. Cases which illustrate the copyrightability of video games are: *Midway Mfg. Co. v. Arctic International*, 685 F. 2d 870 (3rd Cir. 1982), and *Stern Electronics v. Kaufman*, 669 F. 2d 852 (2d Cir. 1982); both of them held that copying an audiovisual display of video games was infringement. *Williams Electronics, Inc. v. Arctic International*, 685 F. 2d 870 (3rd Cir. 1982), held infringement of audiovisual display and underlying computer program. *Midway Mfg. Co. v. Strohon*, 564 F. Supp. 741, 219 U.S.P.Q. 42 (1983), held that copyright in a computer program for a video game was protectable separately from the copyright in the audiovisual work and copyright protection extended to object code stored in a chip. See *Atari v. Oman*, 888 F. 2d 878 (D.C. Cir. 1989); *Sheehan v. MTV*, Copyright Law Rep. 91 26, 886 (S.D.N.Y. 1992) for more recent decisions involving audiovisual works.

3. Section 106(5).

4. The Betamax case did not rule on pay or cable television, organized or informal "tape swapping," tape duplication by groups or corporations, or for use outside the home (such as for use in the schools). Certainly the most controversial case in off-air taping, though with limited precedent, *Universal City Studios, Inc. v. Sony Corporation of America* was the subject of much discussion. Among the books including discussions of Betamax and off-air taping are: (1) Sinofsky, E. (1984). *Off-air videotaping in education: Copyright issues, decisions, implications* (pp. 78–88). New York: R. R. Bowker; (2) Clark, C. (1979-1980). *Universal City Studios, Inc. v. Sony Corporation of America:* Application of the fair use doctrine under the United States Copyright Acts of 1909 and 1976. *New England Law Review* 15, 161–181; (3) Beard, J. (1979-1980). The sale, rental, and reproduction of motion picture videocassettes: Piracy or privilege? *New England Law Review*, 435–484; and (4) Roberts, M. (1980, March). *Disney/Universal v. Sony:* Arguments and conclusions (Special Report). *The Videocassette and CATV Newsletter.*

5. *H. R. 94-1476*, 64.

6. Ibid.

7. *Universal City Studios, Inc. v. Sony Corporation of America.* See note 22, Chapter 2, and note 4, Chapter 5. The court discussed librarying, but found it to be insignificant. However, the BOCES case, see note 4, Chapter 2, found that retention of copies was a cause for infringement. The off-air taping guidelines (see Appendices) prohibit retention of copies.

8. Stanek, D. J. (1986, March). Videotapes, computer programs, and the library. *Information Technology and Libraries*, 42–54. See also Reed, M. H., and D. Stanek (1986, February). Library and classroom use of copyrighted videotapes and computer software. *American Libraries.* Cases which have to do with public exhibition of videos, delineating what constitutes a public performance, are *Columbia Pictures Industries, Inc. v. Aveco, Inc.*, 749 F. 2d 154 (3d Cir. 1984), which dealt with (1) renting viewing rooms and cassettes separately and (2) customer operated videocassette players. Both were considered similar and to be infringements. See also Bruwelheide, J. (1995). *A copyright primer for librarians and educators.* Chicago: American Library Association and the National Education Association.

9. *H. R. 94-1476*, 80.

10. Miller, J. K. (1987). *Using copyrighted videocassettes in classrooms, libraries,*

and training centers (2nd ed.). Friday Harbor, WA: Copyright Information Services.

11. See Sinofsky, E. (1984). *Off-air videotaping in education: Copyright issues, decisions, implications.* New York: R. R. Bowker, 98–102 for a discussion and 121–125 for a list of producers who are not endorsing the guidelines.

12. *Encyclopaedia Britannica Educational Corporation v. Crooks* (1978).

13. Wincor, R. (1982). *Rights contracts in the communications media.* New York: Law and Business.

14. Botterbusch, H. (1996). *Copyright in the age of new technology.* Bloomington, IN: Phi Delta Kappa Foundation.

15. While Section 110 is the section that pertains to off-air taping in the non-profit institution, the *H. R. 94-1476,* 81–88, explains the stipulations of Section 110 more clearly. For a discussion of Section 110 and the off-air taping guidelines, see Miller, J. K. (1984). *Using copyrighted videocassettes in classrooms and libraries.* Champaign, IL: Copyright Information Services; and Billings, R. D. (1977). Off-air video recording, face-to-face teaching, and the 1976 Copyright Act. *Northern Kentucky Law Review* 4, 225–251.

16. While it could be argued that the limited use of closed circuit could be used to transmit a program to a "cluster or campus," the *H. R. 94-1476,* 80–81, specifically prohibits closed circuit. This is, then, an area of contention.

17. See in Lawrence, J. S., and B. Timberg (eds.) (1980). *Fair use and free inquiry.* Norwood, NJ: Ablex, for discussions of off-air taping and television research; Mast, G., Film study and copyright law (pp. 71–80); Kellner, D., Television research and fair use (pp. 90–107); Kies, C., The CBS-Vanderbilt litigation: Taping the evening news (pp. 111–119); and Aleinikoff, E., Fair use and broadcasting (pp. 180–191).

18. See Miller, J. K. *The Video/Copyright Seminar 1986.* Copyright Information Services, for a discussion of the application of the Communications Act to satellite off-air taping; and Bender, I. (1985, November). Copyright implications of satellite transmissions. *TLC Guide,* 8, for another view. While these views do not necessarily conflict, their discussions point out the essential grayness of satellite off-air taping at present.

19. Botterbusch, H. (1996).

20. See in Lawrence, J. S., and B. Timberg (eds.) (1980). *Fair use and free inquiry.* Norwood, NJ: Ablex, for the following: Douglas, J., Seeking copyright clearances for an audiovisual center (pp. 121–125); and Miller, J., The duplication of audiovisual materials for libraries (pp. 127–128).

Chapter 6. Computers

1. Holleyman, R. (1995). Copyright protection for computer software: A global overview. In W. Gilbreth and D. Bender (co-chairs), *Intellectual property law institute 1995.* New York: Practicing Law Institute.

2. Tapper, C. (1982). *Computer law* (2nd ed.). New York: Longman Group. See also CONTU, *Final Report,* 23; objections to the copyrightability of software in Koenig, C. F. (1980). Software copyright: The conflict within CONTU. *Bulletin of the Copyright Society of the U.S.A.* 27, 340–378. Court cases have firmly

established the copyrightability of software. See *Apple Computer Inc. v. Franklin Computer Corporation,* 545 F. Supp. 812 (E.D. Pa. 1982) rev. 714 F. 2d 1240 (3d Cir. 1983), which confirms "categorical" copyrightability of computer programs, "a computer program is a 'work of authorship' subject to copyright"; *Tandy Corporation v. Personal MicroComputers, Inc.,* 524 F. Supp. 171 (N.D. Cal. 1981), copyrightability of ROM; *Williams Electronics, Inc. v. Arctic International, Inc.,* chip duplication as "copy" which Congress clearly intended to protect; and *Apple Computer, Inc. v. Formula International, Inc.,* 725 F. 2d 521 (9th Cir. 1984), in which Apple was granted a preliminary injunction against Formula's selling "Pineapples" that included copies of Apple's "autostart" ROMs. See Latman, Gorman, and Ginsburg, pp. 137–138 for a discussion. However, due to the difficulties of enforcing copyright protection through infringement cases, the number of software patents has increased markedly. See Kennard, W. (1998, January-February). Obtaining and litigating software patents. *IP Litigator,* 1–12.

    3. CONTU, *Final Report,* 38.

    4. *P.L. 96-517, Copyright law amendment for computer programs* (94 Stat. 3028-29), December 12, 1980. Another amendment allowed "mask works" to be copyrighted. *P.L. 98-620, The Semiconductor Chip Protection Act of 1984,* January 23, 1984, provided copyright protection for a new class of writings — mask works. This protection lasts for 10 years from the effective date of registration or from the date of the first commercial exploitation, whichever comes first. For a discussion of this act, see Miller, P. (1985). Computer software and related technology. In M. Goldberg (ed.), *Current developments in copyright law 1985* (pp. 369–422). New York: Practicing Law Institute.

    5. See Patry, W. (1994). *Copyright law and practice.* (3 vols.). Washington, DC: Bureau of National Affairs. This work is, without question, the most complete work on fair use. It also has a 1997 cumulative supplement.

    6. Brooks, D. (1984–1985). Acquisition and exploitation of custom software. In M. Goldberg (ed.), *Computer software 1984: Protection and marketing* (Vols. 1–2, pp. 659–833; p. 765). New York: Practicing Law Institute.

    7. See *Campbell v. Acuff-Rose Music, Inc.,* 114 S. Ct. 1164, 1177 (1994) in which the burden of persuasion to prove that a use is fair and avoid liability is that of the defendant.

    8. Kemp, D. (1990). Limitations upon the software producer's rights: *Vault Corp. v. Quaid Software Ltd., Rutgers Computer & Technology Law Journal* 16(10), 85–128.

    9. Patry, W. (1994). See pp. 213–227 for a discussion of protectibility issues.

    10. Ibid.

    11. *Whelan Associates v. Jaslow Dental Labs,* 797 F.2d 1222 (3d Cir. 1986), cert. denied, 479 U.S. 1031 (1987) and *Computer Associates International, Inc. v. Altai, Inc. ,* 775 F. Supp. 544 (E.D.N.Y. 1991), affirmed, 982 F.2d 693 (2d Cir. 1992), to name just two.

    12. Information Infrastructure Task Force, Working Group on Intellectual Property Rights (1995, September). *Intellectual property and the National Information Infrastructure.* Washington, DC: U.S. Patent and Trademark Office, 65.

    13. Ibid.

    14. See Section 109, and Supp. V, 1993.

    15. *Lewis Galoob Toys, Inc. v. Nintendo of America, Inc.,* N. D. Cal. 1991, 780 F. Supp. 1283, 20 U.S.P.Q. 2d 1662, [main volume] affirmed 964 F. 2d 965, 22

U.S.P.Q. 2d 1857, as amended, certiorari denied 113 S. Ct. 1582, 507 U.S. 985, 123 L. Ed. 2d 149.

16. Working Group on Intellectual Property Rights (1995, September), 71.

17. Section 101 (1988), and Supp. V (1993).

18. Working Group on Intellectual Property Rights (1995, September), 72.

19. *Playboy Enterprises, Inc. v. Frena*, 839 F. Supp. 1552 (M.D. Fla. 1993).

20. Finkel, L. (1985, April-May). Editorial opinion. *Computer-Using Educators, 3.*

21. Patry, W. (1994).

22. Vance, D. (1997). A checklist for license agreements. In *Understanding the intellectual property license* (Co-chairs: L. Pirkey, S. Progoff, B. Weiss, and S. Solomon). New York: Practicing Law Institute.

23. Section 103.

24. Talab, R. (1991). Copyright and other legal considerations in patron software use. *Library Trends* 16(2), 264–274.

25. Copyright law amendment, 1980.

26. Kemp, D. (1990).

27. Section 109.

28. *H. R. 94-1476.*

29. Kemp, D. (1990).

30. Paetzold, R. (1989). Contracts enlarging a copyright owner's rights: A framework for determining unenforceability. *Nebraska Law Review* 68(4), 816–834.

Chapter 7. Electronic Publishing

1. Recent decisions which confirm the copyrightability of databases and compilations are: *Financial Information, Inc. v. Moody's Investors Service, Inc.,* 751 F. 2d 501 (2d Cir. 1984); *Dow Jones and Co., Inc. v. Board of Trade of the City of Chicago,* 546 F. Supp. 113, 217 U.S.P.Q. 901 (1982); *National Business Lists, Inc. v. Dunn and Bradstreet, Inc.,* 552 F. Supp. 89, 215 U.S.P.Q. 595 (1982); *Rand McNally and Co. v. Fleet Management Systems,* 591 F. Supp. 726 (N.D. Ill. 1983). An historic decision that changed copyrightability from protecting "sweat of the brow" to protecting works that require creativity was *Feist Publications, Inc. v. Rural Telephone Service Co.,* 499 U.S. 340 (1991).

2. *H. R. 94-1476,* 54.

3. *Feist Publications, Inc. v. Rural Telephone Service Co.,* 499 U.S. 340 (1991).

4. Baumgarten, J. (1994). Copyright and computer software (including databases and chip technology). In M. Goldberg (ed.), *Computer software 1994: Protection and marketing* (Vol. 1, p. 57). New York: Practicing Law Institute.

5. Fishman, S. (1996). *The copyright handbook* (3rd ed.). Berkeley, CA: Nolo.

6. *Financial Information, Inc. v. Moody's Investors Service, Inc.,* 751 F. 2d 501 (2d Cir. 1984).

7. See *National Business Lists, Inc. v. Dunn and Bradstreet, Inc.,* 552 F. Supp. 89, 215 U.S.P.Q. 595 (1982), which held that "[t]he public interest in dissemination becomes progressively stronger as we move along the spectrum from fancy to fact." *New York Times Co. v. Roxbury Data Interface, Inc.,* 434 F. Supp. 217, 194

U.S.P.Q. 371 (D. NJ. 1977), which held that the use by the defendant to prepare a personal name index to plaintiff's work was fair use.

8. Latman, A., R. Gorman, and J. Ginsburg (1985). *Copyright for the eighties* (2nd ed.). Charlottesville, VA: Michie Bobbs-Merrill, 131.

9. *Brown Bag Software v. Symantec Corp.*, 960 F. 2d 1465 (9th Cir. 1992).

10. *Broderbund Software, Inc. v. Unison World*, 648 F. Supp. 1127 (N.D. Cal. 1986).

11. CONTU, *Final Report*, p. 40.

12. Ibid.

13. "The example of a copyrighted work placed in a computer memory solely to facilitate an individual's scholarly research has been cited as a possible fair use. The Commission agrees that such a use, restricted to individual research, should be considered fair." CONTU, *Final Report*, 40. "Only if information of a substantial amount were extracted and duplicated for redistribution would serious problems exist..." Latman, Gorman, and Ginsburg, 134. In all cases, the records should then be destroyed.

14. Fishman, S. (1996).

15. Section 106(3).

16. Rose, L. (1995). *Netlaw: Your rights in the online world.* New York: Osborne McGraw-Hill, 103–104.

17. Information Infrastructure Task Force, Working Group on Intellectual Property Rights (1995, September). *Intellectual property and the National Information Infrastructure.* Washington, DC: U.S. Patent and Trademark Office, 65.

18. 17 U.S.C. Section 117.

19. Section 101.

20. Fishman, S. (1996).

21. Section 106(6).

22. *Feist Publications, Inc. v. Rural Telephone Service Co.*, 499 U.S. 340 (1991).

Chapter 8. Multimedia and the Fair Use Guidelines for Educational Multimedia

1. DeLoughry, T. (1993a, September 14). Effort to provide scholarly journals by computer tries to retain the look and feel of printed publication. *The Chronicle of Higher Education*, A50.

2. DeLoughry, T. (1993b, September 22). State-of-the-art moot courtroom unveiled at William and Mary. *The Chronicle of Higher Education*, A22–23.

3. *New York Times* (December 20, 1997) as cited in *Edupage* (December 21, 1997) [online], 21 December 1997, educom@educom.unc.edu.

4. Talab, R. (1986). *Commonsense copyright.* Jefferson, NC: McFarland; Talab, R. (1989a). Copyright, CD ROM, and education. *Tech Trends*, 16–18; Talab, R. (1989b). *Copyright and instructional technologies: A guide to fair use and permissions procedures.* Washington, DC: Association for Educational Communications and Technology; Talab, R. (1990). Copyright and multimedia productions. *Tech Trends* 34(1), 13–15; Talab, R. (1992a). General trends in new technology usage: Stages of copyright development on a national level. *Advances in Library Resources Sharing* (Vol. 3). Westport, CT: Meckler; Talab, R. (1992b). Copyright scenarios

for media directors. *Tech Trends* 37(4), 10–12; Talab, R. (1994). Copyright: Legal and ethical considerations on the Internet. *Tech Trends* 40(2), 11–14.

5. Pitler, H. (1994, September-October). A technology magnet school emerges. *Multimedia Schools*, 51–55.

6. Kovalick (1992).

7. Manning, M., G. Manning., and R. Long (1994). *Theme immersion*. Portsmouth, NH: Heinemann.

8. Watkins, B. (1992, June 10). Computerized catalogs extend access to specialized collections. *The Chronicle of Higher Education*, A15–17.

9. Schneebeck, C. (1994). Copyright law: Providing access to information. *Educational Fair Access and the New Media National Conference*. Washington, DC: CCUMC/AIT.

10. *The Chronicle of Higher Education*. (1994, September 22). [online]. p. 23.

11. National Technical Information Association cited in Wilson, D. (1994, January 26). A journal's big break: National Library of Medicine will index an electronic journal on Medline. *The Chronicle of Higher Education*, A23–25; Wilson, D. (1994, May 11). Panel outlines uses of data highway in education and libraries. *The Chronicle of Higher Education*, A18; Consortium of College and University Media Centers/Agency for Instructional Technology. (1994). *Educational Fair Access and the New Media National Conference*. Washington, DC: CCUMC/AIT; EDUCOM. (1993). The bill of rights and responsibilities for electronic learners. *EDUCOM Review* 28(3); Association of American Universities/Association of Research Libraries. (1994). *Reports of the AAU Task Force*. Washington, DC: Association of Research Libraries; Working Group on Intellectual Property Rights of the National Information Infrastructure cited in Deloughry, T. (1994, September 14). Administration panel uses high-tech razzle-dazzle to illustrate promise of the information superhighway. *The Chronicle of Higher Education*, A50.

12. Working Group on Intellectual Property Rights (1994, September). *Working Report*.

13. Working Group on Intellectual Property Rights (1995, July). *Working Report*.

14. Conference on Fair Use (1996, December). *Fair use guidelines for educational multimedia*.

Chapter 9. The Internet and World Wide Web

1. O'Connell, J. (1997, February 2). [online]. cni-copyright@cni.org.

2. *Business Investors Daily*. (1996, October 15).

3. Squeo, M. (1997, October 15). *USA Today*, E1.

4. Tapscott, D. (1996). *Digital economy*.

5. Logan, T. (1997, October 18). [online]. cni-copyright@cni.org

6. Cheng, M. (1997, Fall). *Entertainment Weekly on Campus*.

7. Associated Press. (1998, April 3). Cited in *Edupage* (1998, April 15). [online]. educom@educom.unc.edu.

8. Information Infrastructure Task Force, Working Group on Intellectual Property Rights (1995, September). *Intellectual property and the National Information Infrastructure*. Washington, DC: U.S. Patent and Trademark Office.

9. Fishman, S. (1996). *The copyright handbook: How to protect and use written works.* Berkeley, CA: Nolo.

10. *Lotus Development Corp. v. Borland Intl., Inc.* 49 F. 3rd 807 (1995), affirmed 116 S. Ct. 804 (1996), *Mazer v. Stein,* 347 U.S. 201 (1954) as cited in Oliver, M. (1997, September 11). [online]. cni-copyright@cni.org.

11. Talab, R. (1997, January-February). An educational use checklist for copyright and multimedia. *Tech Trends,* 9–11. See also Talab, R. (1994, November-December). Copyright and multimedia, Part One: Definitions and usage issues in K–12. *Tech Trends,* 9–11; Talab, R. (1995, January-February). Copyright and multimedia, Part Two: Higher education. *Tech Trends,* 9–12; and Talab, R. (1998, January-February). Copyright in network environments. *Tech Trends,* 9–11.

12. Section 501.

13. Templeton, B. [no date]. [online]. www.clarinet/brad/copymyths.html.

14. Harper, G. (1996). Professional fair use after *Texaco.* [online]. www.utsystem.edu/OGC/IntellectualProperty/tex2.htm, on the Web. See also Talab, R. (1998, January-February). Copyright and network environments. *Tech Trends,* 9–11, for a discussion of university networking issues.

15. Crewes, K. (1993). *Copyright, fair use, and the challenge for universities.* Chicago: The University of Chicago Press.

16. Potter, T. (1997, October 27). University subscription increases. *Topeka Capitol Journal.*

17. Keleti, S. (1998, February 12). [online]. cni-copyright@cni.org.

18. Potter, T. (1997, October 14). Professor, university debate creative rights. *Topeka Capitol Journal.*

19. Patry, W. (1994, annual update). *Copyright law and practice* (3 vol.). Washington, DC: Bureau of National Affairs. See also Patry, W. (1997 Supplement). *Copyright law and practice,* for additional case law.

20. *Community for Creative Non-Violence v. Reid,* 490 U.S. 730, 740–41 (1989), *Id.* at 751, as cited in Working Group on Intellectual Property Rights. (1995, September).

21. Ibid.

22. Thompson, T. (1997, March-April). Three futures of the electronic university. *Educom Review,* 34–40. See also Nelson, T. (1998, January-February). Transcopyright: Dealing with the dilemma of digital copyright. *Educom Review,* 32–33.

23. Cangialosi, C. (1989). The electronic underground: Computer piracy and electronic bulletin boards. *Rutgers Computer & Technology Law Journal* 15, 265–301. See also Rose, L. (1995). *Netlaw: Your rights in the online world,* 84–93, for a discussion of case law and illegal use of BBSs.

24. Godwin, M. (1995). Letter of the law. *Internet World* 6(6), 84–86.

25. Title 17, Section 506(a).

26. Cangialosi, C. (1989).

27. Section 504(c).

28. See Porter (1995) and Simons (1995).

29. Association for Computing Machinery, 1995.

30. Ibid.

31. Washington, DC: The world capital of public domain images. http://www.PDImages.com/WEB2.html-ssi.

32. Wertz, S. (1997, October). Public domain and copyright: The final frontier. *Tech Trends*, 9–11.

33. Spaulding, S. (1997). *Internet for kids*. Huntington Beach, CA: Teacher Created Materials, 5.

34. Kirk, C. (1998). *Internet & Web answers! Certified technical support*. Berkeley, CA: Osborne McGraw-Hill, 324.

Chapter 10. Distance Learning

1. Online courses need to look good (1998, February 10). *Chronicle of Higher Education*. Cited in Edupage (February 13, 1998) [online] educom@educom. unc.edu.

2. *The electronic university: A guide to distance learning programs* (1994).

3. Hazel Associates cited in: Weiss, J. (1994). Distance learning: Bridging the gap with technology. *Syllabus* 8(2), 38–40.

4. Bruwelheide, J. (1994). Distance education: Copyright issues. In B. Willis (Ed.), *Distance education: Strategies and tools*. Englewood Cliffs, NJ: Educational Technology Publications, 235.

5. Conference on Fair Use, U.S. Patent and Trademark Office (USPTO) (December, 1996). *CONFU: The conference on fair use: An interim report to the Commissioner*. Washington, D.C.: USPTO. The reports of the many meetings over the four-year period of its existence, which ended in May, 1998, can be found on the USPTO Web site (http://www.uspto.gov/), as well as other Web sites of associations and libraries that have sections devoted to fair use.

6. Lutzker, A., and S. Lutzker (1998, November 18). [online]. Study on distance education and digital technologies at http://www.arl.org/info/recent.html.

7. Miller, J. (1987, October). Using videocasettes in school and libraries. *Tech Trends*, 37.

8. Talab, R., and G. Bailey (1991). Copyright, licensing and contractual issues in distance education course delivery. *Tech Trends*, 63–65. See also Talab, R. (1991). Access, confidentiality, and proprietary issues in distance education research. In *Proceedings of the First Conference on Teaching at a Distance*, Oklahoma State University, 216–220.

9. Sinofsky, E. (1994). *A copyright primer for educational and industrial media producers* (3rd ed.). Washington, DC: Association for Educational Communications and Technology.

10. Regents copyright committee, University of Georgia. [no date]. *Regents guide to understanding copyright and fair use*. http://www.peachnet.edu/admin/legal/copyright/copy.html.

11. Layton, T. [no date]. Cyberschool. (brochure). Eugene, OR: Computing and Information Services, Eugene Public Schools. http://cyberschool.lane.edu. There are other high schools offering this service, as well.

12. Muffoletto, R. (1997, March). Reflections on designing and producing an Internet-based course. *Tech Trends*, 50–53.

13. Parkhurst, T. (1997). *Drafting license agreements*. (3rd ed.). Frederick, MD: Aspen Law and Business.

14. Digital Image Committee. Conference on Fair Use (CONFU). (1996). *CONFU educational fair use guidelines for digital images*. The full text can be found

on the CONFU Web site at the U.S. Patent and Trademark Office (http://www.usp-togov) or other Web sites. These guidelines were not enacted.

15. Kirk, C. (1998). *Internet & Web answers! Certified tech support.* Berkeley, CA: Osborne McGraw-Hill. This book has many other useful tips on using and creating copyrighted materials for use on the Web and Internet.

16. Harper, G. (1998). [online]. General Counsel, University of Texas System. Rules of thumb for digitizing and using images for educational purposes. UT rules of thumb. http://www.utsystem.edu/OGC/IntellectualProperty/.

17. Kirk, C. (1998).

18. Harper, G. (1998). [online].

19. Bruwelheide, J. (1994), 241–242.

Chapter 11. Library Reproduction Rights

1. Lucker, J. K. (1983). Copyright and libraries: A librarian's perspective. In J. Baumgarten and A. Latman (Eds.), *Corporate copyright and information practices* (p. 152). New York: Practicing Law Institute.

2. United States Library of Congress, Copyright Office (1983, January). *Report of the Register of Copyrights: Library reproduction of copyrighted works* (17 U.S.C. 108) (p. viii). Washington, DC: U.S. Government Printing Office. (Hereinafter referred to as *Register's Report*).

3. American Library Association (1983, January). *Comments of the American Library Association on the Report of the Register of Copyrights to Congress: Library reproduction of copyrighted works* (17 U.S.C. 108).

4. Latman, A., and R. Gorman (1985). Copyright for the eighties (2nd ed., p. 522). Charlottesville, VA: Michie Bobbs-Merrill. This is indicated in the *Register's Report* (p. 195).

5. Two sources that indicate this belief are: (1) Martell, C. (1979, July). Copyright one year later: A symposium. *Journal of Academic Librarianship* 5(3), 124–131; (2) Byrd, G. (1981, April). Copyright compliance in health sciences libraries: A status report two years after the implementation of P.L. 94-553. *Bulletin of the Medical Library Association* 69(2), 224–230.

6. Lucker, J. K., 157.

7. *H. R. 94-1476* mentioned libraries or archives in "industrial, profitmaking, or proprietary institutions" (such as the research and development departments of chemical, pharmaceutical, automobile, and oil corporations, the library of a proprietary hospital, the collections owned by a law or medical partnership, etc.)

8. *American Geophysical Union v. Texaco, Inc.,* 37 F. 3d 881 (2d Cir.), rehearing denied, 1994 U.S. App. Lexis 36735 (2d Cir., Dec. 23, 1994), replaced with revised opinion, 60 F. 3d 913 (2d Cir.), cert. dismissed, 116 S. Ct. 592 (1995).

9. See also Patry, W. (1994, annual update). *Copyright law and practice.* (3 vols.). Washington, DC: Bureau of National Affairs, 735, for a listing of applicable case law on this topic; 1997 Cumulative Supplement, 107.

10. See also Gasaway, L., and S. Wiant (1994). *Libraries and copyright: A guide to copyright law in the 1990s.* Washington, DC: Special Libraries Association.

11. As amended by the Copyright Amendments Act of 1992, P.L. 102-307, 106 Stat. 264, 272.

12. Bruwelheide, J. (1995). *The copyright primer for librarians and educators.* (2d ed.). Chicago: American Library Association and the National Education Association, 27.

13. Reed, M. H. (1987). *The copyright primer for librarians and educators* (1st ed.). Chicago: American Library Association and the National Education Association, 10.

14. American Publishers and the Authors League of America (1978). *Photocopying by academic, public, and nonprofit research libraries.* New York: Author, 14.

15. 37 C.F.R. Section 201, 14, 1984.

16. CONTU, 5.

17. *Conference report, House report 94-1733* (Comm. of Conference) (1976, September 29, 94th Congress on S.22), 71–73.

18. American Library Association (1977). *Librarian's copyright kit.* Chicago: ALA.

19. Byrd, G., 226.

20. Martell, C. Copyright and reserve operations: An interpretation. *College and Research Libraries News* 1(1), 1–2.

21. Heller, J., and S. K. Wiant (1984). *Copyright handbook* (AALL Publications Series, p. 23). Littleton, CO: Fred B. Rothman.

22. *H. R. 94-1476,* 72–74.

23. *Register's Report,* 133.

24. *Register's Report,* 136.

25. *Register's Report,* 78.

26. Library of Congress, Copyright Office (1983, March). Warnings of copyright for use by libraries and archives. *Circular R 96* (Section 201.140). Washington, DC: U.S. Government Printing Office.

27. *Register's Report,* 108.

28. *Register's Report,* 110; American Library Association (1982). *Model policy concerning college and university photocopying for classroom, research, and library reserve use.* Chicago: ALA; and Heller, J., and S. K. Wiant (1984), 29; Gasaway, L. (ed.) (1997). *Growing pains: Adopting copyright for libraries, education, and society.* Littleton, CO: Fred B. Rothman.

29. *Register's Report,* 110.

30. This position was originally taken by the American Association of Publishers (AAP) in *Photocopying by academic, public, and nonprofit research libraries* (1978). New York: AAP.

31. Snyder cited a study in 1978 in which 15 out of 27 institutions did not restrict repeated use.

32. Stedman, J. (1978). American library reserves, photocopying and the copyright law. *College and Research Library News* 9, 263, 266; Nimmer, M. (1978). *Nimmer on copyright* (pp. 13–63); see Snyder's article for a thorough examination of reserve room practices in Snyder, F. Copyright and the library reserve room. *Law Library Journal* 73, 702–714. See previous notes for a discussion of other photocopying practice restrictions.

33. *H. R. 94-1476,* 68.

34. *Register's Report,* 72.

35. Ibid.

36. Snyder, F., 713.

37. Heller and Wiant. (1984), 28.

38. ALA.

39. *Register's Report,* 247.

40. Heller and Wiant. (1984), 25.

41. *H. R. 94-1476,* 72.

42. *Pasha Publications, Inc. v. Enmark Gas Corporation*, 22 U.S.P.Q. 2d 1076 (1992).

43. *American Geophysical Union v. Texaco, Inc.*, 37 F. 3d 881 (2d Cir.), rehearing denied, 1994 U.S. App. Lexis 36735 (2d Cir., December 23, 1994), replaced with revised opinion, 60 F. 3d 913 (2d Cir.), cert. dismissed, 116 S. Ct. 592 (1995).

44. *H. R. 94-1476,* 73–74.

45. Bielefield, A., and L. Cheeseman (1993). *Libraries & copyright law.* New York: Neal-Schuman.

46. Copyright Clearance Center, Inc., 21 Congress Street, Salem, MA 01970; (617) 744-3350. See also section on Copyright Clearance Center and *The Bowker annual of library and book trade information* (27th ed.) (1982). New York: R. R. Bowker, for a complete listing of the CCC's services and programs.

47. The *MLA Bulletin* published by the Medical Library Association regularly publishes information on this practice.

48. Information Infrastructure Task Force, Working Group on Intellectual Property Rights (1995, September). *Intellectual property and the National Information Infrastructure.* Washington, DC: U.S. Patent and Trademark Office.

49. Conference on Fair Use (CONFU) (1996, March 5). *Fair-use guidelines for electronic reserve systems.* The draft can be found at http://www.iupui.edu/it/copyinfo/fuguide.html.

50. For excellent information on the electronic reserves and the ARL group, go to the site http://www.columbia.edu/~rosedale. The Columbia Web site also has numerous links to other sites and links to demonstrations of electronic reserve systems. There is also a listserv dedicated to electronic reserves issues and questions. To subscribe, send a message to: listproc@arl.org. To send a message to the list, the address is arl-reserve@arl.org. Another very good site is the ERCOMS Web site. It has information and links on electronic reserves, copyright, electronic copyright management systems, authentification, and electronic payment systems. It is located at http://www.iielr.dmu.ac.uk/Projects/ERCOMS/links.html.

51. *Addison-Wesley Publishers Col., Inc. v. New York University* (settled out of court); *Basic Books, Inc. v. Kinko's Graphics Corporation*, 758 F. Supp. 1522 (S.D.N.Y. 1991); *American Geophysical Union v. Texaco, Inc.*, 37 F. 3d 881 (2d Cir.), rehearing denied, 1994 U.S. App. Lexis 36735 (2d Cir., Dec. 23, 1994), replaced with revised opinion, 60 F. 3d 913 (2d Cir.), cert. dismissed, 116 S. Ct. 592 (1995).; *Princeton University Press v. Michigan Document Services, Inc.*, 37 F. 3d 881 (2nd Cir. 1994); 1996 WL54741 (6th Cir. 1996) [Withdrawn]; 1996 FED App. 0357P 6th Cir. These cases involved coursepaks, supplemental reading materials, and articles copied for research purposes in a library of a for-profit company. These decisions as a whole have changed the definition of fair use for libraries.

52. For information on digital libraries, see the University of Texas Web site by Georgia Harper, General Counsel for the University of Texas, at http://www.utsystem.edu/OGC/IntellectualProperty/l-diglib.htm.

Chapter 12. Library Video Use

1. Stanek, D. J. (1986, March). Videotapes, computer programs, and the library. *Information Technology and Libraries,* 42–54.

2. Letter from Burton H. Hanft to Jerome K. Miller (1983, August 12). Cited in Stanek, D.J.

3. *H. R. 94-1476,* 159.

4. Carter, J. (1995, October). Finding your way through the copyright maze. *Cable in the Classroom,* 5–11. Also see Bruwelheide, J. (1995). *The copyright primer for librarians and educators* (2nd ed.). Chicago: American Library Association and National Education Association.

5. Sinofsky, E. (1984). *Off-air videotaping in education: Copyright issues, decisions, implications.* New York: R. R. Bowker. See also Sinofsky, E. (1994). *A copyright primer for educational and industrial media producers* (3rd ed.). Washington, DC: Association for Educational Communications and Technology.

6. American Library Association (1986, February). *American Libraries.*

7. Ibid.

8. Letter to the author (1985, August 16). MGM/UA.

9. See Stanek, D. J.; and Hutchins, M. R., and D. J. Stanek (1986, February). Library and classroom use of copyrighted videotapes and computer software. *American Libraries.* For further discussion of exhibition, see: *Columbia Pictures Industries, Inc. v. Aveco, Inc.,* 612 F. Supp. 315 (M.D. Pa. 1985), in which the Nickelodeon Video Showcase operated similarly to Maxwell's, except that (1) it rented viewing rooms and cassettes separately, (2) Nickelodeon customers operated the videocassette players on their own, and (3) Nickelodeon yielded physical possession of the videotapes to customers.

10. Bielefield, A., and L. Cheeseman (1993). *Libraries and copyright law.* New York: Neal-Schuman.

11. American Library Association (1986, February). *American Libraries,* 12–14.

Chapter 13. Library Software and Internet Use

1. Bell, T. (1983, November). Copying computer software for educational purposes: Is it allowed? *Personal Computing,* 236–242. See also Talab, R. (1984, Summer). Copyright, microcomputer software, and the library media center. *School Library Media Quarterly,* 285–288.

2. Pattie, K. (1985, October). Copyright abuse: No need for lawsuits. *Tech Trends,* 40.

3. Personal communication of Kenton Pattie to the author (1985, November).

4. International Council on Computers in Education (ICCE) (1983, July 1). *ICCE policy statement on network and multiple machine software.*

5. San Diego County Instructional Resource Center (1982, December). Request for examination of copyrighted coursework. *The Computing Teacher,* 41.

6. *1986 ICCE policy statement on software copyright.* See also Finkel, L. (1985, March). Software copyright interpretation. *The Computing Teacher,* 10.

7. OTA Intellectual Property Rights Questionnaire (1985, March). *The Computing Teacher*, 11. See also The new agenda on intellectual property rights, *Tech Trends*, May-June, 1986, 3–6, for a discussion of the results of this study.

8. Department of Commerce (1998, April). *The emerging digital economy.* Washington, DC: U.S. Government Printing Office.

9. *New York Times* (1997, December 20). Untitled article cited in *Edupage*, written by J. Gehl and S. Douglas [online], educom@educom.unc.edu.

10. Bruwelheide, J. (1995). *The copyright primer for librarians and educators* (2nd ed.). Chicago: American Library Association and the National Education Association.

11. Harper, G. (1997, March 3). Copyright in the library: The digital library. [online] http://www.utsystem.edu/OGC/IntellectualProperty/. See also Information Infrastructure Task Force, Working Group on Intellectual Property Rights. (1995, September). *Intellectual property and the National Information Infrastructure.* Washington, DC: U.S. Patent and Trademark Office, 92.

12. Working Group on Intellectual Property Rights (1995, September).

13. *Screen Gems-Columbia Music, Inc. v. Mack-fi Records,* F. Supp. at 791, 792 (as cited by *Universal City Studios,* 480 F. Supp. at 460). A discussion of contributory infringement is in Latman and Gorman's *Copyright in the eighties,* 532–533.

14. Neumeyer, V. (1989). Software copyright law: The enforceability sham. *Loyola Law Review* 35(2), 485–507.

15. Kennard, W. (1998, January-February). Obtaining and litigating software patents. *IP Litigator,* 1–12.

16. Copyright Act. Section 107 to 118.

17. Quint (1989).

18. *H. R. 5316,* Title 8.

19. American Library Association (1991). Washington, DC: ALA. See Henderson (1990). See also Flagg (1991).

20. Sinofsky, E. (1995, November-December). The water's not safe yet! *Tech Trends,* 12–14.

21. Templeton, B. [no date, online]. Ten big myths about copyright explained. http://www.clarinet.com/brad/copymyths.html.

Chapter 14. Permissions

1. *H. R. 94-1476,* p. 67.

2. Section 504(c).

3. Carnahan, W. (1972). Copyright in our realm of learning. *The College Counsel* 71(1), 445.

4. J. Douglas has works on this subject: (1) Copyright as it affects instructional development. (1974, December). *Audiovisual Instruction,* 37–38; and (2) Seeking copyright clearances for an audiovisual center (1980). In J. Lawrence and B. Timberg (eds.), *Fair use and free inquiry; copyright law and the new media* (pp. 121–126). Norwood, NJ: Ablex. See also Mucklow, E. (1977, March). Steps for resolving the duplication dilemma. *Community and Junior College Journal,* 14–17.

5. American Association of Publishers/Authors League (1978). *A guide to permissions.* New York: American Association of Publishers/Authors League.
6. *H. R. 94-1476*, 14.
7. Gross, L., and W. Millington (1978, February). Coping with the new copyright law. *Change Magazine*, 24–26.
8. Johnson, B. (1993). *How to acquire legal copies of video programs: Resource information.* San Diego, CA: Video Resource Enterprises.

Chapter 15. Policy Development

1. Vlcek, C. (1993, March). Copyright policy development. *Tech Trends*, 13–14.
2. Vlcek, C. (1992). *Copyright policy development and adoptable copyright policy.* Friday Harbor, WA: Copyright Information Services.
3. Vlcek, C. (1993, March).
4. Sellers, S. (1995). *News release: SPA to target Internet and international piracy in 1995.*
5. Section 107.
6. Section 108.
7. Vlcek, C. (1993, March).
8. Section 108.
9. Bruwelheide, J. (1997). *Copyright policy outline.* Unpublished paper presented at the Assoc. for Educational Communications & Technology Conference, Albuquerque, NM.

Chapter 16. Alternatives and Scenarios for Media Center Directors

1. Wertz, S., and M. Chase (1994, April-May). *Tech Trends*, 7–8.
2. Wertz, S. (1984). *Knowledge of the 1976 general revision of the copyright law P.L. 94-553 by college and university media center directors in the United States.* University of South Carolina.
3. Chase, M. (1993). Unpublished directed study. University of Pittsburgh, Pittsburgh, Pennsylvania.
4. Kemp, D. (1990). Limitations upon the software producer's rights: *Vault Corp. v. Quaid Software Ltd. Rutgers Computer & Technology Law Journal* 16(10), 85–127.
5. United States Congress, P.L. 101-650. Computer Software Rental Amendments Act of 1990, December 1, 1990.
6. Cangialosi, C. (1989). The electronic underground: Computer piracy and electronic bulletin boards. *Rutgers Computer & Technology Law Journal* 15, 265–301.
7. Section 506, Title 17(a).
8. Godwin, M. (1995, June). Letter of the law. *Internet World* 6(6), 84–86.
9. United States Congress, P.L. 101-553. The Copyright Remedy Clarification Act, November 15, 1990.

Resource Guides

Electronic Resources on Copyright

World Wide Web and Internet

Acceptable Use Policy Sites
  ftp://nis.nsf.net/acceptable.use.policies/
  http://chico.rice.edu/armadillo

American Society of Composers, Authors, and Publishers (ASCAP)
  http://www.ascap.com/
  Music resources.

Association of Research Libraries
  http://www.arl.org
  Newsletter — http://www.arl.org/transform/esp/index.html

Benedict O'Mahoney's The Copyright Website!
  http://www.benedict.com/
  Copyright Fundamentals — http://www.benedict.com/fund.htm#Notice
  Homepage — http://www.benedict.com/homepage.htm#home
  Public Domain Material — http://www.benedict.com/public.htm#public

Black, J. "Tell It To the Judge"
  http://www.news.com/Quiz/Entry
  This site has a short test that is very useful for teaching students and educators about copyright and the Web.

Broadcast Music Inc. (BMI)
  http://www.bmi.com/
  Music resources.

Cable in the Classroom
  http://www.ciconline.com
  School use of cable programming. Excellent site with taping information.

Coalition for Networked Information
  http://www.cni.org
  This site has a compilation of information policies and pertinent facts.

Communications/Information Law Web Server
http://www.commlaw.com/

Conference on Fair Use of New Technological Works (CONFU) Sites
http://oregon.uoregon.edu/~csundt/CONFUweb.htm
Christine Sundt compiled this CONFU Documents Page that has information on guidelines, the comments-gathering process, the endorsement process, recommendations, and decisions.

Consortium for Educational Technology in University Systems (CETUS): California State University/State University of NY/City University of NY Educational Technology Site
http://www.cetus.org

and

CETUS Discussion Series:
Fair Use of Copyrighted Works
The Academic Library in the Information Age
Information Resources and Library Services for Distance Learners
Ownership of Intellectual Property
http://www.cetus.org/fairindex.html
Contains the pamphlet, "Fair Use of Copyrighted Works: A Crucial Element in Educating America," by CETUS; as well as a few links on copyright, the Copyright Clearance Center, CCC online copyright information and registration. A fair use listserv is maintained at fairuse-talk@cal-state.edu with related information available on the Web site. To sign on to the listserv send an e-mail message with the word "subscribe" as the body of the message.

Copyright Clearance Center (CCC)
http://www.copyright.com/
A not-for-profit organization created at the suggestion of Congress to help organizations comply with U.S. copyright law. Short explanation of the Center's services, charges, and a free demo.

Copyright for Music Librarians (Music Library Association)
http://www.music.indiana.edu/tech_s/mla/legcom/copyhome.htm

Copyright for Researchers and Students
http://www.umi.com/hp/Support/DServices/copyright

Copyright, Intellectual Property Rights, and Licensing Issues
http://sunsite.berkeley.edu/Copyright/index.html

Copyright Issues Related to Distance Learning and Multimedia Development
http://www.lib.siu.edu/regional/copyright.html

Copyright Legislation
http://www.cic.org/

Copyright Management Center: Indiana Univ./Purdue Univ. at Indianapolis
http://www.iupui.edu/it/copyinfo/

Copyright Office: Washington State University
http://publications.urel.wsu.edu/Copyright/Copyright.html

Copyright Permissions Web Site: Professional Center Library for Law and Management at Wake Forest University
> http://www.law.wfu.edu/library/copyright
> This contains links to publishing and journal copyright permission pages. It was designed to make it easier for law faculty to contact copyright holders to obtain permission to use copyrighted materials in scholarly writing and teaching. Nonlegal publishers are included.

Copyright Policy and Universities
> Stanford University
> http://www.portfolio.stanford.edu/101242
> The Association of University Technology Managers
> http://autm.rice.edu/autm/index.html
> Association for Computing Machinery
> http://www.acm.org.pubs/copyright_policy/#Reserves

Copyright Resources Online
> http://www.library.yale.edu:80/~okerson/copyproj.html
> Excellent sources! Much information on a variety of topics for colleges and universities, including model policies of various sorts.

Cornell Legal Information Institute
> http://www.law.cornell.edu/topics/copyright.html#menu

Crews, Kenneth D. "Copyright and Distance Education: Lawful Uses of Protected Works"
> http://www.ind.net/IPSE/fdhandbook/copyrt.html

Crews, Kenneth D. "Fair Use: Overview and Meaning for Higher Education"
> http://www.iupui.edu/it/copyinfo/highered.html

Cyberlaw Periodical
> http://www.cyberlaw.com/

Cyberspace Law Center with Search Engine
> http://www.cybersquirrel.com/clc/
> or
> http://www.cybersquirrel.com/clc/clcindex.html

Cyberspace Law Institute
> http://www.cli.org/

Cyberspace Laws: Providing Links and Information About Internet Laws Free of Charge
> http://www.cyberspacelaws.com/

David Loundy's E-LAW Web Page
> http://www.leepfrog.com/E-Law/

Distance Learning Initiative Home Page
> http://www.uncg.edu/cex/dli

Dolak, Fritz. "A Selective List of Copyright Do's and Don't's for Distance Education"
> http://www.bsu.edu/library/services/dist/copyright.html

Educational Multimedia Fair Use Guidelines
> http://www.libraries.psu.edu/avs/fairuse/default.html

Electronic Frontier Foundation (EFF)
> http://www.eff.org
> or
> gopher.eff.org
> Internet address is eff@eff.org.
> The Electronic Frontier Foundation (EFF) is an advocacy group promoting online civil rights and public interest legislation. It publishes an electronic newsletter on online legal developments called *EFFector*. It offers archives of legal and regulatory materials.

Electronic Reserves Clearinghouse
> http://www.cc.columbia.edu:80/~rosedale/

Europa
> http://europa.eu.int/index.htm
> Information, news, conferences, special interest groups, and the European Commission are to be found here.

Fair Use Guidelines for Educational Multimedia
> http://www.indiana.edu/~ccumc/
> This is the entire document of the "Fair Use Guidelines for Educational Multimedia."

Fair Use in the Electronic Age: Serving the Public Interest
> http://arl.cni.org/scomm/copyright/uses.html

FindLaw Internet Legal Resources
> http://www.findlaw.com/01topics/23intellectprop/index.html
> Supreme Court Decisions back to 1937.

> and

> http://www.findlaw.com/casecode/supreme.html
> Findlaw's database of Supreme Court decisions can be searched for the topic of copyright.

The FPLC Intellectual Property Mall Homepage
> http://www.ipmall.fplc.edu/pointbox/pointbox.htm

Guidelines on Photocopying under Interlibrary Loan Arrangements National Commission on New Technological Uses of Copyright Works (CONTU)
> http://www.cni.org/docs.infopols/www/CONTU.html

Harper, Georgia. "Fair Use of Copyrighted Works"
> http://www.utsystem.edu/OGC/IntellectualProperty/copypol2.htm

The Harry Fox Agency, Inc. (NMPA/Harry Fox Agency)
> http://www.nmpa.org/hfa.html
> The Agency represents more than 19,000 American music publishers and licenses a large percentage of music in the U.S. through various licensing agreements.

HyperLaw, Inc.
> http://www.hyperlaw.com/

Image Search Tools Ramapo Catskill Internet Guides
> http://www.rcls.org/psearch.htm

Information Law Alert
  http://infolawalert.com/

Institute for Learning Technologies (ILT) Web Copyright Resources for Education Online: The ILT Guide to Copyright
  http://www.ilt.columbia.edu/projects/copyright/index.html
  General information, fair use, copyright and the library, multimedia, enforcement, organizations, print bibliographies, online information servers, other resources, and links to other sites.

Intellectual Property: An Annotated Bibliography with Links to Other Sources
  http://ils.unc.edu/harrj/cpyrtbib.htm
  Law and other documents (Berne Convention, some Copyright Office circulars, a few cases), university and university library model policies, recent Supreme Court copyright decisions, primers, web articles, organizations, web bibliographies of copyright resources, *Copyright for computer authors* (Terry Carroll), and links to other sites.

Intellectual Property Center
  http://www.ipcenter.com/

Intellectual Property Magazine
  http://www.ipmag.com/
  Law and policy for high technology.

Intellectual Property "Primer"
  Learning the Ropes: Intellectual Property at UCLA
  http:www.research.ucla.edu/guide/ROPEsa.htm

International Federation of Library Associations (IFLA) and Institutions: Information Policy — Copyright and Intellectual Property
  http://www.nlc-bnc.ca/ifla/ll/cpyright.htm
  Excellent list of sites, alphabetized by author, of various papers, periodicals, Web sites, articles, monographs, organizations, and policies, of interest to university personnel, academic librarians, and scholars.

Internet Law Simplified
  http://home.earthlink.net/~ivanlove/book.html
  Ivan Love, attorney, has written "The Use of Protected Material in Multimedia Projects" in the section about Internet and electronic rights issues.

Journal of Library Services for Distance Education
  http://www.westga.edu/library/jlsde/

Juris Diction Home Page
  http://www.JurisDiction.com/indexip.htm

Kohn on Music Licensing
  http://www.kohnmusic.com
  This is an excellent site for all performance music needs. It has links to music licensing questions, copyright, music rights clearance organizations, music performing rights societies, songwriter organizations, music publishers organizations, and so forth. It also has a free question-and-answer section and an online update.

Kuester Law Technology Law Resource
  http://www.kuesterlaw.com/

Law Journal Extra Site
  http://www.ljx.com/copyright/index.html
  This site has law journals, some articles of which deal with copyright issues.

Law Journal Seminars Press
  http://www.lawcatalog.com/

Law Journal Web Site
  http://gort.ucsd.edu/newjour
  This includes the California Education Law Report, Cardozo Electronic Law Journal, Computer Law Report, Internet Law Journal, and others.

Lawmarks
  http://www.cclabs.missouri.edu/

Liblicense: Licensing Digital Information
  http://www.library.yale.edu/~llicense/index.shtml

Libraries and the National Information Infrastructure
  http://iitcat.nist.gov:94/doc/Library.html

Mountain View College
  http://www.mvc.dcccd.edu/
  Click on Instructional Departments; Arts and Sciences; English; Copyright Information.

Multimedia Law Sites
  http://www.batnet.com/oikoumene/
  This includes developments in electronic commerce, copyrights, and patent law in the U.S., Europe, and Japan.

  Legal Site Search Engines
    http://www.batnet.com/oikoumene/mmlinks.html#engines
    This site includes legal site search engines.

  Internet Legal Forms
    http://www.batnet.com/oikoumene/b4access.html
    This site has Internet legal forms for Internet business and 22 sample print and electronic contracts.

Music Educators National Conference (MENC)
  http://www.menc.org
  It has a copyright booklet and other guides and information for music teachers.

Music Librarians Association: Legislation Committee of Music Librarians.
  http://www.musiclibraryassoc.org/Copyright/copyhome.htm
  Excellent bibliography of print and nonprint materials, current issues in copyright and copyright guidelines.

National Information Infrastructure Web Site
  http://www.nii.doc.gov
  or
  http://www.uspto.gov/text/pto/nii/ipwg.html

National Research Council
    http://www.nap.edu/bookstore/isbn/0309056357.html
    Report entitled "Bits of Power: Issues in Global Access to Scientific Data".
    This is a pre-publication copy of a report on the European Union's Legal
    Protection of Databases Directive and other database protection proposals.

National Writers Union Home Page
    http://www.nwu.org/nwu/

Net Bill
    http://thomas.loc.gov/

Net Rights, Ltd.
    http://www.netrights.com
    Net Rights is a system that fosters relationships between copyright owners
    and developers. At the same time it actualizes the concept of a virtual
    copyright clearinghouse by way of linked Web pages of private learn-
    ing organizations, maintaining their own databases.

New York Law Journal
    http://www.ljx.com/nylj/

Nimmer on Copyright
    http://www.ipmag.com/animmer.html

Oppendahl, Carl, and Marina Larson. "May I Freely Copy, Print, and E-mail
    Things I Find on the Web?"
    http://www.patents.com/weblaw.sht#cpe

Public Access to Government Materials
    http://www.freenet.seri.fsu.edu/

Richmond Journal of Law & Technology
    http://www.urich.edu/~jolt/current.html

Software Copyright Case Summaries
    http://www.sgpdlaw.com/software_copyright/

Software Protection
    http://www.softwareprotection.com/

Software Publishers Association
    http://www.spa.org/project/edu_copyright/cptop.htm
    or
    http://www.spa.org
    Information on copyright for school administrators, teachers, software pol-
    icy statements, sample code of ethics, auditing and inventory software.
    It is a great site for K–12.

Stanford University Library Copyright and Fair Use Site
    http://fairuse.stanford.edu
    It has a search engine, statutes, judicial opinions, regulations, treaties and
    conventions, current legislation, cases and issues (including multime-
    dia), the NII, resources including library copyright guidelines, articles,
    Web sites and mailing lists, and an overview of copyright law. Internet
    resources include college university copyright policies, computers and

the law, copyright and ethical use, copyright and the World Wide Web, and so forth. Includes a good list of organizational web sites. Select Library Copyright Guidelines for several policy pointers.

Student Permissions for Web Publishing
http://www.siec.k12.in.us/~west/online/copy2.htm
This has good information on how to obtain student permission and what information should and should not be placed on the Web.

Task Force for Responsibility and Freedom on the Internet: Church of Scientology — "Netsurfer's Simple Guide to Copyright"
http://www.theta.com/trfn/

Templeton, B. "Ten Big Myths About Copyright Explained"
http://www.templetons.com/brad/copymyths.html
This site has explanations for the most common copyright myths or misconceptions.

Terry Carroll Copyright FAQ
http://www.aimnet.com/~carroll/copyright/faqhome.html

Thomas Legislation Site
http://thomas.loc.gov/
This site has a complete listing of all new and pending copyright legislation.

United States Constitution in html
http://www.law.cornell.edu/constitution/constitution.article.html#section8

United States Copyright Office of the Library of Congress
http://lcweb.loc.gov/
It has research tools (catalogs, databases, and Internet resources), links to the Copyright Office, the Global Legal Information Network (a database of national laws from 35 contributing countries and more are being added), and Civilization (periodical).

U.S. Copyright Office Home Page
http://lcweb.loc.gov/copyright/
Speeches and testimony, press releases, information, publications, registrations, form letters, fax on demand (copyright information via fax), pending legislation, Internet resources related to copyright, treaties, and so forth.

U.S. Copyright Office FAQ Site
http://lcweb.loc.gov/copyright/faq.html
This site has questions and answers to 60 commonly asked copyright questions.

United States House of Representatives Internet Law Library: Intellectual Property
http://law.house.gov/105.htm
Information on copyrights, patents, trademarks, intellectual property law collections by various copyright attorneys, some international copyright laws, various legal articles, the NII "Green Paper," "White Paper," and other general legal resources.

U.S. House of Representatives Internet Law Library: Treaties and International Law

http://law.house.gov/89.htm
Great source of treaties and international conventions.

United States House of Representatives Report on the Activities
http://thomas.loc.gov/
This gives the Nonlegislative Report adopted on September 27, 1996, by the
Subcommittee on Courts and Intellectual Property, Committee of the
Judiciary, U.S. House of Representatives.

United States Patent and Trademark Office
http://www.uspto.gov/web/ipnii
Conference on Fair Use: A Report to the Commissioner — U.S. Patent and
Trademark Office Site
http://www.uspto.gov/web/offices/dcom/olia/confu/
This includes the complete "Phase One CONFU Report to the Commissioner."

United States Patent, Trademark, & Copyright Information, Franklin Pierce Law
Center
http://www.fplc.edu/tfield/order.htm
Basic information for artists, inventors, programmers & small business owners, related web sources, information for the legal profession.

United States Public Policy Office of the Association for Computing Machinery
(ACM)
http://www.acm.org/usacm/
or
http://www.acm.org/pubs/copyright_policy.html
They have developed a copyright policy and copyright guidelines, including
statements on the use of "hyperlinks."

University of Georgia Regents Guide to Understanding Copyright and Educational Fair Use
http://www.peachnet.edu/admin/legal/copyright/copy.html
Excellent guide to copyright and fair use with examples, question-and-answer
sections, and scenarios by media type.

University of Iowa Libraries: Gateway to the Internet
http://www.arcade.uiowa.edu/proj/webbuilder/copyright.html

Visual Resources
http://oregon.uoregon.edu/~csundt/vrcfu.htm
Special issue of Visual Resources titled "Copyright and Fair Use: The Great
Image Debate," February 4, 1997.

Visual Resources Association
http://www.oberlin.edu/~art/vra/vra.html
This is an excellent resource for the visual arts, with information on copyright and other topics.

Web Site Registration
http://www.patents.com/oandl.sht#copyrights>
or
http://www.patents.com/weblaw.sht#lo>

World Intellectual Property Organization (WIPO) Site
http://www.wipo.org/
This gives in-depth information about WIPO and the WIPO Copyright Treaty.

Magazine — http://www.loc.gov/copyright/wipo.html

Treaty, Commentary, and Patent and Trademark Office Federal Register
Notices — http://www.public-domain.org/

Treaty (Science Magazine Policy Forum) — http://www.sciencemag.org/fea
ture/data/forum.shl
April 11, 1997, *Science Magazine* policy forum on the WIPO treaty,
drafted by Jukka Liedes, Chairman of the Expert Committee that drafted
the treaty.

CD-ROM Resources

BNA Books, Inc. (1998). *Patent, trademark, and copyright laws and regulations on
CD.* Washington, D.C.: BNA Books, Inc., a division of the Bureau of National
Affairs, Inc.

Goldstein, P. (1997–   ). *Goldstein on Copyright.* New York: Aspen Law and Business. (Cumulative updates.)

Online Discussion Group

CNI Copyright Discussion Group
Sponsored by the Coalition for Networked Information. To join, send an e-
mail to listproc@cni.org and type: subscribe CNI-Copyright [your name].

CNI Copyright Archive
gopher://gopher.cni.org/ll/cniwg/forums/cni-copyright

CNI Frequently Asked Questions on Copyright and Links to Other Sites
gopher://gopher.cni.org/ll/cniwg/forums/cni-copyright/other
Association of Research Libraries Copyright Information, Terry Carroll's FAQs,
various articles, law-related resources on the Internet and elsewhere, NII
comments and testimony, Working Group on Intellectual Property, the
National Information Infrastructure, as well as links to other sites.

Online Periodicals

American Library Association Washington Office (Alawon)
Contact webmaster@alawash.org
Alawon is a periodic listserv. To contact: listproc@ala.org.
To subscribe: Ala-wo [firstname lastname]
It is free and comes out on a nonscheduled basis.

Edupage
Internet address is http://www.educause.edu/.
Edupage is a bi-weekly listserv maintained by EDUCAUSE (from merger of
CAUSE and Educom). This listserv covers technology and copyright
news in education, business and industry. To subscribe to Edupage,

send mail to edupage-subscribe@educause.unc.edu with the message: subscribe edupage [your name]. It is free and comes out twice monthly.

General Resources

See also the references for each chapter, which provide numerous other sources.

Print Resources

American Library Association (1995, February 8). *Working document: Fair use in the electronic age: Serving the public interest.* ALA Council Document 20.10. Philadelphia, PA: ALA.

Association of American Publishers, et al. (1997, September.) *Questions and answers on copyright for the campus community; includes software and Internet issues.* Oberlin, Ohio: National Association of College Stores.

Becker, G. (1992). *Copyright: A guide to information and resources.* Available from Gary Becker, P.O. Box 951870, Lake Mary, FL 32795-1870; phone (407) 333-2037.

Bielefield, A., and L. Cheeseman (1993). *Libraries and copyright law.* New York: Neal-Schuman.

Botterbusch, H. (1996). *Copyright in the age of new technology.* Bloomington, IN: Phi Delta Kappa Educational Foundation. (Fastback #405).

Brinson, J., and M. Radcliffe. (1994). *Multimedia law handbook: A practical guide for developers and publishers.* Menlo Park, CA: Ladera.

Bruwelheide, J. (1997). Copyright and distance education: Issues for librarians and practitioners. In *Library acquisitions: Practice and theory.* Elsevier.

_____ (1997). Copyright myths and misperceptions. In L. Gasaway (ed.), *Growing pains: Adopting copyright for libraries, education, and society.* Littleton, CO: Fred B. Rothman.

_____ (1997). Copyright: Opportunities and restrictions for the teleinstructor. In T. E. Cyrs (Ed.), *New directions for teaching and learning: Teaching at a distance.* San Francisco: Jossey-Bass.

_____ (1995–1996). Copyright issues for the electronic age. In *Educational media and technology yearbook.* Littleton, CO: Libraries Unlimited.

_____ (1995). *The copyright primer* (2nd ed.). Chicago: American Library Association. Washington, DC: National Education Association.

_____ (1994). Distance education: Copyright issues. In *Distance education: A practical approach.* Englewood Cliffs: Educational Technology Publications.

Cavazos, E. A., and M. Gavino (1994). *Cyberspace and the law: Your rights and duties in the online world.* Cambridge: MIT Press.

Chee, L. (1977). How to research copyright law. *Law Library Journal* 70:171–183.

Copyright Law of the United States of America (Circular 92).

Crews, K. D. (1997, November–December). Fair use and higher education: Are guidelines the answer? *ACADEME*, 38–40.

_____ (1996). *Copyright law and graduate research: New media, new rights, and your new dissertation.* Ann Arbor: University of Michigan.

_____ (1993). *Copyright, fair use, and the challenge for universities: Promoting the progress of higher education.* Chicago: University of Chicago Press.

Delta, F., and J. Matsuura (1998). *Law of the Internet.* Frederick, MD: Aspen Law & Business.

DuBoff, L. (1995). *The law (in plain English) for writers.* (2nd. ed.) New York: John Wiley and Sons.

Dukelow, R. (1992). *The library copyright guide.* Washington, DC: Association for Educational Communications and Technology.

Fishman, S. (1996). *The copyright handbook: How to protect and use written works.* Berkeley, CA: Nolo.

Gasaway, L. N., and S. K. Wiant (1994). *Libraries and copyright: A guide to copyright law in the 1990's.* Washington: Special Libraries Association.

Johnson, B. (1993). *How to acquire legal copies of video programs.* San Diego, CA: Video Resources Enterprise.

Lawrence, J. S., and B. Timberg (1980). *Fair use and free inquiry: Copyright law and the new media.* Norwood, NJ: Ablex.

Lee, L., and J. Davidson (1997). *Intellectual property for the Internet.* Somerset, NJ: Wiley.

Lee, R. (1997). *A copyright guide for authors.* Stamford, CT: Kent.

Lerner, R., and J. Bresler (1992 update). *Art law: The guide for collectors, investors, dealers, and artists.* New York: Practicing Law Institute.

Lutzker, A. (1997). *Copyrights and trademarks for media professionals.* Newton, MA: Butterworth-Heinemann.

Mann, C. (1994). *Copyright for school libraries.* Worthington, OH: Linworth Publishing.

McDonald, S. (1997, October 31). The laws of cyberspace: What colleges need to know. *The Chronicle of Higher Education,* A68.

Miller, J. (1987). *Video copyright permissions: A guide to securing permisssion to retain, perform, and transmit television programs videotaped off the air.* Friday Harbor, WA: Copyright Information Services.

_____ (1987). *Using copyrighted videocassettes in classrooms, libraries, and training centers.* Friday Harbor, WA: Copyright Information Services.

Perritt, H., Jr. (1996). *Law and the information superhighway: Privacy, access, intellectual property, commerce and liability.* Somerset, NJ: Wiley.

Rose, L. (1995). *Netlaw: Your rights in the online world.* Berkeley: Osborne McGraw-Hill.

Sinofsky, E. (1994). *A copyright primer for educational and industrial media producers.* (3rd. ed.) Washington, DC: Association for Educational Communications and Technology.

_____ (1984). *Off-air taping in education: Copyright issues, decisions, implications.* New York: R. R. Bowker.

Sivin, J., and E. Bialo (1992, May). *Ethical use of information technologies in education: Important issues for America's schools.* Washington, DC: U.S. Department of Justice.

Steinbach, S. E., and A. V. Lupo (1998, Feb. 2). The hidden legal traps in distance-learning programs. *The Chronicle of Higher Education,* A52.

Strong, W. (1992). *The copyright book.* Cambridge, MA: MIT Press.

Talab, R. (1998, January/February). Copyright in network environments. *Tech Trends,* 9–11.

_____ (1997, January/February). An educational use checklist for copyright and multimedia. *Tech Trends,* 9–11.

_____ (1995). Contributor/reviewer. In *Technology and teaching.* Office of Technology Assessment. Washington, D.C.: U.S. Government Printing Office.

_____ (1995). In *What's fair? A report on the Proceedings of the National Conference on Educational Fair Access and the New Media* (pp. 79, 88). Bloomington, IN: Agency for Instructional Technology.

_____ (1995, January/February). Copyright and multimedia; Part Two: Higher education. *Tech Trends*, 11–13.

_____ (1994, November). Copyright and multimedia; Part One: K–12. *Tech Trends*, 13–15.

_____ (1994, June). Delegate and Working Committee Member (by invitation). *Report of the Copyright and Fair Access Conference.* Washington, DC: Consortium of College and University Media Centers and the Agency for Instructional Television.

_____ (1992). Digital information. In *Finding a balance: Computer software, intellectual property, and the challenge of technological change.* Office of Technology Assessment, U.S. Congress. Washington, DC: U.S. Government Printing Office.

_____ (1992). Copyright appendix. In B. Heinich, M. Russell, and B. Molenda (eds.), *Instructional media and the new technologies of instruction.* New York: Macmillan.

_____ (1992). General trends in new technology usage: Stages of copyright development on a national level. In D. Graves (ed.), *Issues in library resource sharing,* Vol. III (pp. 76–81). Connecticut: Meckler.

_____ (1992). Copyright scenarios for media center directors ... help with handling tough questions. *Tech Trends* 37(4): 10–13.

_____ (1992). Copyright and other legal considerations in patron software use. *Library Trends* 16(2): 264–274.

_____ (1991). Access, confidentiality and proprietary issues in distance education research. In *Proceedings of the First Conference on Teaching at a Distance* (pp. 216–220). Stillwater: Oklahoma State University.

_____ (1989). *Copyright and educational media: A guide to fair use and permissions procedures.* Washington, DC: Association for Educational Communications and Technology.

_____ (1987, April). Backups: A necessary — but controversial — aspect of software collections. *Small Computers in Libraries,* 34–37.

_____ (1986). *Commonsense copyright: A guide to the new technologies.* Jefferson, NC: McFarland.

_____ (1985, November). Copyright and database downloading. *School Library Journal,* 124–127.

_____ (1985, November). Copyright and database downloading. *Library Journal,* 144–147. (Special Microcomputing Section).

_____ (1982, January). Microcomputers and copyright in education. *Phi Delta Kappan,* 316–317.

_____ (1980, May). Commonsense photocopying. *Phi Delta Kappan,* 619–620.

_____, and G. Bailey (1991, February). Copyright, licensing, and contractual issues in distance education course delivery. *Tech Trends* 36: 16–17.

_____, Bender, I., M. H. Reed, and J. K. Miller (1989). Video in schools and libraries: A look at the issues. *Tech Trends.*

Vlcek, C. W. (1992). *Adoptable copyright policy: Copyright policy and manuals designed for adoption by schools, colleges, & universities.* Association for Educational Communications and Technology, 1025 Vermont Avenue, Suite 820, Washington, DC 20005.

_____ (1986). *Copyright policy development: A resource book for educators.* Copyright Information Services, P. O. Box 1460-D, Friday Harbor, WA 98250.

Library of Congress Information and Internet Address

It is anticipated that regulations may change in the future, with the enormous progress being made by online retrieval mechanisms, consortia, and micrographics. Aside from the information that can be obtained from library periodicals, the Copyright Office also has a free periodic mailing list that can be requested on subjects of interest by phoning (202) 707-3000 or by writing to Information and Publications Section, LM-455, Copyright Office, Library of Congress, Washington DC 20559. The Copyright Office also answers questions by phone. Trained information specialists will answer copyright questions on a phone-in basis. Depending on the request, such as music, video, print materials, they will often send appropriate documents and information free of charge. The Forms Hotline number is (202) 707-9100. This number is available 24 hours a day to request application forms for registration or information circulars. If unsure of the form or circular number, call the Public Information Office number. A Copyright Forms Hotline is also available for registration: (202) 287-9100.

Free from the U.S. Copyright Office are: FL102 — Fair Use; Circular 1 *Copyright Basics*; Circular 2 *Publications on Copyright;* Circular 2b *Bibliographies, Selected*; Circular 4 Copyright Fees; Circular 21 *Reproduction of Copyrighted Works by Educators and Librarians*; and the *Copyright Act of 1976.* Other forms are available, as well.

The Copyright Office cannot: 1) compare works for similarities, 2) advise on possible infringement or prosecution of violations, 3) provide contract terms, 4) enforce contracts or recover manuscripts, 5) recommend publishers, agents, etc., 6) aid in the publication of a work, or 7) "grant permission to use a copyrighted work" (Circular 1b).

The Copyright Office also has Internet addresses for information. Frequently requested Copyright Office circulars, announcements, and the most recent proposed final regulations are available through **lc marvel**. How to connect: Telnet to marvel.loc.gov and login as "marvel" to access the system. Select the copyright menu. It is available 24 hours a day, and there is no charge. To receive Copyright Office files: COHM, which contains all original and renewal registrations except serials; COHD, which contains documents; and COHS, which contains serials. How to connect: locis.loc.gov, or go to the numeric address 140.147.254.3, or gain access through **lc marvel** Telnet to marvel.loc.gov or go to the numeric address 140.147.215 and login as "marvel" to access the system. Then select the Copyright menu.

See http://lcweb.loc.gov/ for the Library of Congress Web site. It has research tools (catalogs, databases, and Internet resources) and links to the Copyright Office.

See the Web site http://thomas.loc.gov for new and pending legislation. Also, the Office of the Federal Registry, Washington, DC, phone (202) 523-5230, provides copies of new legislation.

Video, Cable, and Satellite Resources

In making and acquiring legal copies of video and off-air programs, there are some very good resources that offer help for permissions, sample educational program inquiry forms, policies, services, and directories. The materials provided below are provided as a selected guide to copyright for the layman. The list is not meant to be complete. For other sources, please consult the chapter references.

AIME (Association for Information Media and Equipment). The association provides a Copyright Hotline to members to learn about usage and to report violation (1-800-444-4203). Membership is $150 a year for schools, universities, and libraries and is based on revenues for companies. With membership comes a 21-minute video, "Copyright Law: What Every School, College, and Public Library Should Know," information packet, and a year's subscription to the AIME Newsletter. The packet is $19.95; the video is $64.95 (plus $5 for shipping and handling); and a one-year subscription to the newsletter is $20. Their address is P. O. Box 1173, Clarkdale, Mississippi, phone (662) 624-9355, fax (662) 624-9366. The AIME Copyright Hotline number is 1-800-444-4203. Go to http://www.aime.org to see their Web site.

All About Copyright. Twelve-page guide to off-air taping produced in cooperation with KIDSNET. Copies may be downloaded from the Discovery Web site.

Association of American Publishers, and Software Publishers Association. (1997). *A shared set of values: Copyright and intellectual property in the academic community.* (12-minute video). New York: AAP; Washington, DC: SPA.

Cable in the Classroom. Monthly, except summer. Excellent listing of programs, news, and articles. Its Web site also has a section on which users may input a program, including closed caption, day of the week, how long you wish to retain the program, and use information will be provided. http://www.ciconline.com.

How to Acquire Legal Copies of Video Programs. Johnson, B. (1993). Learning Resource Center, San Diego State University, San Diego, CA, 92182. Has information on free programs, resources, "off-air" licensing opportunities, sources for individual programs, sample forms, information on how to approach producers for copies, negotiation, and a recommended resource library.

PBS Video. 475 L'Enfant Plaza, S.W., Washington, DC, 20024; 1-800-424-7963 information, 1-800-344-3337 ordering and customer service. Puts out the PBS Video Catalog free of charge and arranges for licensing of "off-air" copies of programs for $125 for most programs. Some of the programs include teachers' guides. For extended instructional television off-air recording retention rights, PBS Educational Services (1-800-257-2578) can be contacted. It publishes a monthly newsletter, *PBS Video News,* at no charge. It also publishes the biannual periodical, *PBS Training Guide,* for staff development purposes. The PBS Business Channel phone number is 1-888-822-8229.

Phillips Satellite Industry Directory (annual). Phillips Publishing, 7811 Montrose Road, Potomac, MD, 20854. Programming services, program descriptions and formats, business and information services, and satellite operators are provided. This is the most complete guide.

Sat Guide: Cable's Satellite Magazine. Sat-Guide, POB 29, Boise, ID, 83707. Provides listings of programmers, programming categories (movies, educational, ethnic), contact persons, addresses and affiliate costs, if any.

Video Source Book. Updated yearly. Gale Research Company, Book Tower, Detroit, MI, 48226. Has synopses and evaluations (including sources) of over 40,000 videos from 800 sources.

Computer Software Copyright Resource

The Software Publishers Association has a packet, free of charge, which includes press releases about violations, brochures, a self-audit kit, and other items of interest. A 12-minute video, "It's Just Not Worth the Risk" can also be purchased. The SPA Web site, http://www.spa.org, has information, as well. Their toll-free hotline number is 1-800-388-7478. A representative can be requested to speak at your institution.

Print Periodicals with Copyright Information

Educom Review. Quarterly. 1112 16th St., N.W., Suite 600, Washington, DC, 20036-4823; phone 1-800-338-3282. It frequently has articles on copyright and intellectual property issues for those in colleges and universities.

Tech Trends. Monthly. 1025 Vermont Ave., N.W., Suite 820, Washington, DC, 20005; phone (202) 347-7834. It has a monthly "Copyright and You" column.

Technology Connection. Monthly, except June through August. Linworth Publishing, 480 East Wilson Bridge Rd., Suite L, Worthington, Ohio, 43085; phone 1-800-786-5017. Go to http://newslin@aol.com to see its Web site. It has a "Copyright Question of the Month" column.

Legal Resources

BNA's Patent, Trademark & Copyright Journal. Weekly periodical.

Delta, G., and J. Matsuura (1998). *Law of the Internet.* New York: Aspen Law and Business.

Epstein, M., and F. Politano (1998). *Drafting license agreements.* New York: Aspen Law and Business. P.O. Box 1311, Stamford, CT, 06904-1311, 1-800-562-1973.

Goldstein, P. (1996). Looseleaf, annual update. *Goldstein on copyright* (2nd ed.). (4 vols.). Boston: Little, Brown.

Information Infrastructure Task Force, Working Group on Intellectual Property Rights (1995). *Report of the Working Group on Intellectual Property Rights, National Information Infrastructure Task Force.* Washington, DC: U.S. Patent and Trademark Office.

IP Litigator. Bimonthly. New York: Aspen Law and Business.

Kohn, A., and B. Kohn (1998). *Kohn on music licensing.* (2nd ed.) New York: Aspen Law and Business. See also http://www.kohnmusic.com for online supplements.

Nimmer, M. B., and D. Nimmer (1988). *Nimmer on copyright: A treatise on the law of literary, musical, and artistic property, and the protection of ideas.* New York: Matthew Bender.

Patry, W. (1994; 1997, cumulative supplements). *Copyright law and practice.* Washington, DC: Bureau of National Affairs.

_____ (1995). *The fair use privilege in copyright law.* (2nd ed.) Washington, DC: Bureau of National Affairs.

Practicing Law Institute. Yearly. *Advanced seminar.* New York: Practicing Law Institute.
Scott, M. Looseleaf, annual update. *Scott on computer law.* New York: Aspen Law and Business.
_____. Looseleaf, annual update. *Scott on multimedia law: Development, protection, distribution.* (2nd ed.) New York: Aspen Law and Business.

Multimedia Copyright Resources

Multimedia

CD ROM Warehouse (1-800-237-6623). http://www.warehouse.com.
Educational Resources (1-800-624-2926). Very complete listing of the best software and compact discs for educational and home use. Has excellent listings of top products by subject and grade level. http://www.edresources.com
EDUCORP (1-800-843-9497). http://www.educorp.com.

Music

American Society of Composers,
 Authors, and Publishers (ASCAP)
One Lincoln Plaza
New York, NY 10023
(212) 595-3050

Broadcast Music, Inc. (BMI)
40 West 57th Street
New York, NY 10019
(212) 586-2000

SESAC, Inc.
156 West 56th Street
New York, NY 10019
(212) 586-3450

Motion Pictures

Motion Picture Association of America (MPAA)
http://www.mpaa.org

California office:
14144 Ventura Blvd.
Sherman Oaks, CA 91423
(818) 995-3600

Washington, D.C. Office:
1600 I Street, N.W.
Washington, DC 20006
(202) 293-1966

New York Office (anti-piracy):
1133 Avenue of the Americas
New York, NY 10036
(718) 518-8800

Music Educators National Conference (MENC)
1806 Robert Fulton Drive
Reston, VA 20191
1-800-336-3768
http://www.menc.org

Music Publishers Association (MPA)
152 West 57th Street, 31st Floor
New York, NY 10019
(212) 327-4044

National Music Publishers Association (NMPA)
NMPA/Harry Fox Agency
205 East 42nd Street
New York, NY 10017
(212) 370-5330
http://www.nmpa.org/hfa.html

Picture Network International
(703) 558-7860

Total Clearance (415) 389-1531

Drama-Musical Works

Rodgers & Hammerstein Library
598 Madison Avenue
New York, NY 10019
(212) 486-7378

Samuel French, Inc.
25 West 45th Street
New York, NY 10036
(212) 206-8990

Audiovisual Clearances

ABC News
(202) 222-7777

ABC News/PRIMETIME LIVE (NY)
Rights and clearances:
(212) 456-7777
Recorded message for clearances:
(212) 456-4059

John Allen (archival laboratory and
  stock footage house)
Park Ridge, NJ
(201) 391-3299
(201) 391-6335 FAX

Archive Films
530 West 25th St.
New York, NY 10001
(212) 620-3955

CBS News Archives (network)
533 West 57th St.
New York, NY 10019
(212)-975-4321
(212)-975-1893 FAX

CNN
Library and Tape Sales
P. O. Box 105366
Atlanta, GA 30348
(404) 827-1335
(404) 827-1840 FAX

Conus Communications
1825 K Street, N.W., Suite 915
Washington, DC 20006
(202) 467-5600
(202) 467-5610 FAX

C-SPAN (DC)
(212) 737-3220

Encyclopaedia Britannica Education
  Corp.
310 S. Michigan Ave.
Chicago, IL 60604
Rights and clearances:
(312) 347-7000

KARK-TV Eyewitness News
201 West 3rd St.
Little Rock, AK 72201
(501) 376-1610
(501) 375-1961 FAX

KPLR Channel 11
4935 Lindell Blvd.
St. Louis, MO 63108
(314) 367-7211
(314) 454-6436 FAX

KTVI (ABC St. Louis)
5915 Berthold Ave.
St. Louis, MO 63110
(314) 647-2222
(314) 647-8960 FAX

National Archives
Motion Picture, Sound & Video
  Branch
Washington, DC 20408
(301) 713-7060
(301) 713-6790 Reference Room
(301) 713-6904 FAX

National Library of Medicine
National Institutes of Health
Historical Audiovisuals Collection
Bethesda, MD 20894
(301) 496-5405 Audiovisuals
(301) 402-0872 FAX
http://www.rulm.nih.gov

NBC News Archives
30 Rockefeller Plaza Room 922
New York, NY 10112
(212) 664-3797
(212) 957-8917 FAX

Reuters
(212) 964-2234

Sherman Grinberg Film Archives
630 9th Ave.
New York, NY 10036
(212) 397-6200 NY
(212) 262-1532 FAX
(818) 709-2450 LA
(818) 709-8540 FAX

UCLA
Los Angeles, CA
(323) 466-8559
(323) 461-6317 FAX

University of South Carolina
Newsfilm Library
Instructional Services Center
Columbia, SC 29208
(803) 777-6841

WABC Channel 7 (NYC Affiliate)
77 West 66th St.
New York, NY 10023-6201
(212) 456-1000

WCBS Channel 2 (NYC Affiliate)
51 West 52nd St.
New York, NY 10019-6101
(212) 975-4321
(212) 975-9387 FAX
(212) 975-2875 (News Archives)

WCVB-Channel 5 (ABC)
5 TV Place
Needham, MA 02492
(781) 449-0400
(781) 449-6681 FAX

WHDH Channel 7 (NBC)
Boston, MA
(617) 725-0876
1-800-642-1551
(617) 248-5480 FAX

WIXT Channel 9 (ABC)
5904 Bridge St.
East Syracuse, NY 13057
(315) 446-9999
(315) 446-9283 FAX

WPA Film Library
12233 S. Pulaski
Alslip, IL 60658
(800) 777-2223

WTVH Channel 5 (Syracuse)
980 James St.
Syracuse, NY 13203
(315) 425-5555
(315) 425-0129 FAX

Part VII
Appendices

Appendix A
Guidelines Charts

Chart 1
Simplified Guidelines for Print Materials and Computer Software in Nonprofit Educational Institutions

Material	Instructor's Copy	Multiple Copies	Cumulative Use Per Class Per Term
Fiction, Nonfiction Textbooks, Theses	1 chapter	1,000-word excerpt or 10%	2
Stories, Essays, Anthologies, Encyclopedias	1 story or essay	2,500-word excerpt or story	2–3
Poetry	1 article	250-word excerpt or poem	2
Periodicals	1 article	2,500-word excerpt or essay	3
Cartoons, Charts Pictures	1 per book	Same as above	2–3
Lectures, Sermons Speeches	1 per book or issue	Same as above	2–3
Computer Software and Documentation	1 archival copy[1]	small excerpts only of documentation[2]	?

*The law permits a combination of nine instances of any of the above usages per course per term; free use may be made of newspapers — no limit; workbooks, manuals, standardized tests, study guides, and so forth, are prohibited.

[1]The same rules apply to the software itself.
[2]Multiple copies may only be made by lease or purchase agreement.

Chart 2*
Simplified Library Duplicating Guidelines

Purpose	Books	Periodical Articles	Musical Works	Cartoons Charts Diagrams Graphics Pictorial Works	Audiovisual News Program	Computer Software and Documentation	Digital Preservation Copies[3]	Unpublished Works
Archival reproduction	yes	yes	yes	yes	yes	yes	yes	yes
Replacement of damaged, stolen or lost copy[1]	yes	yes	yes	yes	yes	yes	yes	yes
Out-of-print work or obsolete equipment[2]	yes	yes	yes	yes	yes	yes	yes	yes
Interlibrary loan	yes	5 per calendar year for last 5 years	yes	yes	yes	yes	yes	yes
Unsupervised photocopiers	The library is not responsible as long as copyright warning sign is posted.							
Teacher-student copy	See Chart 1, Simplified Guidelines, for print materials, music, and multimedia.							
Reserve desk	One copy is permissable, more copies depend on usage and subscription policies.							

(The first four rows are bracketed under the label "One Copy.")

*These guidelines are for small libraries. Academic, special, system, and consortia libraries and archives will have additional guidelines appropriate to type.

[1] If unavailable at a fair price or if in a format that is "no longer manufactured or is no longer reasonably available in the commercial marketplace."

[2] Only a damaged copy may be replaced by an archival copy. The copy is not to be used to extend the life of the original.

[3] Up to 3 digital copies may be made of a work currently in a library or archives collection of published or unpublished works.

Chart 3
Simplified Guidelines for Motion Picture and Television Off-Air Taping

Medium	*PBS Programs Cleared for Taping[2]*	*Commercial Television Programs[3]*	*Television Audiovisual News Programs[4]*	*Cable and Satellite Subscription TV Programs[6,7]*	*Motion Pictures*
Live transmission to classroom	yes	yes	yes	no	no
Teacher's copy for limited period classroom use[1]	yes	yes	no[5]	no	fair use in film or stills

[1]Ten days for a once-only use in instructional activities with a once-only repetition for reinforcement purposes; copy may be held up to 45 days before erasure.

[2]PBS Video has a newsletter on programs available.

[3]"It appears that satellite reception of *broadcast* television programs [simultaneously rebroadcast — ABC, CBS, NBC affiliates which require no fee, for example] may be taped off-air." I. Bender. "Copyright Implications of Satellite Transmissions." *TLC Guide* (November 1985), p. 8.

[4]Does not include magazine-format or documentary news program.

[5]May be retained by a library or archive open to the public for purposes of research, criticism, or comment.

[6]Satellite programming is not subject to fair use. Most cable programming has one year or longer rights for the classroom. The Discovery Channel, The Learning Channel, and other cable programmers provide free or low-cost programming guides. Periodicals for both cable and satellite provide usage information, such as *Cable in the Classroom* and *Sat Guide*. I. Bender. "Finding Your Way Through the Copyright Maze." *Cable in the Classroom* (October 1995), p. 7.

[7]"The fact that cablecasts are not part of the [off-air taping] guidelines does not mean, however, that fair use does not apply. Rather, it means that the extent to which it applies is uncertain ... some cable programmers make their own rules ... and many ... are actually more liberal than the guidelines." I. Bender. "Finding Your Way Through the Copyright Maze." *Cable in the Classroom* (October 1995), p. 7.

Chart 4
Simplified Fair Use Guidelines for Educational Multimedia[1,2,3]

Medium	Database Table	Motion Media	Music	Images	Text	Project Retention Period	Number of Copies
Total Amount Used	10% or 2,500 fields or cells	10% or 3 minutes	10% or 30 seconds of 1 work or several works	5 from 1 artist or 15 images from collective work[4]	10% or 1,000 words	2 years	original[5]
Instructor Use 1. face-to-face instruction 2. directed self-study 3. remote instruction (PIN or password) 4. peer conferences	yes	yes	yes	yes	yes	2 years	original[5]
Professional Portfolio (tenure, personal, or job interviews)	yes	yes	yes	yes	yes	?	original[5]
Student Use (portfolio—job, personal, or academic use)	yes	yes	yes	yes	yes	?	original[5]
Unsecured Network	yes	yes	yes	yes	yes	15 days	original[5]
Media Center Reserve Copy and Archival Copy	yes	yes	yes	yes	yes	2 years	a total of 2 copies

[1]Adapted from "Fair Use Guidelines for Educational Multimedia," adapted by the Subcommittee on Courts and Intellectual Property, Committee on the Judiciary, U.S. House of Representatives, on September 27, 1996.

[2]Permission is required if: 1) noneducational or commercial purposes, 2) portions used beyond guidelines, 3) used on electronic networks.

[3]K–6 Exemptions: "It is understood, however, that students in kindergarten through grade six may not be able to adhere rigidly to the portion limitations in this section."

[4]If each image is copyrighted, then copyright mark must be with each image, or if used for a test and the copyright information would be incompatible with test purposes, then the use of the image should be "compatible with instructional objectives."

[5]In case of joint authors, each may keep a copy.

All projects should include:

1. Credit and copyright information on each screen or on a credit's screen. (The exception would be for images incorporated into the project such that they are attached to the image file and appear on screen when images are viewed.)

2. Notice on opening screen and accompanying materials that "certain materials are included under the fair-use exemption of U.S. copyright law and prepared ... [under] fair-use guidelines and are restricted from further use."

Author's note: The Guideline negotiators may not have been aware that K–6 would likely not be able to read or understand the above statement, particularly at lower grade levels. It is advisable to simply have a "credits" or "bibliography" screen, since K–6 is already exempted from portion limitations.

Chart 5
Simplified Fair Use Guidelines for Educational Multimedia[1,2,3]
Student Form — Example One: Media Contest

Amounts
Students, Teachers and Librarian/Teachers May Use:

Database/ Table	Motion Media	Music	Images	Text
10% or 2,500 fields or cell entries	10% or 3 minutes	10% or 30 seconds from 1 work or extracts from several works	5 from 1 artist or 15 images from a collective work	10% or 1,000 words

Credits
Each project must:
    1. Credit sources.
    2. Display the copyright notice.
    3. Display the copyright ownership information (author, title, producer, year of publication) either on each screen or on a credits screen.
    4. Have screen that states that fair use portions of materials have been made, and further use is restricted.

Performances, Displays, Retention
    Students and teachers may: 1) show student or teacher projects at district inservices, conferences, open house, or in the classroom for two years; 2) keep a project in a teacher or student portfolio for personal use for job, tenure, and graduate school interviews; and 3) perform or display in teaching or self-directed study in remote instruction on a PIN or password network for two years.

K–6 Exemptions
    "It is understood, however, that students in kindergarten through grade six may not be able to adhere rigidly to the portion limitations in this section." "Fair Use Guidelines for Educational Multimedia," 1996 (FUGEM).

[1]"Clip" means a small portion of the work; the amount will vary depending on the medium.

[2]"Instructor" can also mean librarian if the librarian is engaged in teaching "face-to-face systematic instruction in classrooms or similar places."

[3]"or one 250-word poem or three 250-word poems by one poet or five 250-word poems by different poets or one 250-word excerpt or three 250-word excerpts of one poet or five 250-word excerpts from different poets from one anthology" (FUGEM).

Chart 6
Simplified Fair Use Guidelines for Educational Multimedia
Student Form — Example Two: Media Contest

Amount

Your multimedia project to be entered in a contest may use:

Database/ Table	Videotapes, Computer Video	Music	Pictures, Photographs Drawings	Written Words (Text)
10% or 2,500 fields or cell entries	10% or 3 minutes	10% or 30 seconds from 1 work or 30 seconds from several works	5 from 1 artist or 15 images from several artists or works	10% or 1,000 words

Credits

1. When you use someone else's work, give them credit.

2. Place the copyright information (author, singers, band, title of work, producer, record company, motion picture company, year of publication) on a "Bibliography" screen at the end.

3. Make a screen that says: "Fair use amounts used. Further use is restricted."

4. If you follow these rules you may enter your project in a local, state, or national media contest.

Chart 7
Simplified Fair Use Guidelines for Educational Multimedia
Student Form — Example Three: Media Contest

How Much Can I Use?
For your project, try to use:

	Database/ Table	Movie Clips	Music	Pictures, Photographs, Drawings	Words
1 or	2,500 fields or cells	3 minutes	30 seconds	5 from 1 person or 15 from many people	4 pages or 3 short poems from 1 person or 5 short poems from 5 people
2	some fields	a small part of a movie (computer or video)	a little music	some pictures	4 pages or a few poems

Give Credit to Others
Credit who did the music, movie, or pictures on a screen that says:

(Music)   "Everybody," Back Street Boys, *Back Street Boys*, 1998, Jive.
(Picture)   Picture from "The Worst," by Shel Silverstein, *Where the Sidewalk Ends*. New York: Harper Collins, 1974, p. 130.
(Poem)   "Who Pulled the Plug in My Ant Farm?" by Jack Prelutsky, *Something Big Has Been Here*. New York: William Morrow, 1990, p. 70.
(Words)   *I Took My Frog to the Library*, by Eric Kimmel, pictures by Blanche Jims. New York: Viking, 1990, pp. 2–4.

Teacher's Note:
You understand, however, that kindergarten through sixth grade students probably won't adhere strictly to the limitations.

Chart 8
Cable in the Classroom
Copyright Clearances at a Glance*

Programmer	Cable in the Classroom *Programs*	*All Other Programs*
📖 A&E	1 Year	Fair
ABC	---	Fair
AMC	---	Restricted
📖 AT	In development	Free
📖 BET	1 Year	BET-produced programs: 1 year Other programs: Restricted
📖 BRV	1 Year or longer	Fair
📖 C-SPAN	Free	All programs are *Cable in the Classroom*
CBS	---	Fair
📖 CNBC	Free	Free
📖 CNN	Free	Restricted
📖 CTN	2 Years	2 Years
DIS	---	Restricted
📖 DSC	1 Year	Restricted
📖 ESPN 📖 ESPN2	Free	All ESPN- and ESPN2-produced: 3 Years Other programs: Case-by-case basis
📖 F&V	1 Year	Restricted
📖 FAM	1 Year or longer	Restricted
GALA	---	Free
📖 HBO	Some programs available on request	Restricted
📖 HIST	1 Year	Fair
📖 LIFE	1 Year	Fair
MAX	---	Restricted
📖 ME/U	1 Year or longer	Individual program copyrights vary; see monthly schedule
📖 MTV	1 Year	Restricted
NBC	---	Fair
📖 NICK	10 Years	Restricted
📖 NTTV	1 Year	*NTTV: Afternoon Edition/Teen Segment*: 30 days. Other programs: Restricted
📖 PBS	1 Year or longer	Fair or longer
📖 SFC	Free	All SFC-produced programs: Free Other programs: Restricted
📖 SHOW	Some programs available on request	Restricted
TBS	---	*National Geographic Explorer* and *Network Earth*: Fair Other programs: Restricted

(Table continued on next page.)

Programmer	Cable in the Classroom *Programs*	*All Other Programs*
📖 TLC	*The Magic Box*: 1 year *TLC Elementary School*: 2 years	*Teacher TV*: 1 Year Other programs: Restricted
TMC	---	Restricted
TNT	---	Restricted
📖 TOON	Free	Restricted
📖 TVFN	In development	Restricted
📖 TWC	Free	Free
UNI	---	Free
📖 USA	Free	Restricted
📖 WAM	Some programs available on request	Restricted
📖 WGN	1 Year	Restricted

📖 denotes a Cable in the Classroom member.

*Chart taken from:

   Cable in the Classroom (1999) [supplied by CIC]. To search the cable listings by keyword for CIC programs, other programs, and closed caption programs for day of the week and time period for use go to the Web site at http://www.ciconline.com.

Chart 9
The Copyright Mindset
Copyright 1998 by Xerox Corporation

   1. Assume everything is copyrighted.

   2. Just because you *can* copy, scan, or otherwise reproduce a work, doesn't mean you *may* do so.

   3. Copyright is constant. It doesn't disappear when a work changes from one medium to another.

   4. *Classroom use* and *fair use* are NOT synonymous.

   5. *Brevity* and *spontaneity* are key characteristics of fair use.

   6. Most U.S. government (federal) documents are in the public domain. State documents may be copyrighted.

Appendix B
Fair Use Guidelines for Educational Multimedia

Nonlegislative Report of the Subcommittee
on Courts and Intellectual Property
Committee on the Judiciary
U.S. House of Representatives
[Supporting Material for Fair Use Guidelines for Educational Multimedia]

This nonlegislative report was adopted by the Subcommittee on Courts and Intellectual Property, Committee on the Judiciary, U.S. House of Representatives, on September 27, 1996, and relates to Fair Use Guidelines for Educational Multimedia.

Under the Copyright Act of 1976, copyright owners have the exclusive right to reproduce, prepare derivative works, distribute, perform, display, transfer ownership, rent or lend their creations. Under the same act, the "fair use" exemption places a limit on these exclusive rights to promote free speech, learning, scholarly research and open discussion. Accordingly, under the act, educators may use portions of copyrighted material if the purpose and character of the use is educational in nature, previously published, not a substantial part of the entire work and if the marketability of the work is not impaired by the use. These vague standards do not provide much specific guidance for educators, scholars and students, and are fairly subjective in their interpretation.

Because of the vague nature of the exemption, shortly after Congress passed the Copyright Act in 1976, a group of publishers, authors and educators gathered to agree on an interpretation of the fair use exemption which would in turn provide more specific guidelines that educators could follow and be reasonably sure that they would not be in violation of the copyright law. These guidelines were made part of the *Congressional Record* and became an unrelated part of a Judiciary Committee Report.

Many technological developments have occurred since 1976. The fair use exemption contained in the Copyright Act must again be interpreted by copyright owners and the educational community to allow educators to apply the act in light of

217

these new technologies. To that end, the Consortium of College and University Media Centers ("CCUMC") convened a diverse group of interested parties to draft guidelines which would provide guidance on the application of the fair use exemption by educators, scholars and students in creating multimedia projects that include portions of copyrighted works, for their use in noncommercial educational activities, without having to seek the permission of copyright owners. These guidelines form the body of this nonlegislative report.

These guidelines do not represent a legal document, nor are they legally binding. They do represent an agreed-upon interpretation of the fair use provisions of the Copyright Act by the overwhelming majority of institutions and organizations affected by educational multimedia. A list of those organizations who have supplied written endorsements for the guidelines appears at the end of the guidelines. While only the courts can decide whether a particular use of a copyrighted work fits within the fair use exemption, these guidelines represent the participants' consensus view of what constitutes the fair use of a portion of a work which is included in a multimedia educational project. The specific portion and time limitations will help educators, scholars and students more easily identify whether using a portion of a certain copyrighted work in their multimedia program constitutes a fair use of that work. They grant a relative degree of certainty that a use within the guidelines will not be perceived as an infringement of the Copyright Act by the endorsing copyright owners, and that permission for such use will not be required. The more one exceeds these guidelines, the greater the risk that the use of a work is not a fair use, and that permission must be sought.

Along with the U.S. Copyright Office and the U.S. Patent and Trademark Office, whose letters of endorsement for these guidelines are included in this report, the Subcommittee congratulates the CCUMC and the other drafting participants for their hard work and effort, which clearly advances the strength of the U.S. copyright system.

Sincerely,

Carlos J. Moorhead   Patricia Schroeder
Chairman   Ranking Democratic Member

The Register of Copyrights of the
    United States of America
Library of Congress, Department 17
Washington, D.C. 20540
September 4, 1996

Dear Lisa and Ivan:
First, congratulations on completing a most difficult and important project—namely, the creation of new fair use guidelines for the creation of multimedia projects by educators and students who use portions of lawfully acquired copyrighted works. The Consortium of College and University Media Centers (CCUMC) deserves a great deal of credit for its efforts in initiating as well as

coordinating the process of lengthy negotiations that have led to the "Educational Multimedia Fair Use Guidelines" ["Fair Use Guidelines for Educational Multimedia"].

I also congratulate the participating organizations and their representatives for their efforts and for the compromises they made. I include Mary Levering, Associate Register for National Copyright Programs, who served as a resource person in all of the discussions and negotiations over the past two years. I know you found her contributions extremely helpful, and the Copyright Office was pleased to assist in this way.

I believe that experience has demonstrated that guidelines do assist organizations and individuals who wish to comply with the copyright law, and these new multimedia guidelines should be most helpful to educators and educational institutions as they use new technology for teaching and learning purposes.

As you know, the Copyright Office is the office charged with the administration of the copyright law; to that end, we register claims to copyright and record documents as well as collect and distribute statutory license fees and oversee the copyright arbitration royalty panels. The Office also provides information services to the public and technical assistance to the Congress and the Executive Branch agencies. As such, we cannot formally endorse guidelines. Nevertheless, I believe you know how we feel about them — we brought your efforts to the attention of Congressional leaders and urged inclusion of the adopted multimedia guidelines in an appropriate Judiciary Committee report.

I wish you well in your continued efforts.

Sincerely,

Marybeth Peters
Register of Copyrights

Ivan Bender and Lisa Livingston
Co-Chairs, Educational Multimedia
Fair Use Guideline Development Committee

United States Department of Commerce
Patent and Trademark Office
Assistant Secretary of Commerce and
   Commissioner of Patents and Trademarks
Washington, D.C. 20231

August 21, 1996

Ivan R. Bender, Esq.
Attorney at Law
3442 North Hoyne Ave.
Chicago, IL 60618

Dear Mr. Bender:

Thank you for your letter dated July 23, 1996, and the Fair Use Guidelines for Educational Multimedia enclosed therein.

I am delighted that the hard work and diligence of the Consortium of College and University Media Centers (CCUMC) has produced widely acceptable voluntary guidelines. The drafting, and now the endorsement of such guidelines by major players in the user and content provider communities, are very major accomplishments and clearly represent a significant contribution to the overall effort of establishing voluntary guidelines for fair use of digital works in general. With such guidelines adopted by CCUMC, the goal of the Conference on Fair Use, of which CCUMC has been so supportive, has clearly been advanced.

I am encouraged by and supportive of your efforts to submit the guidelines to Congress for attachment to appropriate legislation. I will be encouraging CONFU to do likewise with the guidelines drafted and adopted through that process. I also appreciate your support for the National Information Infrastructure legislation, and I look forward to its timely passage.

If I can be of any further assistance in this matter, please do not hesitate to contact my office.

Sincerely,

Bruce A. Lehman
Assistant Secretary of Commerce and
    Commissioner of Patents and Trademarks

Fair Use Guidelines for Educational Multimedia*

TABLE OF CONTENTS

1.   INTRODUCTION

1.1   Preamble
Fair use is a legal principle that provides certain limitations on the exclusive rights† of copyright holders. The purpose of these guidelines is to provide guidance on the application of fair use principles by educators, scholars, and students who develop multimedia projects using portions of copyrighted works under fair

---

*These Guidelines shall not be read to supersede other pre-existing education fair use guidelines that deal with the Copyright Act of 1976.
†See Section 106 of the Copyright Act.

use rather than by seeking authorization for noncommercial educational uses. These guidelines apply only to fair use in the context of copyright and to no other rights.

There is no simple test to determine what is fair use. Section 107 of the Copyright Act* sets forth the four fair use factors which should be considered in each instance, based on the particular facts of a given case, to determine whether a use is a "fair use": (1) the purpose and character of the use, including whether such use is of a commercial nature or is for nonprofit educational purposes, (2) the nature of the copyrighted work, (3) the amount and substantiality of the portion used in relation to the copyrighted work as a whole, and (4) the effect of the use upon the potential market for or value of the copyrighted work.

While only the courts can authoritatively determine whether a particular use is a fair use, these guidelines represent the participants'† consensus of conditions under which fair use should generally apply and examples of when permission is required. Uses that exceed these guidelines may or may not be fair use. The participants also agree that the more one exceeds these guidelines, the greater the risk that fair use does not apply.

The limitations and conditions set forth in these guidelines do not apply to works in the public domain — such as U.S. government works or works on which the copyright has expired for which there are no copyright restrictions — or to works for which the individual or institution has obtained permission for the particular use. Also, license agreements may govern the uses of some works, and users should refer to the applicable license terms for guidance.

The participants who developed these guidelines met for an extended period of time, and the result represents their collective understanding in this complex area. Because digital technology is in a dynamic phase, there may come a time when it is necessary to review these guidelines. Nothing in these guidelines shall be construed to apply to the fair use privilege in any context outside of educational and scholarly uses of educational multimedia projects.

This Preamble is an integral part of these guidelines and should be included whenever the guidelines are reprinted or adopted by organizations and educational institutions. Users are encouraged to reproduce and distribute these guidelines freely without permission; no copyright protection of these guidelines is claimed by any person or entity.

1.2 Background

These guidelines clarify the application of fair use of copyrighted works as teaching methods are adapted to new learning environments. Educators have traditionally brought copyrighted books, videos, slides, sound recordings and other media into the classroom, along with accompanying projection and playback equipment. Multimedia creators integrated these individual instructional resources with their own original works in a meaningful way, providing compact

---

*The Copyright Act of 1976, as amended, is codified at 17 U.S.C. Sec. 101 et seq.
†The names of the various organizations participating in this dialog appear at the end of these guidelines and clearly indicate the variety of interest groups involved, both from the standpoint of the users of copyrighted material and also from the standpoint of copyright owners.

educational tools that allow great flexibility in teaching and learning. Material is stored so that it may be retrieved in a nonlinear fashion, depending on the needs or interests of learners. Educators can use multimedia projects to respond spontaneously to students' questions by referring quickly to relevant portions. In addition, students can use multimedia projects to pursue independent study according to their needs or at a pace appropriate to their capabilities. Educators and students want guidance about the application of fair use principles when creating their own multimedia projects to meet specific instructional objectives.

1.3 Applicability of These Guidelines

(Certain basic terms used throughout these guidelines are identified in bold and defined in this section.)

These guidelines apply to the use, without permission, of portions of lawfully acquired copyrighted works in educational multimedia projects which are created by educators or students as part of a systematic learning activity by nonprofit educational institutions. **Educational multimedia projects** created under these guidelines incorporate students' or educators' original material, such as course notes or commentary, together with various copyrighted media formats including but not limited to, motion media, music, text material, graphics, illustrations, photographs and digital software which are combined into an integrated presentation. **Educational institutions** are defined as nonprofit organizations whose primary focus is supporting research and instructional activities of educators and students for noncommercial purposes.

For the purposes of these guidelines, **educators** include faculty, teachers, instructors and others who engage in scholarly, research and instructional activities for educational institutions. The copyrighted works used under these guidelines are **lawfully acquired** if obtained by the institution or individual through lawful means such as purchase, gift or license agreement but not pirated copies. Educational multimedia projects which incorporate portions of copyrighted works under these guidelines may be used only for **educational purposes** in systematic learning activities, including use in connection with noncommercial curriculum-based learning and teaching activities by educators to students enrolled in courses at nonprofit educational institutions or otherwise permitted under Section 3. While these guidelines refer to the creation and use of educational multimedia projects, readers are advised that in some instances other fair use guidelines such as those for off-air taping may be relevant.

2. PREPARATION OF EDUCATIONAL MULTIMEDIA PROJECTS USING PORTIONS OF COPYRIGHTED WORKS

These uses are subject to the Portion Limitations listed in Section 4. They should include proper attribution and citation as defined in Section 6.2.

2.1 By Students

Students may incorporate portions of lawfully acquired copyrighted works when producing their own educational multimedia projects for a specific course.

2.2 By Educators for Curriculum-Based Instruction

Educators may incorporate portions of lawfully acquired copyrighted works when producing their own educational multimedia projects for their own teaching tools in support of curriculum-based instructional activities at educational institutions.

3. PERMITTED USES OF EDUCATIONAL MULTIMEDIA PROJECTS CREATED UNDER THESE GUIDELINES

Uses of educational multimedia projects created under these guidelines are subject to the Time, Portion, Copying and Distribution Limitations listed in Section 4.

3.1 Student Use

Students may perform and display their own educational multimedia projects created under Section 2 of these guidelines for educational uses in the course for which they were created and may use them in their own portfolios as examples of their academic work for later personal uses and as job and graduate school interviews.

3.2 Educator Use for Curriculum-Based Instruction

Educators may perform and display their own educational multimedia projects created under Section 2 for curriculum-based instruction to students in the following situations:

3.2.1 for face-to-face instruction,

3.2.2 assigned to students for directed self-study,

3.2.3 for remote instruction to students enrolled in curriculum-based courses and located at remote sites, provided over the educational institution's secure electronic network in real-time, or for after-class review or directed self-study, provided there are technological limitations on access to the network and educational multimedia project (such as a password or PIN) and provided further that the technology prevents the making of copies of copyrighted material.

If the educational institution's network or technology used to access the educational multimedia project created under Section 2 of these guidelines cannot prevent duplication of copyrighted material, students or educators may use the multimedia educational projects over an otherwise secure network for a period of only 15 days after its initial real-time remote use in the course of instruction or 15 days after its assignment for directed self-study. After that period, one of the two use copies of the educational multimedia project may be placed on reserve in a learning resource center, library or similar facility for on-site use by students enrolled in the course. Students shall be advised that they are not permitted to make their own copies of the educational multimedia project.

3.3 Educator Use for Peer Conferences

Educators may perform or display their own educational multimedia projects created under Section 2 of these guidelines in presentations to their peers, for example, at workshops and conferences.

3.4 Educator Use for Professional Portfolio

Educators may retain educational multimedia projects created under Section 2 of these guidelines in their personal portfolios for later personal uses such as tenure review or job interviews.

4.   LIMITATIONS — TIME, PORTION, COPYING AND DISTRIBUTION

The preparation of educational multimedia projects incorporating copyrighted works under Section 2, and the use of such projects under Section 3, are subject to the limitations noted below.

4.1   Time Limitations

Educators may use their educational multimedia projects created for educational purposes under Section 2 of these guidelines for teaching courses, for a period of up to two years after the first instructional use with a class. Use beyond that time period, even for educational purposes, requires permission for each copyrighted portion incorporated in the production. Students may use their educational multimedia projects as noted in Section 3.1.

4.2   Portion Limitations

Portion limitations mean the amount of a copyrighted work that can reasonably be used in educational multimedia projects under these guidelines regardless of the original medium from which the copyrighted works are taken. **In the aggregate** means the total amount of copyrighted material from a single copyrighted work that is permitted to be used in an educational multimedia project without permission under these guidelines. These limitations apply cumulatively to each educator's or student's multimedia project(s) for the same academic semester, cycle or term. All students should be instructed about the reasons for copyright protection and the need to follow these guidelines. It is understood, however, that students in kindergarten through grade six may not be able to adhere rigidly to the portion limitations in this section in their independent development of educational multimedia projects. In any event, each such project retained under Sections 3.1 and 4.3 should comply with the portion limitations in this section.

4.2.1 Motion Media

Up to 10 percent or 3 minutes, whichever is less, in the aggregate of a copyrighted motion media work may be reproduced or otherwise incorporated as part of an educational multimedia project created under Section 2 of these guidelines.

4.2.2 Text Material

Up to 10 percent or 1,000 words, whichever is less, in the aggregate of a copyrighted work consisting of text material may be reproduced or otherwise incorporated as part of an educational multimedia project created under Section 2 of these guidelines. An entire poem of less than 250 words may be used, but no more than three poems by one poet, or five poems by different poets from any anthology may be used. For poems of greater length, 250 words may be used but no more than three excerpts by a poet, or five excerpts by different poets from a single anthology may be used.

4.2.3 Music, Lyrics, and Music Video

Up to 10 percent, but in no event more than 30 seconds, of the music and lyrics from an individual musical work (or in the aggregate of extracts from an individual work), whether the musical work is embodied in copies, or audio or audio-visual works, may be reproduced or otherwise incorporated as a part of a multimedia project created under Section 2. Any alterations to a musical work shall not change the basic melody or the fundamental character of the work.

4.2.4 Illustrations and Photographs

The reproduction or incorporation of photographs and illustrations is more difficult to define with regard to fair use because fair use usually precludes the use of an entire work. Under these guidelines a photograph or illustration may be used in its entirety but no more than 5 images by an artist or photographer may be reproduced or otherwise incorporated as part of an educational multimedia project created under Section 2. When using photographs and illustrations from a published collective work, not more than 10 percent or 15 images, whichever is less, may be reproduced or otherwise incorporated as part of an educational multimedia project created under Section 2.

4.2.5 Numerical Data Sets

Up to 10 percent or 2,500 fields or cell entries, whichever is less, from a copyrighted database or data table may be reproduced or otherwise incorporated as part of an educational multimedia project created under Section 2 of these guidelines. A field entry is defined as a specific item of information, such as a name or Social Security number, in a record of a database file. A cell entry is defined as the intersection where a row and a column meet on a spreadsheet.

4.3   Copying and Distribution Limitations

Only a limited number of copies, including the original, may be made of an educator's educational multimedia project. For all of the uses permitted by Section 3, there may be no more than two use copies, only one of which may be placed on reserve as described in Section 3.2.3.

An additional copy may be made for preservation purposes but may only be used or copied to replace a use copy that has been lost, stolen, or damaged. In the case of a jointly created educational multimedia project, each principal creator may retain one copy but only for the purposes described in Sections 3.3 and 3.4 for educators and in Section 3.1 for students.

5.   EXAMPLES OF WHEN PERMISSION IS REQUIRED

5.1   Using Multimedia Projects for Noneducational or Commercial Purposes

Educators and students must seek individual permissions (licenses) before using copyrighted works in educational multimedia projects for commercial reproduction and distribution.

5.2   Duplication of Multimedia Projects Beyond Limitations Listed in These Guidelines

Even for educational uses, educators and students must seek individual permissions for all copyrighted works incorporated in their personally created educational multimedia projects before replicating or distributing beyond the limitations listed in Section 4.3.

5.3   Distribution of Multimedia Projects Beyond Limitations Listed in These Guidelines

Educators and students may not use their personally created educational multimedia projects over electronic networks, except for uses as described in Section 3.2.3, without obtaining permissions for all copyrighted works incorporated in the program.

6.   IMPORTANT REMINDERS

6.1   Caution in Downloading Material from the Internet

Educators and students are advised to exercise caution in using digital material downloaded from the Internet in producing their own educational multimedia projects, because there is a mix of works protected by copyright and works in the public domain on the network. Access to works on the Internet does not automatically mean that these can be reproduced and reused without permission or royalty payment and, furthermore, some copyrighted works may have been posted to the Internet without authorization of the copyright holder.

6.2   Attribution and Acknowledgement

Educators and students are reminded to credit the sources and display the copyright notice and copyright ownership information if this is shown in the original source, for all works incorporated as part of educational multimedia projects prepared by educators and students, including those prepared under fair use. Crediting the source must adequately identify the source of the work, giving a full bibliographic description where available (including author, title, publisher, and place and date of publication). The copyright ownership information includes the copyright notice (©, year of first publication, and name of the copyright holder). The credit and copyright notice information may be combined and shown in a separate section of the educational multimedia project (e.g., credit section) except for images incorporated into the project for the uses described in Section 3.2.3. In such cases, the copyright notice and the name of the creator of the image must be incorporated into the image when, and to the extent, such information is reasonably available; credit and copyright notice information is considered "incorporated" if it is attached to the image file and appears on the screen when the image is viewed. In those cases when displaying source credits and copyright ownership information on the screen with the image would be mutually exclusive with an instructional objective (e.g., during examinations in which the source credits and/or copyright information would be relevant to the examination questions), those images may be displayed without such information being simultaneously displayed on the screen. In such cases, this information should be linked to the image in a manner compatible with such instructional objectives.

6.3   Notice of Use Restrictions

Educators and students are advised that they must include on the opening screen of their multimedia project and any accompanying print material a notice that certain materials are included under the fair use exemption of the U.S. Copyright Law and have been prepared according to the educational multimedia fair use guidelines and are restricted from further use.

6.4 Future Uses Beyond Fair Use

Educators and students are advised to note that if there is a possibility that their own educational multimedia project incorporating copyrighted works under fair use could later result in broader dissemination, whether or not as commercial product, it is strongly recommended that they take steps to obtain permissions during the development process for all copyrighted portions rather than waiting until after completion of the project.

6.5 Integrity of Copyrighted Works: Alterations

Educators and students may make alterations in the portions of the copyrighted works they incorporate as part of an educational multimedia project only if the alterations support specific instructional objectives. Educators and students are advised to note that alterations have been made.

6.6 Reproduction or Decompilation of Copyrighted Computer Programs

Educators and students should be aware that reproduction or decompilation of copyrighted computer programs and portions thereof, for example, the transfer of underlying code or control mechanisms, even for educational uses, is outside the scope of these guidelines.

6.7 Licenses and Contracts

Educators and students should determine whether specific copyrighted works, or other data or information, are subject to a license or contract. Fair use and these guidelines shall not preempt or supersede licenses and contractual obligations.

APPENDIX A: ORGANIZATIONS ENDORSING THESE GUIDELINES

Agency for Instructional Technology (AIT)
American Association of Community Colleges (AACC)
American Society of Journalists and Authors (ASJA)
American Society of Media Photographers, Inc. (ASMP)
American Society of Composers, Authors, and Publishers (ASCAP)
Association for Educational Communications and Technology (AECT)
Association for Information Media and Equipment (AIME)
Association of American Publishers (AAP)
Association of American Colleges and Universities (AAC&U)
Association of American University Presses, Inc. (AAUP)
Broadcast Music, Inc. (BMI)
Consortium of College and University Media Centers (CCUMC)
Creative Incentive Coalition (CIC)
Educational Testing Service (ETS)
Information Industry Association (IIA)
Instructional Telecommunications Council (ITC)
Iowa Association for Communication Technology (IACT)
Maricopa Community Colleges/Phoenix
Motion Picture Association of America (MPAA)
Music Publishers' Association of the United States (MPA)
National Association of Regional Media Centers (NARMC)
Northern Illinois Learning Resources Consortium (NILRC)
Recording Industry Association of America (RIAA)
Software Publishers Association (SPA)

2. INDIVIDUAL COMPANIES AND INSTITUTIONS ENDORSING THESE GUIDELINES
Houghton Mifflin
John Wiley & Sons, Inc.
McGraw-Hill
Time Warner, Inc.

3. U.S. GOVERNMENTAL AGENCIES SUPPORTING THESE GUIDELINES
U.S. National Endowment for the Arts (NEA)
U.S. Copyright Office
U.S. Patent and Trademark Office

APPENDIX B: ORGANIZATIONS PARTICIPATING IN GUIDELINE DEVELOPMENT
Being a participant does not necessarily mean the organization has or will endorse these guidelines.
Agency for Instructional Technology (AIT)
American Association of Community Colleges (AACC)
American Association for Higher Education (AAHE)
American Library Association (ALA)
American Society of Journalists and Authors (ASJA)
American Society of Media Photographers (ASMP)
Artists Rights Foundation
Association of American Colleges and Universities (AAC&U)
Association of American Publishers (AAP):
    Harvard University Press
    Houghton Mifflin
    McGraw-Hill
    Simon and Schuster
    Worth Publishers
Association of College and Research Libraries (ACRL)
Association for Educational Communications and Technology (AECT)Association for Information Media and Equipment (AIME)
Association of Research Libraries (ARL)
Authors Guild, Inc.
Broadcast Music, Inc. (BMI)
Consortium of College and University Media Centers (CCUMC)
Copyright Clearance Center (CCC)
Creative Incentive Coalition (CIC)
Directors Guild of America (DGA)
European American Music Distributors Corporation
Educational Institutions Participating in Guideline Discussion:
    American University
    Carnegie Mellon University
    City College/City University of New York
    Kent State University
    Maricopa Community Colleges/Phoenix
    Pennsylvania State University
    University of Delaware

Information Industry Association (IIA)
Instructional Telecommunications Council (ITC)
International Association of Scientific, Technical and Medical Publishers
Motion Picture Association of America (MPAA)
Music Publishers Association (MPA)
National Association of State Universities and Land-Grant Colleges (NASULGC)
National Council of Teachers of Mathematics (NCTM)
National Educational Association (NEA)
National Music Publishers Association (NMPA)
National School Boards Association (NSBA)
National Science Teachers Association (NSTA)
National Video Resources (NVR)
Public Broadcasting System (PBS)
Recording Industry Association of America (RIAA)
Software Publishers Association (SPA)
Special Libraries Association (SLA)
Time Warner, Inc.
U.S. Copyright Office
U.S. National Endowment for the Arts (NEA)
Viacom, Inc.

Prepared by the Fair Use Guidelines for Educational Multimedia Development Committee, July 17, 1996.

INFORMATION RELATED TO THE FAIR USE GUIDELINES FOR EDUCATIONAL MULTIMEDIA

The Association of American Publishers (AAP) membership includes over 200 publishers. The Information Industry Association (IIA) membership includes 550 companies involved in the creation, distribution and use of information products, services and technologies. The Software Publishers Association (SPA) membership includes 1,200 software publishers.

The Creative Incentive Coalition membership includes the following organizations:
Association of American Publishers
Association of Independent Television Stations
Association of Test Publishers
Business Software Alliance
General Instrument Corporation
Information Industry Association
Information Technology Industry Council
Interactive Digital Software Association
Magazine Publishers of America
The McGraw-Hill Companies
Microsoft Corporation
Motion Picture Association of America, Inc.
National Cable Television Association

National Music Publisher's Association
Newspaper Association of America
Recording Industry Association of America
Seagram/MCA, Inc.
Software Publishers Association
Time Warner, Inc.
Turner Broadcasting System, Inc.
West Publishing Company
Viacom, Inc.

MULTIMEDIA GUIDELINES WEB SITE

(The final "Fair Use Guidelines for Educational Multimedia" document with a
current list of endorsers can be found on the following Web sites:
   http://www.sju.edu/~lees/FU-let-intro.html
   http://www.libraries.psu.edu/avs./

Appendix C
Principles for Licensing Electronic Resources

Developed jointly by the American Library Association, the American Association of Law Libraries, the Association of Academic Health Science Libraries, the Association of Research Libraries, the Medical Library Association, and the Special Libraries Association.

The 15 principles articulated in the final draft (dated July 15, 1997) are:

1. A license agreement should state clearly what access rights are being acquired by the licensee — permanent use of the content or access rights only for a defined period of time.
2. A license agreement should recognize and not restrict or abrogate the rights of the licensee or its user community permitted under copyright law. The licensee should make clear to the licensor those uses critical to its particular users including, but not limited to, printing, downloading, and copying.
3. A license agreement should recognize the intellectual property rights of both the licensee and the licensor.
4. A license agreement should not hold the licensee liable for unauthorized uses of the licensed resource by its users, as long as the licensee has implemented reasonable and appropriate methods to notify its user community of use restrictions.
5. The licensee should be willing to undertake reasonable and appropriate methods to enforce the terms of access to a licensed resource.
6. A license agreement should fairly recognize those access enforcement obligations the licensee is able to implement without unreasonable burden. Enforcement must not violate the privacy and confidentiality of authorized users.
7. The licensee should be responsible for establishing policies that create an environment in which authorized users make appropriate use of licensed resources and for carrying out due process when it appears that a use may violate the agreement.
8. A license agreement should require the licensor to give the licensee notice

of any suspected or alleged license violations that come to the attention of the licensor and allow a reasonable time for the licensee to investigate and take corrective action, if appropriate.

9. A license agreement should not require the use of an authentication system that is a barrier to access by authorized users.

10. When permanent use of a resource has been licensed, a license agreement should allow the licensee to copy data for the purposes of preservation and/or the creation of a usable archival copy. If a license agreement does not permit the licensee to make a usable preservation copy, a license agreement should specify who has permanent archival responsibility for the resource and under what conditions the licensee may access or refer users to the archival copy.

11. The terms of a license should be considered fixed at the time the license is signed by both parties. If the terms are subject to change (for example, scope of coverage or method of access), the agreement should require the licensor or licensee to notify the other party in a timely and reasonable fashion of any such changes before they are implemented and permit either party to terminate the agreement if the changes are not acceptable.

12. A license agreement should require the licensor to defend, indemnify and hold the licensee harmless from any action based on a claim that use of the resource in accordance with the license infringes any patent, copyright, trademark or trade secret of any third party.

13. The routine collection of use data by either party to a license agreement should be predicated upon disclosure of such collection activities to the other party and must respect laws and institutional policies regarding confidentiality and privacy.

14. A license agreement should not require the licensee to adhere to unspecified terms in a separate agreement between the licensor and a third party unless the terms are fully reiterated in the current license or fully disclosed and agreed to by the licensee.

15. A license agreement should provide termination rights that are appropriate to each party.

More information on these principles and a short bibliography is found at the ALA Washington Office Web site at:

www.ala.org/washoff/ip/license.html

The ARL Web site also contains the text of the principles and other background materials at:

www.arl.org/scomm/licensing/licbooklet.html

The Yale Library Web site contains some examples of "good" licenses for the use of electronic data files and other related information on this important issue, including an excellent commentary by Robert Oakley, at:

www.library.yale.edu/~llicense/index.shtml

Appendix D

Agreement on Guidelines for Classroom Copying in Not-for-Profit Educational Institutions

With Respect to Books and Periodicals

The purpose of the following guidelines is to state the minimum and not the maximum standards of educational fair use under Section 107 of H.R. 2223. The parties agree that the conditions determining the extent of permissible copying for educational purposes may change in the future; that certain types of copying permitted under these guidelines may not be permissible in the future; and conversely that in the future other types of copying not permitted under these guidelines may be permissible under revised guidelines. Moreover, the following statement of guidelines is not intended to limit the types of copying permitted under the standards of fair use under judicial decision and which are stated in Section 107 of the Copyright Revision Bill. There may be instances in which copying which does not fall within the guidelines stated below may nonetheless be permitted under the criteria of fair use.

GUIDELINES

I. Single Copying for Teachers

A single copy may be made of any of the following by or for a teacher at his or her individual request for his or her scholarly research or use in teaching or preparation to teach a class:

A. A chapter from a book.
B. An article from a periodical or newspaper.
C. A short story, short essay or short poem, whether or not from a collective work.
D. A chart, graph, diagram, drawing, cartoon or picture from a book, periodical, or newspaper.

II. Multiple Copies for Classroom Use

Multiple copies (not to exceed in any event more than one copy per pupil in a course) may be made by or for the teacher giving the course for classroom use or discussion, provided that:

A. The copying meeting the tests of brevity and spontaneity as defined below.
B. The copying meets the cumulative effect test as defined below.
C. Each copy includes a notice of copyright.

DEFINITIONS

Brevity
(i) Poetry: (a) A complete poem is less than 250 words and if printed on not more than two pages, or (b) from a longer poem, an excerpt of not more than 250 words.
(ii) Prose: (a) Either a complete article, story or essay of less than 2,500 words, or (b) an excerpt from any prose work of not more than 1,000 words or 10 percent of the work, whichever is less, but in any event a minimum of 500 words. (Each of the numerical limits stated in "i" and "ii" above may be expanded to permit the completion of an unfinished line of a poem or of an unfinished prose paragraph.)
(iii) Illustration: one chart, graph, diagram, drawing, cartoon or picture per book or periodical issue.
(iv) "Special" works: Certain works in poetry, prose or in "poetic prose" which often combine language with illustrations and which are intended sometimes for children and at other times for a more general audience fall short of 2,500 words in their entirety. Paragraph "ii" above notwithstanding such "special works" may not be reproduced in their entirety; however, an excerpt comprising not more than two of the published pages of such special work and containing not more than 10 percent of the words found in the text thereof, may be reproduced.

Spontaneity
(i) The copying is at the instance and inspiration of the individual teacher, and
(ii) the inspiration and decision to use the work and the moment of its use for maximum teaching effectiveness are so close in time that it would be unreasonable to expect a timely reply to a request for permission.

Cumulative Effect
(i) The copying of material is for only one course in the school in which the copies are made.
(ii) Not more than one short poem, article, story, essay, or two excerpts may be copied from the same author, not more than three from the same collective work or periodical volume during one class term.
(iii) There shall not be more than one instance of such multiple copying for one course during one class term. The limitations stated in "ii" and "iii" above shall not apply to current new periodicals and newspapers and current news sections of other periodicals.

III. Prohibitions as to I and II Above

Notwithstanding any of the above, the following shall be prohibited:

A. Copying shall not be used to create or to replace or substitute for anthologies, compilations or collective works. Such replacement or substitution may occur whether copies of various works or excerpts therefrom are accumulated or reproduced and used separately.

B. There shall be no copying from works intended to be "consumable" in the course of study or of teaching. These include workbooks, exercises, standardized tests and test booklets and answer sheets and like consumable material.

C. Copying shall not:

  a. substitute for the purchase of books, publishers' reprints or periodicals;

  b. be directed by higher authority;

  c. be repeated with respect to the same item by the same teacher from term to term;

  d. no charge shall be made to the student beyond the actual cost of the photocopying.

Appendix E
Guidelines for
Educational Use of Music

The purpose of the following guidelines is to state the minimum and not the maximum standards of educational fair use under Section 107 of H.R. 2223. The parties agree that the conditions determining the extent of permissible copying for educational purposes, may change in the future; that certain types of copying permitted under these guidelines may not be permissible in the future, and conversely that in the future other types of copying not permitted under these guidelines may be permissible under revised guidelines.

Moreover, the following statement of guidelines is not intended to limit the types of copying permitted under the standards of fair use under judicial decision and which are stated in Section 107 of the Copyright Revision Bill. There may be instances in which copying which does not fall within the guidelines stated below may nonetheless be permitted under the criteria of fair use.

A. Permissible Uses
  1. Emergency copying to replace purchased copies which for any reason are not available for an imminent performance provided purchased replacement copies shall be substitutes in due course.
  2. (a) For academic purposes other than performance, single or multiple copies of excerpts of works may be made, provided that the excerpts do not comprise a part of the whole which would constitute a performable unit such as a selection, movement, or aria, but in no case more than 10 percent of the whole work. The number of copies shall not exceed one copy per pupil.*
     (b) For academic purposes other than performance, a single copy of an entire performable unit such as a section, movement, or aria, that is (1) confirmed by the copyright proprietor to be out of print or (2) unavailable except in a larger work, may be made by or for a teacher solely for the purpose of his or her scholarly research or in preparation to teach a class.
  3. Printed copies which have been purchased may be edited or simplified provided that the fundamental character of the work is not distorted or the lyrics, if any, altered or lyrics added if none exist.

---

*Section 2a as amended in the *Congressional Record*, September 22, 1976, p. 31,980.

4. A single copy of a recording of performances by students may be made for evaluation or rehearsal purposes and may be retained by the educational institution or individual teacher.
5. A single copy of a sound recording (such as a tape, disc or cassette) of copyrighted music may be made from sound recordings owned by an educational institution or an individual teacher. (This pertains only to the copyright of the music itself and not to any copyright which may exist in the sound recording.)

B. Prohibitions
1. Copying to create or replace or substitute for anthologies, compilations, or collective works.
2. Copying from works intended to be "consumable" in the course of study or of teaching, such as workbooks, exercises, standardized tests and answer sheets and like material.
3. Copying for the purpose of performance, except as in A.1. above.
4. Copying for the purpose of substituting for the purchase of music, except as in A.1. and A.2. above.
5. Copying without inclusion of the copyright notice which appears on the printed copy.

Appendix F
Guidelines for Off-Air Recording of Broadcast Programming for Educational Purposes

In accordance with what we believe was (the) intent, the Negotiating Committee has limited its discussion to nonprofit educational institutions and to television programs broadcast for reception by the general public without charge. Within the guidelines, the Negotiating Committee does not intend that off-air recordings by teachers under fair use be permitted to be intentionally substituted in the school curriculum for a standard practice of purchase or license of the same educational material by the institution concerned.

1. The guidelines were developed to apply only to off-air recordings by non-profit educational institutions.
2. A broadcast program my be recorded off-air simultaneously with broadcast transmission (including simultaneous cable retransmission) and retained by a nonprofit educational institution for a period not to exceed the first forty-five (45) consecutive calendar days after date of recording. Upon conclusion of such retention period, all off-air recordings must be erased or destroyed immediately. "Broadcast programs" are television programs transmitted by television stations for reception by the general public without charge.
3. Off-air recordings may be used once by individual teachers in the course of relevant teaching activities, and repeated once only when instructional reinforcement is necessary, in classrooms and similar places devoted to instruction within a single building, cluster or campus, as well as in the homes of students receiving formalized home instruction, during the first ten (10) consecutive school days in the forty-five (45) day calendar day retention period.
4. Off-air recordings may be made only at the request of and used by individual teachers, and may not be regularly recorded in anticipation of requests. No broadcast program may be recorded off-air more than once

at the request of the same teacher, regardless of the number of times the program may be broadcast.

5. A limited number of copies may be reproduced from each off-air recording to meet the legitimate needs of teachers under these guidelines. Each such additional copy shall be subject to all provisions governing the original recording.

6. After the first ten (10) consecutive school days, off-air recordings may be used up to the end of the forty-five (45) calendar day retention period only for teacher evaluation purposes, i.e., to determine whether or not to include the broadcast program in the teaching curriculum, and may not be used in the recording institution for student exhibition or any other non-evaluation purpose without authorization.

7. Off-air recordings need not be used in their entirety, but the recorded programs may not be altered from their original content. Off-air recordings may not be physically or electronically combined or merged to constitute teaching anthologies or compilations.

8. All copies of off-air recordings must include the copyright notice on the broadcast program as recorded.

9. Educational institutions are expected to establish appropriate control procedures to maintain the integrity of these guidelines.

The Bill of Rights and Responsibilities for Electronic Learners

A model computer and computer network policy addressing the rights and responsibilities of individuals, schools and colleges in the twenty-first century.

PREAMBLE

In order to protect the rights and recognize the responsibilities of individuals and institutions, we, the members of the educational community, propose this Bill of Rights and Responsibilities for the Electronic Community of Learners. These principles are based on a recognition that the electronic community is a complex subsystem of the educational community founded on the values espoused by that community. As new technology modifies the system and further empowers individuals, new values and responsibilities will change this culture. As technology assumes an integral role in education and lifelong learning, technological empowerment of individuals and organizations becomes a requirement and right for students, faculty, staff, and institutions, bringing with it new levels of responsibility that individuals and institutions have to themselves and to other members of the educational community.

ARTICLE I: INDIVIDUAL RIGHTS

The original Bill of Rights explicitly recognized that all individuals have certain fundamental rights as members of the national community. In the same way, the citizens of the electronic community of learners have fundamental rights that empower them.

Section 1.
A citizen's access to computing and information resources shall not be denied or removed without just cause.

Section 2.
The right to access includes the right to appropriate training and tools required to effect access.

Section 3.
All citizens shall have the right to be informed about personal information that is being and has been collected about them, and have the right to review and correct that information. Personal information about a citizen shall not be used for other than the expressed purpose of its collection without the explicit permission of that citizen.

Section 4.
The constitutional concept of freedom of speech applies to citizens of electronic communities.

Section 5.
All citizens of the electronic community of learners have ownership rights over their own intellectual works.

ARTICLE II: INDIVIDUAL RESPONSIBILITIES

Just as certain rights are given to each citizen of the electronic community of learners, each citizen is held accountable for his or her actions. The interplay of rights and responsibilities within each individual and within the community engenders the trust and intellectual freedom that form the heart of our society. This trust and freedom are grounded on each person's developing the skills necessary to be an active and contributing citizen of the electronic community. These skills include an awareness and knowledge about information technology and the uses of information and an understanding of the roles in the electronic community of learners.

Section 1.
It shall be each citizen's personal responsibility to actively pursue needed resources: to recognize when information is needed, and to be able to find, evaluate, and effectively use information.

Section 2.
It shall be each citizen's personal responsibility to recognize (attribute) and honor the intellectual property of others.

Section 3.
Since the electronic community of learners is based upon the integrity and authenticity of information, it shall be each citizen's personal responsibility to be aware of the potential for and possible effects of manipulating electronic information; to understand the tangible nature of electronic information; and to verify the integrity and authenticity, and assure the security of information that he or she compiles or uses.

Section 4.
Each citizen, as a member of the electronic community of learners, is responsible to all other citizens in that community: to respect and value the rights of privacy

for all; to recognize and respect the diversity of the population and opinion in the community; to behave ethically; and to comply with legal restrictions regarding the use of information resources.

Section 5.
Each citizen, as a member of the electronic community of learners, is responsible to the community as a whole to understand what information technology resources are available, to recognize that the members of the community share them, and to refrain from acts that waste resources or prevent others from using them.

ARTICLE III: INSTITUTIONAL RIGHTS

Educational institutions have legal standing similar to that of individuals. Our society depends upon educational institutions to educate our citizens and advance the development of knowledge. However, in order to survive, educational institutions must attract financial and human resources. Therefore, society must grant these institutions the rights to the electronic resources and information necessary to accomplish their goals.

Section 1.
The access of an educational institution to computing and information resources shall not be denied or removed without just cause.

Section 2.
Educational institutions in the electronic community of learners have ownership rights over the intellectual works they create.

Section 3.
Each educational institution has the authority to allocate resources in accordance with its unique institutional mission.

ARTICLE IV: INSTITUTIONAL RESPONSIBILITIES

Just as certain rights are assured to educational institutions in the electronic community of learners, so too each is held accountable for the appropriate exercise of those rights to foster the values of society and to carry out each institution's mission. This interplay of rights and responsibilities within the community fosters the creation and maintenance of an environment wherein trust and intellectual freedom are the foundation for individual and institutional growth and success.

Section 1.
The institutional members of the electronic community of learners have a responsibility to provide all members of their community with legally acquired computer resources (hardware, software, networks, databases, etc.) in all instances where access to or use of the resources is an integral part of active participation in the electronic community of learners.

Section 2.
Institutions have a responsibility to develop, implement, and maintain security procedures to insure the integrity of individual and institutional files.

Section 3.
The institution shall treat electronically stored information as confidential. The institution shall treat all personal files as confidential, examining or disclosing the contents only when authorized by the owner of the information, approved by the appropriate institutional official, or required by local, state or federal law.

Section 4.
Institutions in the electronic community of learners shall train and support faculty, staff, and students to effectively use information technology. Training includes skills to use the resources, to be aware of the existence of data repositories and techniques for using them, and to understand the ethical and legal uses of the resources.

The Bill of Rights and Responsibilities project is affiliated with the American Association for Higher Education (AAHE). It was begun in 1990 as part of the Educational Uses of Information Technology program of EDUCOM. For more information contact: **Frank W. Connolly, 125 Clark Hall, The American University, Washington, D.C. 20016. Internet: FRANK@American.EDU. Phone: (202) 885-3164.**

Appendix H
The Copyright Act, Transitional Supplements, Provisions and Amendments

The Copyright Law of the United States of America is incorporated in Title 17 of the United States Code. The text printed herein includes the Act for the General Revision of the Copyright Law, being Chapters 1 through 8 of Title 17 of the United States Code, together with Transitional and Supplementary Provisions, enacted as Public Law 94-553, 90 Stat. 2541, on October 19, 1976. Also incorporated herein and listed below in chronological order of their enactment are subsequent amendments to the said General Revision of the Copyright Law as embodied in Title 17 of the United States Code.

- Act of August 5, 1977 (Amendment to section 203, Title 17, U.S. Code, being the Act of 1909, as amended, and to section 708, Title 17, U.S. Code, being the Copyright Act of 1976, regarding the deposit of monies by the Register of Copyrights in the Treasury of the United States), P.L. 95-94, 91 Stat. 653, 682.

- Act of November 6, 1978 (Amendment of section 201(e), Title 17, U.S. Code, to permit involuntary transfer under the Bankruptcy Law), P.L. 95-598, 92 Stat. 2549, 2676.

- Act of December 12, 1980 (Amendment of sections 101 and 117, Title 17, U.S. Code, regarding computer programs), P.L. 96-517, 94 Stat. 3015, 3028.

- Act of May 24, 1982 ("Piracy and Counterfeiting Amendments Act of 1982," amending Title 18, U.S. Code, in section 2318, and by adding a new section 2319, and also by amending section 506(a), Title 17, U.S. Code), P.L. 97-180, 96 Stat. 91, 93.

- Act of July 13, 1982 (Amendment of manufacturing clause in chapter 6, Title 17, U.S. Code), P.L. 97-215, 96 Stat. 178.

- Act of October 25, 1982 (Amendments to sections 708 and 110, Title 17, U.S. Code, regarding the redesignation of registration fees as filing fees, and the exemption from copyright liability of certain performances of nondramatic literary or musical works), P.L. 97-366, 96 Stat. 1759.

- Act of October 4, 1984 ("Record Rental Amendment of 1984," amending sections 109 and 115, Title 17, U.S. Code, with respect to rental, lease, or lending of sound recordings), P.L. 98-450, 98 Stat. 1727.

- Act of August 27, 1986 (Amendments to sections 801 and 111, Title 17, U.S. Code, to clarify the definition of the local service area of a primary transmitter in the case of a low-power television station), P.L. 99-397, 100 Stat. 848.

- Act of October 31, 1988 ("Berne Convention Implementation Act of 1988"), P.L. 100-568, 102 Stat. 2853. (See Appendix of Circular 92, *infra*, for the text of certain non-amendatory provisions of the Berne Convention Implementation Act of 1988.)

- Act of November 5, 1988 ("Extension of Record Rental Amendment"), P.L. 100-617, 102 Stat. 3194.

- Act of November 16, 1988 ("Satellite Home Viewer Act of 1988"), being Title II of P.L. 100-667, 102 Stat. 3935, 3949.

- Act of July 3, 1990 ("Copyright Fees and Technical Amendments Act of 1989"), P.L. 101-318, 104 Stat. 287.

- Act of July 3, 1990 ("Copyright Royalty Tribunal Reform and Miscellaneous Pay Act of 1989"), P.L. 101-319, 104 Stat. 290.

- Act of November 15, 1990 ("Copyright Remedy Clarification Act"), P.L. 101-553, 104 Stat. 2749.

- Act of December 1, 1990 ("Visual Artists Rights Act of 1990"), being Title VI of the "Judicial Improvements Act of 1990," P.L. 101-650, 104 Stat. 5089, 5128.

- Act of December 1, 1990 ("Architectural Works Copyright Protection Act"), being Title VII of the "Judicial Improvements Act of 1990," P.L. 101-650, 104 Stat. 5089, 5133.

- Act of December 1, 1990 ("Computer Software Rental Amendments Act of 1990"), being Title VIII of the "Judicial Improvements Act of 1990," P.L. 101-650, 104 Stat. 5089, 5134.

- Act of June 26, 1992 ("Copyright Amendments Act of 1992," Title III of which repealed subsection 108(i), Title 17, U.S. Code, in its entirety), P.L. 102-307, 106 Stat. 264, 272.

- Act of June 26, 1992 ("Copyright Renewal Act of 1992,") being Title I of the "Copyright Amendments Act of 1992," P.L. 102-307, 106 Stat. 264.

- Act of October 24, 1992 (Amendment of section 107, Title 17, U.S. Code, regarding unpublished works), P.L. 102-492, 106 Stat. 3145.

- Act of October 28, 1992 (Amendments of section 2319, Title 18, U.S. Code, regarding criminal penalties for copyright infringement), P.L. 102-561, 106 Stat. 4233.

- Act of October 28, 1992 ("Audio Home Recording Act of 1992," amending Title 17, U.S. Code, by the addition of a new Chapter 10), P.L. 102-563, 106 Stat. 4237.

- Act of December 8, 1993 ("North American Free Trade Agreement Implementation Act," amending section 109 of the Copyright Act and adding a new section 104A to the same act), P.L. 103-182, 107 Stat. 2057, 2114, and 2115.

- Act of December 17, 1993 ("Copyright Royalty Tribunal Reform Act of 1993," amending, *inter alia*, Chapter 8 of the Copyright Act), P.L. 103-198, 107 Stat. 2304.

- Act of December 8, 1994 ("Uruguay Round Agreements Act," Title V, Subtitle A of which amends section 104A of the Copyright Act, and, *inter alia*, adds a new Chapter 11 to the same act), P.L. 103-465, 108 Stat. 4809, 4973. (See Appendix of Circular 92, *infra*, for the text of certain non-amendatory provisions of the Uruguay Round Agreements Act of December 8, 1994.)

- Act of November 1, 1995 ("Digital Performance Right in Sound Recordings Act of 1995," amending, *inter alia*, sections 114 and 115 of the Copyright Act), P.L. 104-39, 109 Stat. 336.

- Act of July 2, 1996 ("Anticounterfeiting Consumer Protection Act of 1996," amending section 603(c) of Title 17 and section 2318 of Title 18, U.S. Code), P.L. 104-153, 110 Stat. 1386, 1388.

- Act of September 16, 1996 ("Legislative Branch Appropriations Act, 1997," which, *inter alia*, added a new section 121 to Title 17, U.S. Code, concerning the limitation on exclusive copyrights for literary works in specialized format for the blind and disabled), P.L. 104-197, 110 Stat. 2394, 2416.

- Act of November 13, 1997 ("Copyright Technical Amendments Act," 1997, P.L. 105-80).

- Act of October 27, 1998 ("Sonny Bono Copyright Term Extension Act, 1998, P.L. 105-278).

- Act of October 8, 1998 ("Digital Millenium Copyright Act, 1998," P.L. 105-304).

Footnotes to the text refer to the amendments where they occur.

Note: Title 17 of the United States Code was also amended by the Act of November 8, 1984, P.L. 98-620, 98 Stat. 3347, 3356, which added to Title 17, Chapter 9 thereof, entitled "Protection of Semiconductor Chip Products." The provisions of Chapter 9, are not a part of the Copyright Law. The amendatory act states that it may be cited as the "Semiconductor Chip Protection Act of 1984." Copies may be obtained free of charge from the Copyright Office.

Appendix I

Sonny Bono Copyright Term Extension Act

To amend the provisions of Title 17, United States Code, with respect to the duration of copyright, and for other purposes.

Be it enacted by the Senate and House of Representatives of the United States of America in Congress assembled,

TITLE I — COPYRIGHT TERM EXTENSION

SEC.101.SHORT TITLE.

This title may be referred to as the "Sonny Bono Copyright Term Extension Act."

SEC.102.DURATION OF COPYRIGHT PROVISIONS.

(a) PREEMPTION WITH RESPECT TO OTHER LAWS.— Section 301(c) of Title 17, United States Code, is amended by striking "February 15, 2047" each place it appears and inserting "February 15, 2067."

(b) DURATION OF COPYRIGHT: WORKS CREATED ON OR AFTER JANUARY 1, 1978.— Section 302 of Title 17, United States Code, is amended —

(1) in subsection (a) by striking "fifty" and inserting "70";

(2) in subsection (b) by striking "fifty" and inserting "70";

(3) in subsection (c) in the first sentence —

(A) by striking "seventy-five" and inserting "95"; and

(B) by striking "one hundred" and inserting "120"; and

(4) in subsection (e) in the first sentence —

(A) by striking "seventy-five" and inserting "95";

(B) by striking "one hundred" and inserting "120"; and

(C) by striking "fifty" each place it appears and inserting "70."

(c) DURATION OF COPYRIGHT: WORKS CREATED BUT NOT PUBLISHED OR COPYRIGHTED BEFORE JANUARY 1, 1978.— Section 303 of Title 17, United States Code, is amended in the second sentence by striking "December 31, 2027" and inserting "December 31, 2047."

(d) DURATION OF COPYRIGHT: SUBSISTING COPYRIGHTS.—

(1) IN GENERAL.— Section 304 of Title 17, United States Code, is amended —

    (A) in subsection (a)—

        (i) in paragraph (1)—

            (I) in subparagraph (B) by striking "47" and inserting "67"; and

            (II) in subparagraph (C) by striking "47" and inserting "67";

        (ii) in paragraph (2)—

            (I) in subparagraph (A) by striking "47" and inserting "67"; and

            (II) in subparagraph (B) by striking "47" and inserting "67"; and

        (iii) in paragraph (3)—

            (I) in subparagraph (A)(i) by striking "47" and inserting "67"; and

            (II) in subparagraph (B) by striking "47" and inserting "67";

    (B) by amending subsection (b) to read as follows:

"(b) COPYRIGHTS IN THEIR RENEWAL TERM AT THE TIME OF THE EFFECTIVE DATE OF THE SONNY BONO COPYRIGHT TERM EXTENSION ACT.— Any copyright still in its renewal term at the time that the Sonny Bono Copyright Term Extension Act becomes effective shall have a copyright term of 95 years from the date copyright was originally secured";

    (C) in subsection (c)(4)(A) in the first sentence by inserting "or, in the case of a termination under subsection (d), within the five-year period specified by subsection (d)(2)," after "specified by clause (3) of this subsection"; and

    (D) by adding at the end the following new subsection:

"(d) TERMINATION RIGHTS PROVIDED IN SUBSECTION (C) WHICH HAVE EXPIRED ON OR BEFORE THE EFFECTIVE DATE OF THE SONNY BONO COPYRIGHT TERM EXTENSION ACT.— In the case of any copyright other than a work made for hire, subsisting in its renewal term on the effective date of the Sonny Bono Copyright Term Extension Act for which the termination right provided in subsection (c) has expired by such date, where the author or owner of the termination right has not previously exercised such termination right, the exclusive or nonexclusive grant of a transfer or license of the renewal copyright or any right under it, executed before January 1, 1978, by any of the persons designated in subsection (a)(1)(C) of this section, other than by will, is subject to termination under the following conditions:

    "(1) The conditions specified in subsections (c) (1), (2), (4), (5), and (6) of this section apply to terminations of the last 20 years of copyright term as provided by the amendments made by the Sonny Bono Copyright Term Extension Act.

    "(2) Termination of the grant may be effected at any time during a period of 5 years beginning at the end of 75 years from the date copyright was originally secured."

    (2) COPYRIGHT AMENDMENTS ACT OF 1992.— Section 102 of the Copyright Amendments Act of 1992 (Public Law 102-307; 106 Stat. 266; 17 U.S.C. 304 note) is amended —

(A) in subsection (c)—
   (i) by striking "47" and inserting "67";
   (ii) by striking "(as amended by subsection (a) of this section)"; and
   (iii) by striking "effective date of this section" each place it appears and inserting "effective date of the Sonny Bono Copyright Term Extension Act"; and
(B) in subsection (g)(2) in the second sentence by inserting before the period the following: "except each reference to forty-seven years in such provisions shall be deemed to be 67 years."

TITLE II — MUSIC LICENSING EXEMPTION FOR FOOD SERVICE OR DRINKING ESTABLISHMENTS

SEC.201.SHORT TITLE.
   This title may be cited as the "Fairness in Music Licensing Act of 1998."

SEC.202.EXEMPTIONS.
   (a) EXEMPTIONS FOR CERTAIN ESTABLISHMENTS.— Section 110 of Title 17, United States Code, is amended—
   (1) in paragraph (5)—
   (A) by striking "(5)" and inserting "(5)(A) except as provided in subparagraph (B)"; and
   (B) by adding at the end the following:
   "(B) communication by an establishment of a transmission or retransmission embodying a performance or display of a nondramatic musical work intended to be received by the general public, originated by a radio or television broadcast station licensed as such by the Federal Communications Commission, or, if an audiovisual transmission, by a cable system or satellite carrier, if—
   "(i) in the case of an establishment other than a food service or drinking establishment, either the establishment in which the communication occurs has less than 2,000 gross square feet of space (excluding space used for customer parking and for no other purpose), or the establishment in which the communication occurs has 2,000 or more gross square feet of space (excluding space used for customer parking and for no other purpose) and—
   "(I) if the performance is by audio means only, the performance is communicated by means of a total of not more than 6 loudspeakers, of which not more than 4 loudspeakers are located in any 1 room or adjoining outdoor space; or
   "(II) if the performance or display is by audiovisual means, any visual portion of the performance or display is communicated by means of a total of not more than 4 audiovisual devices, of which not more than 1 audiovisual device is located in any 1 room, and no such audiovisual

device has a diagonal screen size greater than 55 inches, and any audio portion of the performance or display is communicated by means of a total of not more than 4 loudspeakers are located in any 1 room or adjoining outdoor space;

"(ii) in the case of a food service or drinking establishment, either the establishment in which the communication occurs has less than 3,750 gross square feet of space (excluding space used for customer parking and for no other purpose), or the establishment in which the communication occurs has 3,750 gross square feet of space or more (excluding space used for customer parking and for no other purpose) and —

"(I) if the performance is by audio means only, the performance is communicated by means of a total of not more than 6 loudspeakers, of which not more than 4 loudspeakers are located in any 1 room or adjoining outdoor space; or

"(II) if the performance or display is by audiovisual means, any visual portion of the performance or display is communicated by means of a total of not more than 4 audiovisual devices, of which not more than one audiovisual device is located in any 1 room, and no such audiovisual device has a diagonal screen size greater than 55 inches, and any audio portion of the performance or display is communicated by means of a total of not more than 6 loudspeakers, of which not more than 4 loudspeakers are located in any 1 room or adjoining outdoor space;

"(iii) no direct charge is made to see or hear the transmission or retransmission;

"(iv) the transmission or retransmission is not further transmitted beyond the establishment where it is received; and

"(v) the transmission or retransmission is licensed by the copyright owner of the work so publicly performed or displayed"; and

(2) by adding after paragraph (10) the following:
"The exemptions provided under paragraph (5) shall not be taken into account in any administrative, judicial, or other governmental proceeding to set or adjust the royalties payable to copyright owners for the public performance or display of their works. Royalties payable to copyright owners for any public performance or display of their works other than such performances or displays as are exempted under paragraph (5) shall not be diminished in any respect as a result of such exemption."

(b) EXEMPTION RELATING TO PROMOTION. — Section 110(7) of Title 17, United States Code, is amended by inserting "or of the audiovisual or other devices utilized in such performance," after "phonorecords of the work."

SEC. 203.LICENSING BY PERFORMING RIGHTS SOCIETIES.

(a) In General. — Chapter 5 of Title 17, United States Code, is amended by adding at the end of the following:

"§512. Determination of reasonable license fees for individual proprietors

"In the case of any performing rights society subject to a consent decree which provides for the determination of reasonable license rates or fees to be charged by the performing rights society, notwithstanding the provisions of that consent decree, an individual proprietor who owns or operates fewer than 7 non-publicly traded establishments in which nondramatic musical works are performed publicly and who claims that any license agreement offered by that performing rights society is unreasonable in its license rate or fee as to that individual proprietor, shall be entitled to determination of a reasonable license rate or fee as follows:

"(1) The individual proprietor may commence such proceeding for determination of a reasonable license rate or fee by filing an application in the applicable district court under paragraph (2) that a rate disagreement exists and by serving a copy of the application on the performing rights society. Such proceeding shall commence in the applicable district court within 90 days after the service of such copy, except that such 90-day requirement shall be subject to the administrative requirements of the court.

"(2) The proceeding under paragraph (1) shall be held, at the individual proprietor's election, in the judicial district of the district court with jurisdiction over the applicable consent decree or in that place of holding court of a district court that is the seat of the Federal Circuit (other than the Court of Appeals for the Federal Circuit) in which the proprietor's establishment is located.

"(3) Such proceeding shall be held before the judge of the court with jurisdiction over the consent decree governing the performing rights society. At the discretion of the court, the proceeding shall be held before a special master or magistrate judge appointed by such judge. Should that consent decree provide for the appointment of an advisor or advisors to the court for any purpose, any such advisor shall be the special master so named by the court.

"(4) In any such proceeding, the industry rate shall be presumed to have been reasonable at the time it was agreed to or determined by the court. Such presumption shall in no way affect a determination of whether the rate is being correctly applied to the individual proprietor.

"(5) Pending the completion of such proceeding, the individual proprietor shall have the right to perform publicly the copyrighted musical compositions in the repertoire of the performing rights society by paying an interim license rate or fee into an interest bearing escrow account with the clerk of the court, subject to retroactive adjustment when a final rate or fee has been determined, in an amount equal to the industry rate, or, in the absence of an industry rate, the amount of the most recent license rate or fee agreed to by the parties.

"(6) Any decision rendered in such proceeding by a special master or magistrate judge named under paragraph (3) shall be reviewed by the judge of the court with jurisdiction over the consent decree governing the performing rights society. Such proceeding, including such review, shall be concluded within 6 months after its commencement.

"(7) Any such final determination shall be binding only as to the individual proprietor commencing the proceeding, and shall not be applicable to any other proprietor or any other performing rights society, and the performing rights society shall be relieved of any obligation of nondiscrimination among similarly situated music users that may be imposed by the consent decree governing its operations.

"(8) An individual proprietor may not bring more than one proceeding provided for in this section for the determination of a reasonable license rate or fee under any license agreement with respect to any one performing rights society.

"(9) For purposes of this section, the term 'industry rate' means the license fee a performing rights society has agreed to with, or which has been determined by the court for, a significant segment of the music user industry to which the individual proprietor belongs."

(b) TECHNICAL AND CONFORMING AMENDMENT.— The table of sections for Chapter 5 of Title 17, United States Code, is amended by adding after the item relating to section 511 the following: "512. Determination of reasonable license fees for individual proprietors."

SEC.204.PENALTIES.

Section 504 of Title 17, United States Code, is amended by adding at the end the following:

"(d) ADDITIONAL DAMAGES IN CERTAIN CASES.— In any case in which the court finds that a defendant proprietor of an establishment who claims as a defense that its activities were exempt under section 110(5) did not have reasonable grounds to believe that its use of a copyrighted work was exempt under such section, the plaintiff shall be entitled to, in addition to any award of damages under this section, an additional award of two times the amount of the license fee that the proprietor of the establishment concerned should have paid the plaintiff for such use during the preceding period of up to 3 years."

SEC.205.DEFINITIONS.

Section 101 of Title 17, United States Code, is amended —

(1) by inserting after the definition of "display" the following:

"An 'establishment' is a store, shop, or any similar place of business open to the general public for the primary purpose of selling goods or services in which the majority of the gross square feet of space that is nonresidential is used for that purpose, and in which nondramatic musical works are performed publicly.

"A 'food service or drinking establishment' is a restaurant, inn, bar, tavern, or any other similar place of business in which the public or patrons assemble for the primary purpose of being served food or drink, in which the majority of the gross square feet of space that is nonresidential is used for that purpose, and in which nondramatic musical works are performed publicly";

(2) by inserting after the definition of "fixed" the following:

"The 'gross square feet of space' of an establishment means the entire interior space of that establishment, and any adjoining outdoor space used to serve patrons, whether on a seasonal basis or otherwise";

(3) by inserting after the definition of "perform" the following:

"A 'performing rights society' is an association, corporation, or other entity that licenses the public performance of nondramatic musical works on behalf of copyright owners of such works, such as the American Society of Composers, Authors and Publishers (ASCAP), Broadcast Music, Inc. (BMI), and SESAC, Inc."; and

(4) by inserting after the definition of "pictorial, graphic and sculptural works" the following:

"A 'proprietor' is an individual, corporation, partnership, or other entity, as the case may be, that owns an establishment or a food service or drinking establishment, except that no owner or operator of a radio or television station licensed by the Federal Communications Commission, cable system or satellite carrier, cable or satellite carrier service or programmer, provider of online services or network access or the operator of facilities therefore, telecommunications company, or any other such audio or audio-visual service or programmer now known or as may be developed in the future, commercial subscription music service, or owner or operator of any other transmission service, shall under any circumstances be deemed to be a proprietor."

SEC.206.CONSTRUCTION OF TITLE.

Except as otherwise provided in this title, nothing in this title shall be construed to relieve any performing rights society of any obligation under any State or local statute, ordinance, or law, or consent decree or other court order governing its operation, as such statute, ordinance, law, decree, or order is in effect on the date of the enactment of this act, as it may be amended after such date, or as it may be issued or agreed to after such date.

SEC.207.EFFECTIVE DATE.

This title and the amendments made by this title shall take effect 90 days after the date of the enactment of this act.

Speaker of the House of Representatives.

*Vice President of the United States and
President of the Senate.*

Appendix J
Selected Excerpts from the Digital Millennium Copyright Act

Excerpt 1

DIGITAL MILLENNIUM COPYRIGHT ACT

OCTOBER 8, 1998.—Ordered to be printed

MR. COBLE, from the committee of conference,
submitted the following

CONFERENCE REPORT

[To accompany H.R. 2281]

The committee of conference on the disagreeing votes of the two Houses on the amendment of the Senate to the bill (H.R. 2281), to amend Title 17, United States Code, to implement the World Intellectual Property Organization Copyright Treaty and Performances and Phonograms Treaty, and for other purposes, having met, after full and free conference, have agreed to recommend and do recommend to their respective Houses as follows:

That the House recede from its disagreement to the amendment of the Senate and agree to the same with an amendment as follows:

In lieu of the matter proposed to be inserted by the Senate amendment, insert the following:

SEC. 1. SHORT TITLE.

This Act may be cited as the "Digital Millennium Copyright Act."

SEC. 2. TABLE OF CONTENTS.

Sec. 1. Short title.
Sec. 2. Table of contents.

Excerpt 2

"(d) EXEMPTION FOR NONPROFIT LIBRARIES, ARCHIVES, AND EDUCATIONAL INSTITUTIONS. — (1) A nonprofit library, archives, or educational institution which gains access to a commercially exploited copyrighted work solely in order to make a good faith determination of whether to acquire a copy of that work for the sole purpose of engaging in conduct permitted under this title shall not be in violation of subsection (a)(1)(A). A copy of a work to which access has been gained under this paragraph —

"(A) may not be retained longer than necessary to make such good faith determination; and

"(B) may not be used for any other purpose.

"(2) The exemption made available under paragraph (1) shall only apply with respect to a work when an identical copy of that work is not reasonably available in another form.

"(3) A nonprofit library, archives, or educational institution that willfully for the purpose of commercial advantage or financial gain violates paragraph (1)—

"(A) shall, for the first offense, be subject to the civil remedies under section 1203; and

"(B) shall, for repeated or subsequent offenses, in addition to the civil remedies under section 1203, forfeit the exemption provided under paragraph (1).

"(4) This subsection may not be used as a defense to a claim under subsection (a)(2) or (b), nor may this subsection permit a nonprofit library, archives, or educational institution to manufacture, import, offer to the public, provide, or otherwise traffic in any technology, product, service, component, or part thereof, which circumvents a technological measure.

"(5) In order for a library or archives to qualify for the exemption under this subsection, the collections of that library or archives shall be—

"(A) open to the public; or

"(B) available not only to researchers affiliated with the library or archives or with the institution of which it is a part, but also to other persons doing research in a specialized field.

Excerpt 3

"(d) INFORMATION LOCATION TOOLS.— A service provider shall not be liable for monetary relief, or, except as provided in subsection (j), for injunctive or other equitable relief, for infringement of copyright by reason of the provider referring or linking users to an online location containing infringing material or infringing activity, by using information location tools, including a directory, index, reference, pointer, or hypertext link, if the service provider—

"(1)(A) does not have actual knowledge that the material or activity is infringing;

"(B) in the absence of such actual knowledge, is not aware of facts or circumstances from which infringing activity is apparent; or

"(C) upon obtaining such knowledge or awareness, acts expeditiously to remove, or disable access to, the material;

"(2) does not receive a financial benefit directly attributable to the infringing activity, in a case in which the service provider has the right and ability to control such activity; and

"(3) upon notification of claimed infringement as described in subsection (c)(3), responds expeditiously to remove, or disable access to, the material that is claimed to be infringing or to be the subject of infringing activity, except that, for purposes of this paragraph, the information described in subsection (c)(3)(A)(iii) shall be identification of the reference or link, to material or activity claimed to be infringing, that is to be removed or access to which is to be disabled, and information reasonably sufficient to permit the service provider to locate that reference or link.

"(e) LIMITATION ON LIABILITY OF NONPROFIT EDUCATIONAL INSTITUTIONS. — (1) When a public or other nonprofit institution of higher education is a service provider, and when a faculty member or graduate student who is an employee of such institution is performing a teaching or research function, for the purposes of subsections (a) and (b) such faculty member or graduate student shall be considered to be a person other than the institution, and for the purposes of subsections (c) and (d) such faculty member's or graduate student's knowledge or awareness of his or her infringing activities shall not be attributed to the institution, if —

"(A) such faculty member's or graduate student's infringing activities do not involve the provision of online access to instructional materials that are or were required or recommended, within the preceding 3-year period, for a course taught at the institution by such faculty member or graduate student;

"(B) the institution has not, within the preceding 3-year period, received more than 2 notifications described in subsection (c)(3) of claimed infringement by such faculty member or graduate student, and such notifications of claimed infringement were not actionable under subsection (f); and

"(C) the institution provides to all users of its system or network informational materials that accurately describe, and promote compliance with, the laws of the United States relating to copyright.

"(2) INJUNCTIONS. — For the purposes of this subsection, the limitations on injunctive relief contained in subsections (j)(2) and (j)(3), but not those in (j)(1), shall apply.

Excerpt 4

SEC. 404. EXEMPTION FOR LIBRARIES AND ARCHIVES.

Section 108 of Title 17, United States Code, is amended —

(1) in subsection (a) —

(A) by striking "Notwithstanding" and inserting "Except as otherwise provided in this title and notwithstanding";

(B) by inserting after "no more than one copy or phonorecord of a work" the following: ", except as provided in subsections (b) and (c)"; and

(C) in paragraph (3) by inserting after "copyright" the following: "that appears on the copy or phonorecord that is reproduced under the provisions of this section, or includes a legend stating that the work may be protected by copyright if no such notice can be found on the copy or phonorecord that is reproduced under the provisions of this section";

(2) in subsection (b) —

(A) by striking "a copy or phonorecord" and inserting "three copies or phonorecords";

(B) by striking "in facsimile form"; and

(C) by striking "if the copy or phonorecord reproduced is currently in the collections of the library or archives." and inserting "if —

"(1) the copy or phonorecord reproduced is currently in the collections of the library or archives; and

"(2) any such copy or phonorecord that is reproduced in digital format is not otherwise distributed in that format and is not made available to the public in that format outside the premises of the library or archives"; and

(3) in subsection (c)—

(A) by striking "a copy or phonorecord" and inserting "three copies or phonorecords";

(B) by striking "in facsimile form";

(C) by inserting "or if the existing format in which the work is stored has become obsolete," after "stolen"; and

(D) by striking "if the library or archives has, after a reasonable effort, determined that an unused replacement cannot be obtained at a fair price," and inserting "if—

"(1) the library or archives has, after a reasonable effort, determined that an unused replacement cannot be obtained at a fair price; and

"(2) any such copy or phonorecord that is reproduced in digital format is not made available to the public in that format outside the premises of the library or archives in lawful possession of such copy"; and

(E) by adding at the end the following:

"For purposes of this subsection, a format shall be considered obsolete if the machine or device necessary to render perceptible a work stored in that format is no longer manufactured or is no longer reasonably available in the commercial marketplace."

Appendix K
Teacher Survey on Copyright Allowances for Education

Survey by Vicki Pillard, Marysville, Kansas
vpillard@cjnetworks.com

Please don't throw this away yet. If you can find a few minutes to complete this survey concerning general knowledge of copyright limitations and allowances in regard to activities of teachers and students, I would be very grateful. And in the process, you might learn something, too (I know I certainly have). The data collected will comprise part of a project for one of the classes I'm taking. The correct answers to the following questions will be sent to you on e-mail after all surveys have been returned. I need a good response rate, so I hope you will participate. Thank you for your time and your promptness in returning this survey.

Copyright applications for *print materials*:

1. A teacher copies two encyclopedia articles, totaling 3,000 words, and distributes them to students in a class as part of their study. Is this permissible?
   Yes   No

2. May a teacher make transparencies of two or more maps from a book to illustrate changes in a country's borders?   Yes   No

3. A teacher encourages students to collect current event clippings from newspapers or magazines which will eventually be gathered, copied, and distributed to all members of the class. Is this acceptable?   Yes   No

4. A teacher copies two photographs from a magazine and distributes them to students in a class for evaluation purposes. Is this allowable?   Yes   No

5. Is the teacher justified in cutting costs for students by making just enough copies of a workbook so each student can have a copy free?   Yes   No

6. If a teacher who is developing a new course wants to "create" his own textbook by compiling published poems, stories, or articles that he or she wants to use with students, is this allowable?   Yes   No

259

Copyright applications for *music*:
1. May a choir teacher edit and simplify purchased sheet music?   Yes   No
2. May a music teacher make a sound recording of a contemporary song for the students to study the use of lyrics?   Yes   No
3. When teachers or students make a multimedia presentation or a videotape for educational use in an educational setting, can they use entire songs as background music without getting permission?   Yes   No
4. May a teacher record small excerpts onto an audiotape to demonstrate various music styles to a class?   Yes   No

Copyright applications for *videotapes*:
1. At home, a teacher begins to watch a television program and discovers that it is relevant to what he or she is currently teaching. Can the teacher record the program to show to his students the next day?   Yes   No
2. As a reward, the teacher or one of his students brings a purchased or rented videotape that the entire class can watch for enjoyment. Is this permissible? Yes   No
3. Can a teacher make a videotape of small clips from television shows to illustrate a point of instruction?   Yes   No
4. Can a teacher or librarian duplicate a purchased videotape for the purpose of having a backup copy?   Yes   No

Copyright applications for *computer software*:
1. A computer disk does not allow the teacher to make a normal backup copy. Is it okay for the teacher to use an anti-lock software program in order to make one archival copy of the original disk?   Yes   No
2. If the original computer disk goes bad, can the teacher make a second backup copy from the one remaining backup?   Yes   No
3. The teacher received one manual with a software program, but would like to reproduce it so that each student in the class can have his/her own manual. Is this acceptable?   Yes   No

Copyright applications for *multimedia presentations*:
1. If students use proper portions of copyrighted materials and give proper credit in their multimedia projects for a class, may they keep their presentations in their personal portfolios for later use with a job interview or graduate school application?   Yes   No
2. If, for instructional purposes, a teacher creates a multimedia presentation which has proper portions of copyrighted works and which gives proper credit, can the teacher use the presentation for as long as he or she teaches the course? Yes   No

Answers to Survey Questions

Print materials:
1. Yes. Although the guidelines for fair use copying of short stories, essays, encyclopedias, or anthologies are 2,500 words, this slight exception would probably go unnoticed unless the amount was habitually exceeded.
2. No. The rule for maps, charts, graphs, or cartoons is one per book or per issue

if a periodical is used. Two would be permissible on a rare basis. Otherwise, ask permission before copying more than what is allowed.

3. Yes. Unlimited copying of newspapers or current events items in magazines is allowed.

4. Yes. As long as neither picture has its own copyright. Pictures that are individually copyrighted may not be reproduced without permission.

5. No. Workbooks, study guides, manuals, and so forth, are not included under fair use guidelines and, therefore, cannot be reproduced.

6. No. A teacher may not "create" and distribute his own "textbook" for students by copying selected works already published. This would harm the market of published anthologies or textbooks.

Music:

1. Yes. A choir teacher may edit and simplify purchased sheet music as long as the piece is not distorted or the lyrics altered.

2. Yes. A copied sound recording may be used in aural exercises or examinations.

3. Yes. Entire songs can be used as background music in multimedia presentations by teachers or students if the presentation is for an educational use in an educational setting.

4. Yes. Small excerpts of music recorded on an audiotape may be used for educational purposes.

Videotapes:

1. Yes. The spontaneity of recording an off-air broadcast that coincides with an instructional unit already in progress is considered fair use. The tape can be used only during the current unit and then must be erased.

2. No. Rented or purchased videos must be an integral part of "systematic instructional activities," and never used only as recreational diversions.

3. Yes. A teacher may record small clips from television shows to illustrate an instructional point.

4. No. Making a backup copy of a purchased videotape is not considered fair use.

Computer software:

1. Yes. Even if a computer program does not allow copying in the normal fashion to produce a backup, a person may use anti-lock software to make one backup per disk.

2. No. If the original disk fails to work and the backup disk needs to be used, it is time to consider purchasing an upgrade of the program. Making another backup copy is not considered fair use.

3. No. One archival copy may be made of a computer manual. For multiple copies, the teacher may select only small excerpts of the documentation to reproduce.

Multimedia presentations:

1. Yes. Students may keep their presentations for later use in job interviews or graduate school applications if proper portions of copyrighted material and proper credits have been included.

2. No. A teacher may keep her or his instructional presentation for two years if

proper portions of copyrighted material and proper credits have been included. After that, the teacher needs to acquire permission for each copyrighted portion incorporated. The teacher can, however, retain the presentation for a professional portfolio or graduate school.

Appendix L
What Students Need to Know About Copyright

Lesson Plan
by Lynette Kracht, Marysville, Kansas
lkracht@cjnetworks.com

Summary
In this five-session unit, students experience what it feels like to be a creator of intellectual property (contributing to a class journal) and not to receive credit for their work. In class discussion, students relate this experience to the concept of *intellectual property*. The class also discusses the concept of compensation for intellectual property and the negative effects of unauthorized copying of intellectual property. Students discuss the idea that laws can be passed to protect intellectual property. And finally, students will view two Software Publishers Association videos. [See Resource Guides, pp. 191, 198–201 for ordering information.]

Learning Objectives
Students will:
• Become familiar with the concept of *intellectual property*.
• Experience a sense of ownership over their ideas and intellectual creations, and develop respect for the intellectual property of others.
• Experience the negative impact of unauthorized copying of intellectual property, and relate it to their own lives.
• Appreciate the value of laws to protect intellectual property.
• Become familiar with U.S. copyright law as a means of protecting intellectual property.

Prerequisite Skills
Students should know how to use word-processing and graphics software for artwork and design.

Materials Needed
Computer, word-processing and graphics software. Software Publishers Association (SPA) videos, *Don't Copy That Floppy* and *It's Just Not Worth the Risk*.

Time Required
Five 45-minute class sessions. Sessions 1 and 2 should take place back-to-back,

with Sessions 3, 4, and 5 taking place at least one week after Session 2. Some students may want extra, out-of-class time to complete their creative projects.

Sessions 1 and 2

Preactivity and Teacher Preparation
Get computers, word-processing, and graphics software ready for Sessions 1 and 2.

Student Activity
Explain to students that they have been identified as a talented group of student authors, artists, designers, and innovators. They have been selected to create a journal to display their talents. Explain that each student is required to complete at least one artistic contribution to the journal that involves writing and creating a graphic (using a computer and word-processing/graphics software).
Allow students to use two class periods and their own time (if they wish) to develop their own individual contributions to the journal. Give the students a deadline to complete their work. Collect the students' creations prior to Session 3.

Session 3

Preactivity Teacher Preparation
Develop a draft version of the journal that includes creations from each student in class. Deliberately *omit* any mention of the individual student contributors and any reference to the class. Prepare copies of the journal for distribution to the class. Get VCR ready to show two videos.

Whole Class Discussion
Distribute copies of the draft version of the journal to your students for their review. After the students have had an opportunity to examine the journal, lead a class discussion that focuses on intellectual property issues. Questions you might ask include:

> "How does it feel to have your work distributed without you receiving any credit?"
> "How should the journal be revised?"
> "Suppose we were going to sell this journal to students and parents. Who should receive the money from the sale of the journal?"
> "If the journal is published, and people copy the journal rather than pay for it, who loses? Why?"
> "What guarantee do you have that the journal will not be copied by others? How can you ensure it will not be copied by others?"

Introduce the concept of *intellectual property* and have students relate it to their experience with the journal. Then move the discussion to other situations in which students have experienced people copying the work of others without permission. Likely examples include: homework, in-class assignments, exams, computer software, music audiocassettes, videocassettes, and pages from books. If computer software is not specifically mentioned by students, direct the discussion toward software as a form of intellectual property.

Finally, ask students: "What laws should be created to protect people who develop creative works?"

Homework Assignment

Have students identify businesses, industries, and jobs that were not discussed in class for which protecting intellectual property is important (e.g., photography, music publishing). For each business, industry, or job, have students describe the kinds of intellectual property that might need protection.

Session 4

Preactivity Teacher Preparation

Gather together the packaging and or documentation from several popular educational software programs, making sure that the materials include copyright information. Prepare copies of the background information on U.S. copyright law, the district copyright policy statement, and examples of school software copyright policy statements or guidelines for distribution to students. [See Appendices for examples.]

Whole Class Discussion

Identify the copyright symbol and explain what it represents. Point out that sometimes software publishers use the word *copyright* to indicate that a program is protected by copyright law, and sometimes they use the copyright symbol instead.

Student Activity

Distribute the packaging and documentation for several of the students' favorite software programs. Have the students locate the word *copyright* or the copyright symbol for several different products.

Distribute the background material on U.S. copyright law. Then lead a discussion on how the law protects intellectual property, in general, and computer software specifically. Make sure that students understand the purpose and use of back-up or archival copies of software programs.

Distribute the district copyright policy statement and examples of school software copyright protection policy statements or guidelines.

Follow-up Activity

Distribute copies of several publishers' licensing agreements. Review these agreements with your students.

Session 5

Student Activity

Distribute SPA pamphlets, *Software Use and the Law* and *Is It Okay to Copy My Colleague's Software?* Read and discuss.

As a final part of the unit, show students the SPA videos *Don't Copy That Floppy*, and *It's Just Not Worth the Risk.*

Follow-up Activity

Ask students to develop their own copyright warnings for the work they have done. Alone or in teams, students could do research on copyright, electronic commerce, new technologies, software, or other intellectual property topics.

Appendix M
Copyright and Trademark Issues

Lesson Plan
by Adrienne Mammen, C.J.E.
Salina High School Central
Salina, Kansas

Lesson Guidelines and Enrichment Ideas

Goals and Objectives
- Students will gain an understanding of the concept of copyright.
- Students will gain an understanding of the principle of fair use.
- Students will learn what constitutes a trademark.
- Students will develop an understanding of the penalties for copyright and trademark infringement.
- Students will become aware of the need to obtain permission for use from the copyright or trademark owner.
- Students will identify types of material not requiring permission.
- Students will practice gaining permission.

Student Handout
- Chapter 3, "Copyright and Trademark Issues," from *Taking Issue* published by Jostens, pp. 10–15. [Teacher and student versions, $1.00 each, 1-800-972-5628.]

Areas for Further Research and Discussion
Beyond Material Presented in the Student Handout
- Does copyright limit free access to materials? Discuss the concept of copyright with regard to photocopying materials used in class.
- Since the materials are being used for educational purposes, is it fair use? Does duplicating material deny the artist just compensation for his work? If duplication is not available, how can students without the means to purchase materials have access?
- A few years ago, Sony tried to introduce the digital audiotape (DAT) audiocassette. Because the audio reproduction quality was so high on this cassette, the music industry blocked its introduction on the grounds that people would copy

266

music rather than pay for it. Have students research these issues. Should copyright concerns block public access to a superior product?

- Discuss the issue of videotaping movies and programs. Does this constitute fair use? How can artists be compensated for materials taped by consumers?
- Choose some copyrighted material and have students practice writing for permission to use the material. Use a variety of materials (song lyrics, magazine articles, photography, quotes from literary works, graphics).

Appendix N
American Library Association Copyright Term Extension Act Guide

Copyright Term Extension Act Guide

PURPOSE: To extend by 20 years the length of protection afforded to works created by both individuals and corporate copyright holders.

FUTURE LIBRARY ROLE: By taking full advantage of the limited but important exemption described below, libraries, archives, and nonprofit educational institutions can minimize the practical impact of this unfortunate legislation.

KEY PROVISIONS:
- Extends the term of copyright from "life + 50 years" to "life + 70 years" for individual authors and to 95 years from 75 years for corporate "creators";
- Applies both prospectively and to all works still under copyright on the bill's effective date;
- Includes an exception permitting libraries, archives, and nonprofit educational institutions to treat a copyrighted work in its last (new) 20 years of protection as if it were in the public domain for noncommercial purposes, provided that: 1) a good faith investigation has determined that the work is "not subject to normal commercial exploitation," and 2) such use of the work stops if the copyright owner provides notice to the contrary (even if the work had never before been exploited).

Appendix O
American Library Association Digital Millennium Copyright Act Guide

PURPOSE: Update the current Copyright Act for the digital environment and conform U.S. law to the requirements of new World Intellectual Property Organization (WIPO) treaties negotiated in Geneva in December 1996.

FUTURE LIBRARY ROLE: As detailed below, assuring that all kinds of copyrighted works remain available for fair use (and other lawful uses). The adoption of the Digital Millennium Copyright Act could depend in large part upon the success of librarians and library supporters in collecting and organizing evidence of the law's adverse or potentially adverse effects. In addition, librarians will have the opportunity to assist the Register of Copyrights in making recommendations to Congress early in 1999 as to whether (and, if so, how) the Copyright Act should be updated to better facilitate distance education.

KEY PROVISIONS: ALA, together with other major national library associations and its partners in the Digital Future Coalition, has struggled to maintain the traditional balance in copyright law between protecting information and affording access to it by: 1) helping Congress to craft an entirely new law with this balance in mind; and 2) updating information users' existing rights and privileges to take changed technologies and practices into account. These efforts necessarily implicated many parts of the Digital Millennium Copyright Act identified with separate headings below.

TITLE I: NEW PROHIBITIONS ON CIRCUMVENTION OF PROTECTION TECHNOLOGIES

- Prohibits the "circumvention" of any effective "technological protection measure" (e.g., a password or form of encryption) used by a copyright holder to restrict access to its material;

- Prohibits the manufacture of any device, or the offering of any service, primarily designed to defeat an effective "technological protection measure";
- Defers the effective date of these prohibitions for two years and 18 months, respectively;
- During those two years, and then every three years thereafter, requires the Librarian of Congress (through the office of the Register of Copyrights), to conduct a formal "on the record" rulemaking proceeding to determine whether the "anti-circumvention" prohibition will "adversely affect" information users' (both individuals and institutions) "ability to make noninfringing uses" of "a particular class of copyrighted works" (NOTE: The term "class" was deliberately left undefined, but is intended to be fairly narrow, e.g., history texts, digital maps, or personal finance software.);
- Requires that the Librarian issue a three-year waiver from the anti-circumvention prohibition with respect to any class of work to which the new law has adversely affected (or is likely to affect) access for fair use and other noninfringing uses;
- Exempts nonprofit libraries, archives and educational institutions from criminal penalties and allows for nullification of any civil fine when such an institution can demonstrate that it had no reason to be aware that its actions violated the new law;
- Expressly states that many valuable activities based on the Fair Use Doctrine (including reverse engineering, security testing, privacy protection, and encryption research) will not constitute illegal "anti-circumvention";
- Makes no change to the Fair Use Doctrine, or to other information user privileges and rights.

TITLE II: LIMITATIONS ON
ONLINE SERVICE PROVIDER LIABILITY

- Exempts any "online service provider" or carrier of digital information (including libraries) from copyright liability based solely on the content of a transmission made by a user of the provider's or carrier's system (e.g., the user of a library computer system);
- Establishes a mechanism for avoiding copyright infringement liability based upon the storage of infringing information on an online service provider's own computer system, or upon the use of "information location tools" and hyperlinks, if the provider acts "expeditiously to remove or disable access to" infringing material identified in a formal notice by the copyright holder.

[Author's note: For purposes of this book, TITLE III is not applicable.]

TITLE IV: INCLUDES DIGITAL PRESERVATION
AND DISTANCE EDUCATION

DIGITAL PRESERVATION
Updates the current preservation provision of the Copyright Act (Sec. 108) to:

- Expressly permit authorized institutions to make up to three digital preservation copies of an eligible copyrighted work;
- Electronically "loan" those copies to other qualifying institutions;
- Permit preservation, including by digital means, when the existing format in which the work has been stored becomes obsolete.

DISTANCE EDUCATION

- Charges the Register of Copyrights with reporting to Congress within six months of the bill's effective date on "how to promote distance education through digital technologies";
- Encourages the Register to formulate such recommendations as statutory proposals
- Specifies eight factors to be considered by the Register, including: "the extent to which the availability of licenses for the use of copyrighted works in distance education through interactive digital networks should be considered in assessing eligibility for any distance education exemption."

Appendix P
Library Preservation: Changes Incorporated in H.R. 2281, the Digital Millennium Copyright Act of 1998 (P.L. 105-304)

Section 108 Privileges

Section 108 of the Copyright Act provides for limitations on the exclusive rights of proprietors to permit certain reproduction by libraries and archives. These limitations are separate from the Section 107 fair use privileges, and do not depend on application of the four factors listed as determining whether a use is "fair." Section 108 specifies that it does not affect the right of fair use, and its privileges may or may not go beyond what might otherwise be determined to be fair use.

Because Section 108 privileges are set out in a separate section, they provide predictability for libraries and archives under certain circumstances for preservation, for interlibrary loan, and for immunity from liability for the unsupervised use of on-site reproduction equipment.

Section 108 deals with the right of reproduction for certain library and archival purposes. The right of distribution in Section 108 is limited to interlibrary loan, or to the equivalent of interlibrary loan for a copy of an unpublished work or a replacement preservation copy. Other distribution is limited to what might be permitted under fair use or other provisions of the law. Systematic reproduction or distribution of single or multiple copies is prohibited except for interlibrary arrangements that do not have the effect of substituting for subscription or purchase.

Why Change in Section 108 Was Needed

Previous law allowed libraries and archives, when an unused replacement at a fair price could not be obtained, to make one "facsimile" copy for preservation purposes,

272

such as when paper in books was too brittle for use, or when a phonorecord was damaged by a user. The "one facsimile copy" was interpreted by some to refer only to the print environment, and to potentially restrict preservation in digital form or replacement of digital formats themselves, which quickly become obsolete and readable only by obsolete hardware and software. For some materials and preservation methods, state-of-the-art technique requires an "iron mountain" copy, a master copy, and a use copy, with only the use copy accessible at any one time.

Library groups proposed language in 1997, incorporated in bills introduced by Senator Ashcroft, Representative Boucher and Representative Campbell (S. 1146 and H.R. 3048), that would allow libraries and archives to make three copies of endangered materials for preservation purposes, and to use digital and successor technologies for preservation.

Negotiated Changes Incorporated in the Bill

On April 23, 1998, the Senate Judiciary Committee approved revisions to Section 108 that had been negotiated on April 21 in a hastily called session with Senate committee staff and representatives of the Copyright Office, the Association of American Publishers, the American Library Association, and counsel representing several library groups (American Association of Law Libraries, American Library Association, Association of Research Libraries, Medical Library Association, and Special Libraries Association). On April 30, the Committee approved the bill, S. 2037, the Digital Millennium Copyright Act of 1998, with several changes to Section 108 of the Copyright Act. These changes remained in the Senate-passed bill, were also incorporated in the House-passed H.R. 2281, and thus retained in the final House-Senate conference version. Specifically, the revisions are as follows:

- The required notice of copyright on a reproduction or distribution under Section 108 is clarified to include a requirement for a legend stating that the work may be protected by copyright (if no copyright notice can otherwise be found).
- The number of copies or phonorecords that may be made for preservation purposes is increased from one to three (for both published and unpublished works).
- The words "in facsimile form" are deleted, whether referring to published or unpublished works.
- For preservation replacements of unpublished works, "any such copy or phonorecord that is reproduced in digital format is not otherwise distributed in that format and is not made available to the public in that format outside the premises of the library or archives."
- For preservation replacements of published works, "any such copy or phonorecord that is reproduced in digital format is not made available to the public in that format outside the premises of the library or archives in lawful possession of such copy."
- For published works for which an unused replacement at a fair price is not available, an added reason for which reproduction for preservation purposes is allowed is "if the existing format in which the work is stored has become obsolete." A format is "considered obsolete if the machine or device

necessary to render perceptible a work stored in that format is no longer
manufactured or is no longer reasonably available in the commercial marketplace."

Impact of Revisions to Section 108

These negotiated revisions update Section 108 in critically needed ways. First, the
number of copies that can be made for preservation purposes is increased from
one to three. Second, it is absolutely clear that Section 108 applies to digital formats — through deletion of references to "facsimile form," through specific references to digital formats in subsections referring to preservation of both
unpublished and published works, and through the addition of the new concept
of preservation because a format has become obsolete (which happens more
quickly with digital formats than with any previous formats).

While there are limitations on the distribution of preservation copies in digital
formats, these limitations are consistent with the long-standing and continuing
prohibition in Section 108 against "systematic reproduction or distribution" except
for certain interlibrary arrangements. The limitations on the distribution of preservation copies in digital formats specifically allow for interlibrary loan in the subsections relating to the preservations of both unpublished and published works.

Appendix Q
School Sample
Permission Forms

Bellingham (WA) Public Schools
Parent Permission Form
for World Wide Web:
Publishing of Student Work

Name of Student _____

School _____ Name of Parent _____

We understand that our daughter or son's art work, or writing, is under consideration for publication on the World Wide Web, a part of the Internet. We further understand that the work will appear with a copyright notice prohibiting the copying of such work without express written permission. In the event anyone requests such permission, those requests will be forwarded to us as parents. No home address or telephone number will appear with such work.

We grant permission for the World Wide Web publishing as described above until June of 1999. A copy of all such publishing will be printed out and brought home for us to see.

Name _____ Date _____

Name _____ Date _____

I, the student, also give my permission for such publishing.

Name _____ Date _____

Bellingham (WA) Public Schools
Parent Permission Letter:
Internet and Electronic Mail Permission Form

We are pleased to offer students of the Bellingham Public Schools access to the district computer network for electronic mail (e-mail) and the Internet. To gain access to e-mail and the Internet, all students under the age of 18 must obtain parental permission and must sign and return this form to the LIBRARY MEDIA SPECIALIST. Students 18 and over may sign their own forms.

Access to e-mail and the Internet will enable students to explore thousands of libraries, databases, and bulletin boards while exchanging messages with Internet users throughout the world. Families should be warned that certain material accessible via the Internet may contain items that are illegal, defamatory, inaccurate or potentially offensive to some people. While our intent is to make Internet access available to further educational goals and objectives, students may find ways to access other materials as well. We believe that the benefit to students from access to the Internet, in the form of information resources and opportunities for collaboration, exceed any disadvantages. But ultimately, parents and guardians of minors are responsible for setting and conveying the standards that their children should follow when using media and information sources. To that end, the Bellingham Public Schools support and respect each family's right to decide whether or not to apply for access.

DISTRICT INTERNET AND E-MAIL RULES

Students are responsible for good behavior on school computer networks just as they are in a classroom or a school hallway. Communications on the network are often public in nature. General school behavior and communications apply.

The network is provided for students to conduct research and communicate with others. Access to network services is given to students who agree to act in a considerate and responsible manner. Parent permission is required. Access is a privilege — not a right. Access entails responsibility.

Individual users of the district computer networks are responsible for their behavior and communications over those networks. It is presumed that users will comply with district standards and will honor the agreements they have signed. Beyond the clarification of such standards, the district is not responsible for restricting, monitoring, or controlling the communications of individuals utilizing the network.

Network storage areas may be treated like school lockers. Network administrators may review files and communications to maintain system integrity and insure that users are utilizing the system responsibly. Users should not expect that files stored on district servers will always be private.

Within reason, freedom of speech and access to information will be honored. During school, teachers of younger students will guide them toward appropriate materials. Outside of school, families bear the same responsibility for such guidance as they exercise with information sources such as television, telephones, movies, radio and other potentially offensive media.

As outlined in Board policy and procedures on student rights and responsibilities (3200), copies of which are available in school offices, the following are not permitted:

- Sending or displaying offensive messages or pictures
- Using obscene language
- Harassing, insulting or attacking others
- Damaging computers, computer systems or computer networks
- Violating copyright laws
- Using another's password
- Trespassing in another's folders, work or files
- Intentionally wasting limited resources
- Employing the network for commercial purposes.

Violations may result in a loss of access as well as other disciplinary or legal action.

User Agreement and Parent Permission Form

As a user of the Bellingham Public Schools computer network, I hereby agree to comply with the above stated rules — communicating over the network in a reliable fashion while honoring all relevant laws and restrictions.

Student Signature _____

As the parent or legal guardian of the minor student signing above, I grant permission for my son or daughter to access networked computer services such as electronic mail and the Internet. I understand that individuals and families may be held liable for violations. I understand that some materials on the Internet may be objectionable, but I accept responsibility for guidance of Internet use — setting and conveying standards for my daughter or son to follow when selecting, sharing or exploring information and media.

Parent Signature _____ Date _____

Name of Student _____

School _____ Grade _____

Soc. Sec. # _____ Birth Date _____

Street Address _____

Home Telephone _____ Work Telephone _____

Issaquah (WA) Copyright Permission Letter

DIRECTIONS: Whenever a student or staff member wishes to "re-publish" someone else's writing or graphics on an Issaquah Public School Web site, explicit permission must be obtained from the owner of copyright or evidence must be provided that the materials are "in the public domain." The form below may be copied and pasted into an e-mail message sent to the owner of the site and or the owner of copyright. An e-mail reply which answers all questions fully and grants permission should be printed out and presented along with any Web pages being submitted to the library media specialist for publication. Every Web page containing such items must provide full credit to the source, indicate that permission was granted and include a notice clarifying that all rights are still reserved by the copyright owner.

ISSAQUAH SCHOOLS COPYRIGHT PERMISSION REQUEST

[Type Name of Site here]
[Type Name of Site Manager here]
[Type e-mail address of Site Manager here]
[Type URL(s) (addresses) of Web page containing desired item(s)]

Dear (insert name of Site Manager):

I am a (insert either "student" or "teacher") in the Issaquah (WA) Public Schools creating Web pages for a school project. My school is (insert name of school). My e-mail address is (insert full e-mail address).

We are currently engaged in a project which (insert description of the project and its goals here).

While doing research for this project, I visited your excellent site and was very much impressed with what you have done.

I am interested in gaining permission to "re-publish" the following material from your Web site on our school's Web site:

(describe first item)
(describe additional items)

Are you the holder of a copyright for these materials?

_____ Yes _____ No

If you are not the holder of a copyright, can you identify the owner and supply an e-mail address so that I may contact the owner?

_____

If you are the holder of copyright, may we "republish" these items, including at the bottom of the Web page a clear notice that we are "re-publishing" the item with your permission, with all rights reserved?

_____ I give my permission.

_____ I do not give my permission.

Please write the words you wish for us to place at the bottom of the page describing your copyright restrictions.

_____

Thanks so much for your time and assistance. We appreciate your contribution to the development of excellent content on the Web. Please send back this whole message with your name and title at the bottom so that we can identify the source of permission.

Schools and nonprofit organizations may copy and make use of these materials within their own school districts or may republish the pages on their Web sites provided that a clear notice of source is included on the Web page.

Cupertino Union (CA) School District Web Page Standards

ADMINISTRATOR'S CHECKLIST

A sign-off sheet for administrators to evaluate and approve a Web Site for public release.

- ☐ I have reviewed the entire Web site and I am familiar with its workings and content.
- ☐ The Web site is in accordance with the CUSD Web Page Guidelines.
- ☐ The Web site is in support of my school's/department's overall mission and objectives.
- ☐ I am aware that I must approve future modifications to the Web site prior to publication on the Internet.

I give authorization for our Web site to be published on the Internet.

_____
(Principal's or Administrator's Signature)

_____
(Principal's or Administrator's Position/Title)

_____
(Date)

Please return this completed form to the manager of the Data Center.

Blanket Parent Agreement for Portal School (WA)

This Agreement has been signed only after reading, understanding, and considering the following:

I am aware that my child is participating in (name of project, date) _____
_____.

I hereby grant permission to anyone authorized to use and reproduce any and all video and photographic film, prints, tapes, audio recordings, and or other audiovisual media taken of my child, as well as my child's name and likeness, for any and all documentation and promotional purposes solely in conjunction with the _____ project.

All video and photographic film, prints, tapes, audio recordings, and or other audiovisual media shall constitute the sole and exclusive property of _____
_____.

I give my permission for my child to participate in all of the project's activities which may include videotaping, interviews, publicity, and pictures.
I give my permission for any videotapes, interviews, or pictures of my child to be used for publicity by the print, broadcast, or telecommunications media.
Please sign this agreement and return to Portal School.

_____
CHILD'S NAME

_____
PARENT/GUARDIAN SIGNATURE

_____
DATED

Montgomery County (VA) Public Schools
Appropriate Usage Agreements

Using the Internet at (Name of School) Grades 2–5

If I read these pages carefully, and after my parent or guardian signs the second sheet, I may be allowed to use a computer at (name of school) to look at the Internet and send messages to people around the world. But I also know that if I do not use the Internet in the right way, my teacher or principal may need to punish me. In fact, I may not be allowed to use the Internet again at school.

I will read the rules for using the Internet that are given below and will ask an adult at my school if I do not understand what any of them mean.

- I will be polite to other people when writing to them (or talking with them) while I am on the Internet. I will not use curse words or any language that my teacher or parent would not want me to use in my classroom.
- I will never give my name, my home address, any personal information about me or my family, or my telephone number to anyone I write to or talk with on the Internet. I know that almost anyone I contact is a stranger to me, and that I don't share personal information with strangers no matter how nice they seem to be.
- I know that my teacher and my principal want me to use the Internet to learn more about the subjects I am studying in my classroom. I will not use the Internet for any other reason. For example, I will not search for a comic book site when I am supposed to be looking for something in science.
- Because the people I write to or talk with on the Internet cannot see me, they will not know what I look like or even how old I am. When I am on the Internet, I promise never to tell people that I am someone else. And I will never send them personal information, such as a picture or my name, by using an envelope and stamp.
- I understand that sometimes I may see a site on the Internet that has pictures or words that my teacher or parents would not want me to see. I will not try to find those sites and, if I come across one of them by accident, I will leave it as soon as I can. For example, suppose I am searching for a type of animal and find a picture that only adults should see. I quickly use my forward or backward keys to take me to another site. I will not continue to look at the site with the bad picture and will not show it to others around me. I also will not print it out or save the picture.
- I agree that I cannot use the words or pictures I see on an Internet site without giving credit to the person who owns the site. For example, I will not copy information from the Internet and hand it in to my teacher as my own work.
- I may be given a password — a special word that only I know. I may have to use this password to sign onto a computer or to send mail over the Internet. I know that I must never tell a friend what that password is. My password should be known only by me. And I know that I should never use a password for myself if that password belongs to someone else. For example,

John asks me to loan him my password so he can send someone an e-mail message. John cannot remember what password he was given. I would not loan my password to him and would never ask to use his.

Student's Agreement (for Students in the Second Grade or Above)
I have read the information that is written above. If I did not understand the meaning of part of it, I asked an adult to explain it to me. I agree to follow these rules at all times when I use the Internet at school.

_____

Signature

_____

Date

Parent or Guardian
My son or daughter, who has signed above, understands the rules that he or she is to follow in using the Internet at school. I have talked to him or her to make sure that those rules are understood. I realize that teachers and other school officials will try their best to provide only educationally sound material from the Internet to my child and that, should objectionable pictures or information appear by accident, they will take immediate action to correct that situation. I give my permission to Montgomery County Public Schools for my son or daughter to use the Internet while on school property.

_____

Signature

_____

Date

ACCEPTABLE USE POLICY FOR INTERNET ACCESS GRADES 6–12

With the permission of your parent or guardian, (name of school) offers you an opportunity to use the Internet at school. We expect you to use the Internet while in our building only for educational purposes approved by (name of school). This use is a privilege, not a right, and we may discipline you or take away your right to use the Internet at school if you misuse this privilege. You are responsible for your own actions while you are on the Internet at (name of school) and are also accountable for any online activities that occur by others because you have allowed them to use your account.

As a student, you should read the following regulations and then sign this form to show that you understand your responsibilities in using the Internet at this school.

While using the Internet from school properties:

- While online, I will not use language which may be offensive to other users. I will treat others with respect. The written and verbal messages I send while on the Internet will not contain profanity, obscene comments, sexually explicit material, nor expressions of bigotry, racism, and hate.

- I will not place unlawful information on the Internet, nor will I use the Internet illegally in any way that violates federal, state, or local laws or statutes. I will never falsify my identity while using the Internet.
- I will not use the Internet for non-school related activities.
- I will not send chain letters nor any pyramid scheme either to a list of people or to an individual, nor will I send any other type of communication that might cause a congestion of the Internet or interfere with the work of others.
- I will not use the Internet to buy or sell, or to attempt to buy or sell, any service or product.
- I will not change any computer file that does not belong to me.
- I will not use copyrighted materials from the Internet without permission of the author. I will cite the source where appropriate.
- I will never knowingly give my password to others, nor will I use another person's password.
- I will never use the Internet to send or obtain pornographic or inappropriate material or files.
- Except for the usual information contained in the headers of my electronic mail, I will never give out personal information such as name, address, phone number, or gender.
- I will never knowingly circumvent, or try to circumvent, security measures on either Montgomery County Public Schools' computers or on computers at any remote site.
- I will never attempt to gain unlawful access to another person's or organization's resources, programs, or data.
- I will not make, or attempt to make, any malicious attempt to harm or destroy data of another user on the Internet, including the uploading, downloading, or creation of computer viruses.

Student's Agreement
I have read the Acceptable Use Policy for Internet Access, as written above, and understand fully and agree to follow the principles and guidelines it contains.

_____
Signature

_____
Date

Parent's Agreement
As the parent or guardian of this student, I have read the Acceptable Use Policy for Internet Access as written above. I understand that Internet access at school for students of Montgomery County Public Schools is provided for educational purposes only. I understand that employees of the school system will make every reasonable effort to restrict access to all controversial material on the Internet, but

I will not hold them responsible for materials my son or daughter acquires or sees as a result of the use of the Internet from school facilities. I give my permission to (name of school) to allow the student above to use the Internet on computers at the school.

_____

Signature

_____

Date

Index

There is much information to be found in the Notes beginning on page 161 and the Resource Guides beginning on page 185; neither is indexed. The appendices are indexed.